The Beatles
Yellow Submarine

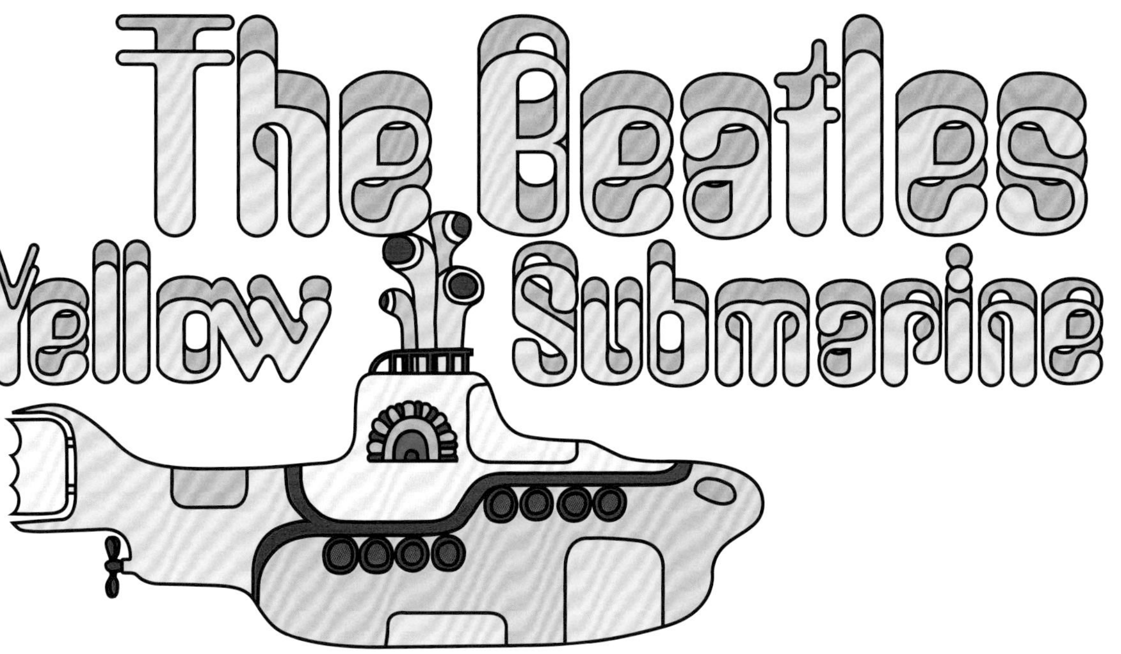

TITAN COMICS

TITAN COMICS

SENIOR EDITOR Martin Eden

EDITORIAL ASSISTANT Jake Devine

PRODUCTION CONTROLLER Peter James

PRODUCTION SUPERVISOR Maria Pearson

SENIOR PRODUCTION CONTROLLER Jackie Flook

ART DIRECTOR Oz Browne

SENIOR SALES MANAGER Santosh Maharaj

PRESS OFFICER Will O'Mullane

COMICS BRAND MANAGER Chris Thompson

ADS & MARKETING ASSISTANT Bella Hoy

DIRECT SALES & MARKETING MANAGER Ricky Claydon

COMMERCIAL MANAGER Michelle Fairlamb

HEAD OF RIGHTS Jenny Boyce

PUBLISHING MANAGER Darryl Tothill

PUBLISHING DIRECTOR Chris Teather

OPERATIONS DIRECTOR Leigh Baulch

EXECUTIVE DIRECTOR Vivian Cheung

PUBLISHER Nick Landau

THANK YOU TO: Joe Marziotto, Barry Linton and all at Apple Corps Ltd.

For rights information contact:
jenny.boyce@titanemail.com

Published by Titan Comics
A division of Titan Publishing Group Ltd.
144 Southwark St.
London, SE1 0UP

A CIP catalogue record for this title is available from the British Library
First edition: August 2018

ISBN (regular edition): 9781785863943
ISBN (limited edition): 9781785863967
ISBN (Newbury edition): 9781785869563

10 9 8 7 6 5 4 3 2 1

Printed in China

Yellow Submarine graphic novel, published by Titan Comics. Titan Comics is a registered trademark of Titan Publishing Group Ltd. 144 Southwark Street, London SE1 0UP
© 2018 Subafilms Ltd, A Yellow Submarine™ Product, ™ Trade Mark of Subafilms Ltd
© 1968, Authorised BEATLES ™ Merchandise.

www.beatles.com

Beatles
Yellow Submarine

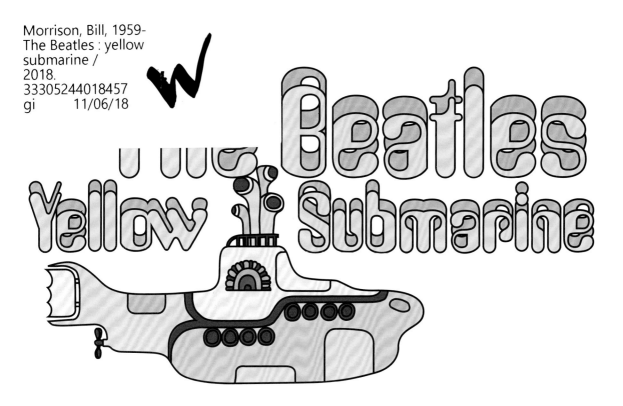

BASED ON A SONG BY JOHN LENNON AND PAUL MCCARTNEY

STORY ADAPTATION BY
BILL MORRISON
from the Screenplay by Lee Minoff,
Al Brodax, Jack Mendelsohn and Erich Segal.
With thanks to Roger McGough

ARTWORK ADAPTED BY
BILL MORRISON
from the design and artwork of Heinz Edelmann

INKERS (P25 to 96)
ANDREW PEPOY
with TONE RODRIGUEZ

COLORS
NATHAN KANE

LETTERING
ADITYA BIDIKAR

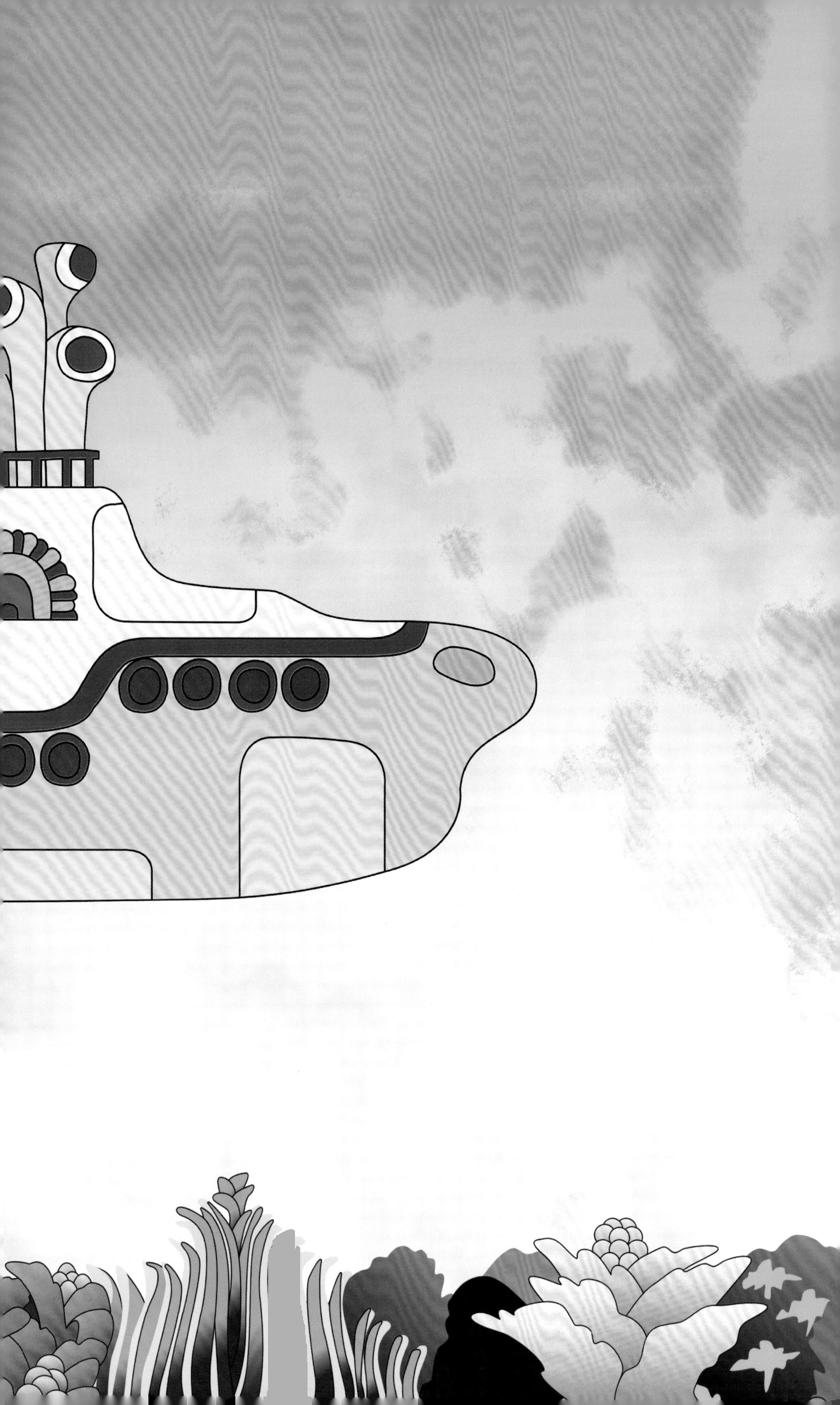

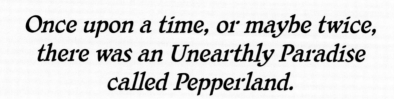

*Once upon a time, or maybe twice,
there was an Unearthly Paradise
called Pepperland.*

*Eighty thousand leagues
beneath the sea it lay... or lie.*

I'm not too sure.

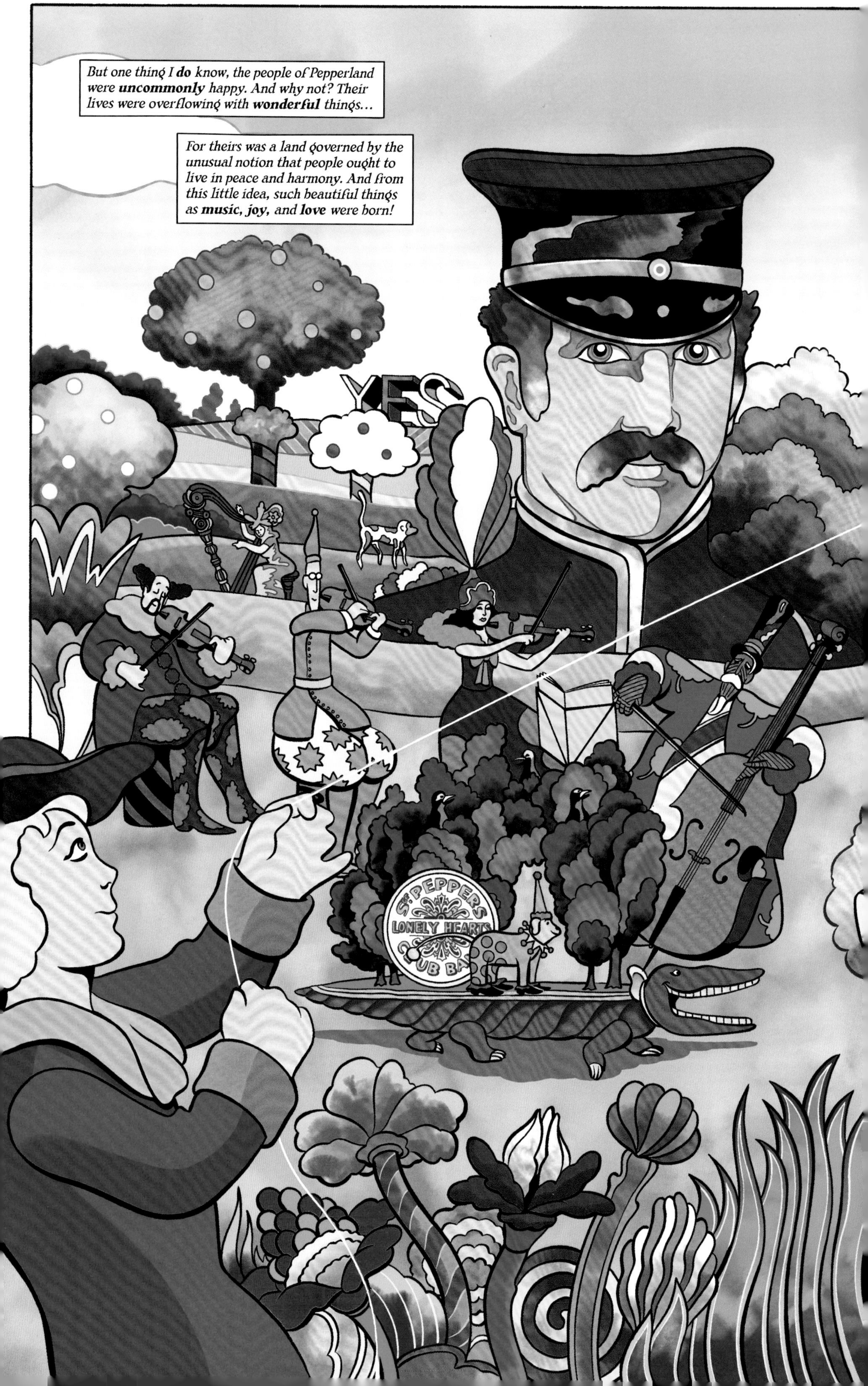
But one thing I **do** know, the people of Pepperland were **uncommonly** happy. And why not? Their lives were overflowing with **wonderful** things...
For theirs was a land governed by the unusual notion that people ought to live in peace and harmony. And from this little idea, such beautiful things as **music**, **joy**, and **love** were born!
YES
LONELY HEARTS

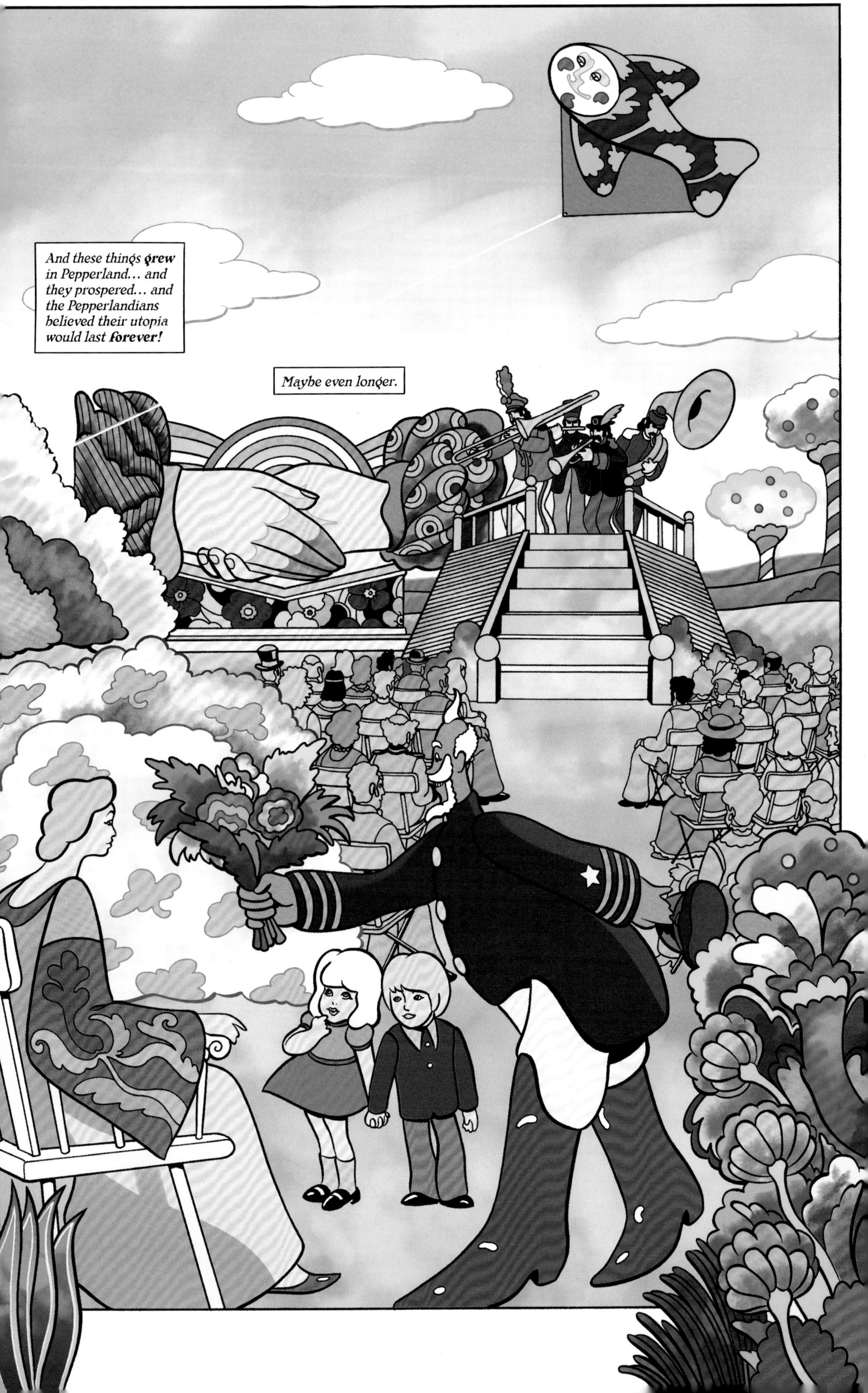

*And these things **grew** in Pepperland… and they prospered… and the Pepperlandians believed their utopia would last **forever!***
Maybe even longer.

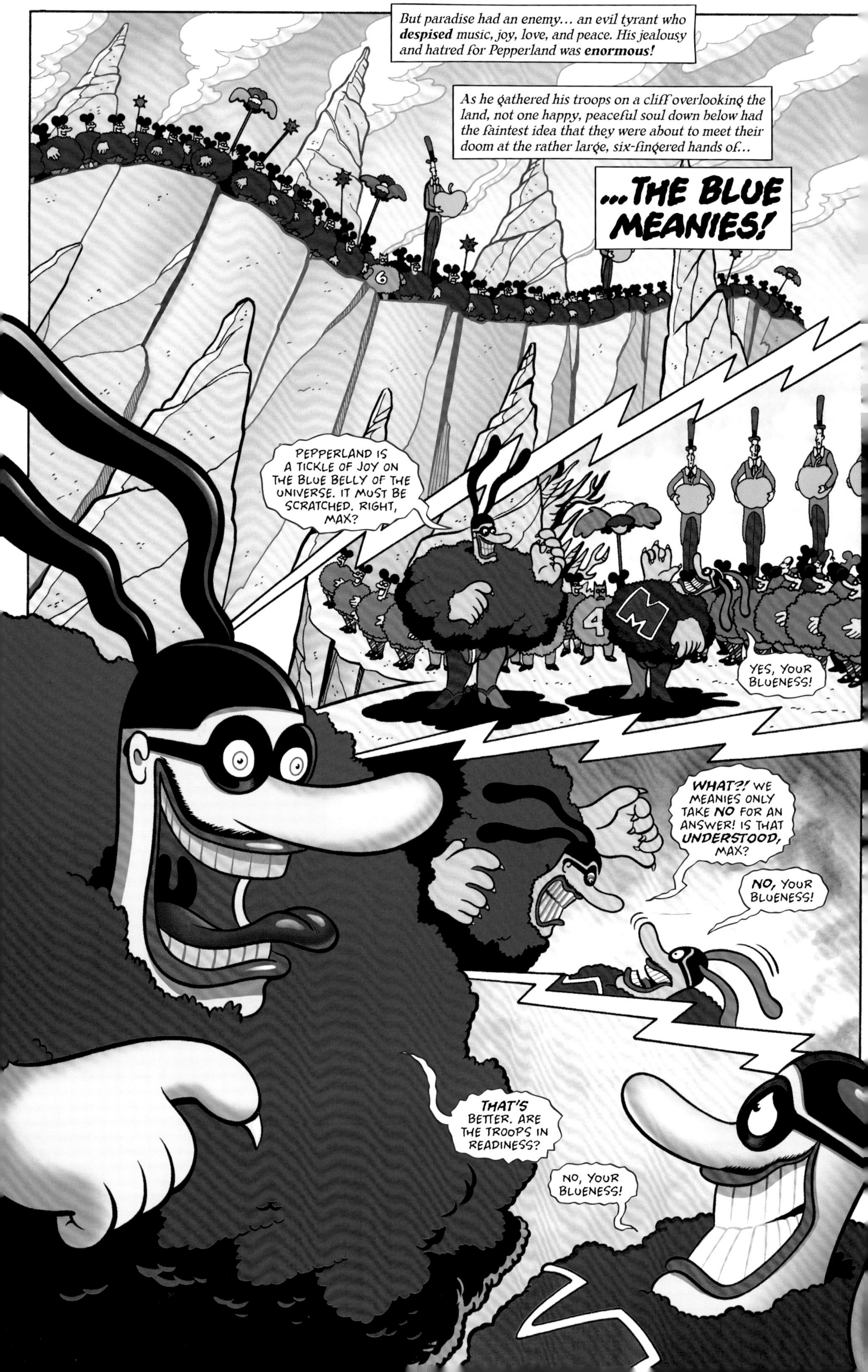
But paradise had an enemy... an evil tyrant who **despised** music, joy, love, and peace. His jealousy and hatred for Pepperland was **enormous!**
As he gathered his troops on a cliff overlooking the land, not one happy, peaceful soul down below had the faintest idea that they were about to meet their doom at the rather large, six-fingered hands of...
...THE BLUE MEANIES!
PEPPERLAND IS A TICKLE OF JOY ON THE BLUE BELLY OF THE UNIVERSE. IT MUST BE SCRATCHED. RIGHT, MAX?
YES, YOUR BLUENESS!
WHAT?! WE MEANIES ONLY TAKE NO FOR AN ANSWER! IS THAT UNDERSTOOD, MAX?
NO, YOUR BLUENESS!
THAT'S BETTER. ARE THE TROOPS IN READINESS?
NO, YOUR BLUENESS!

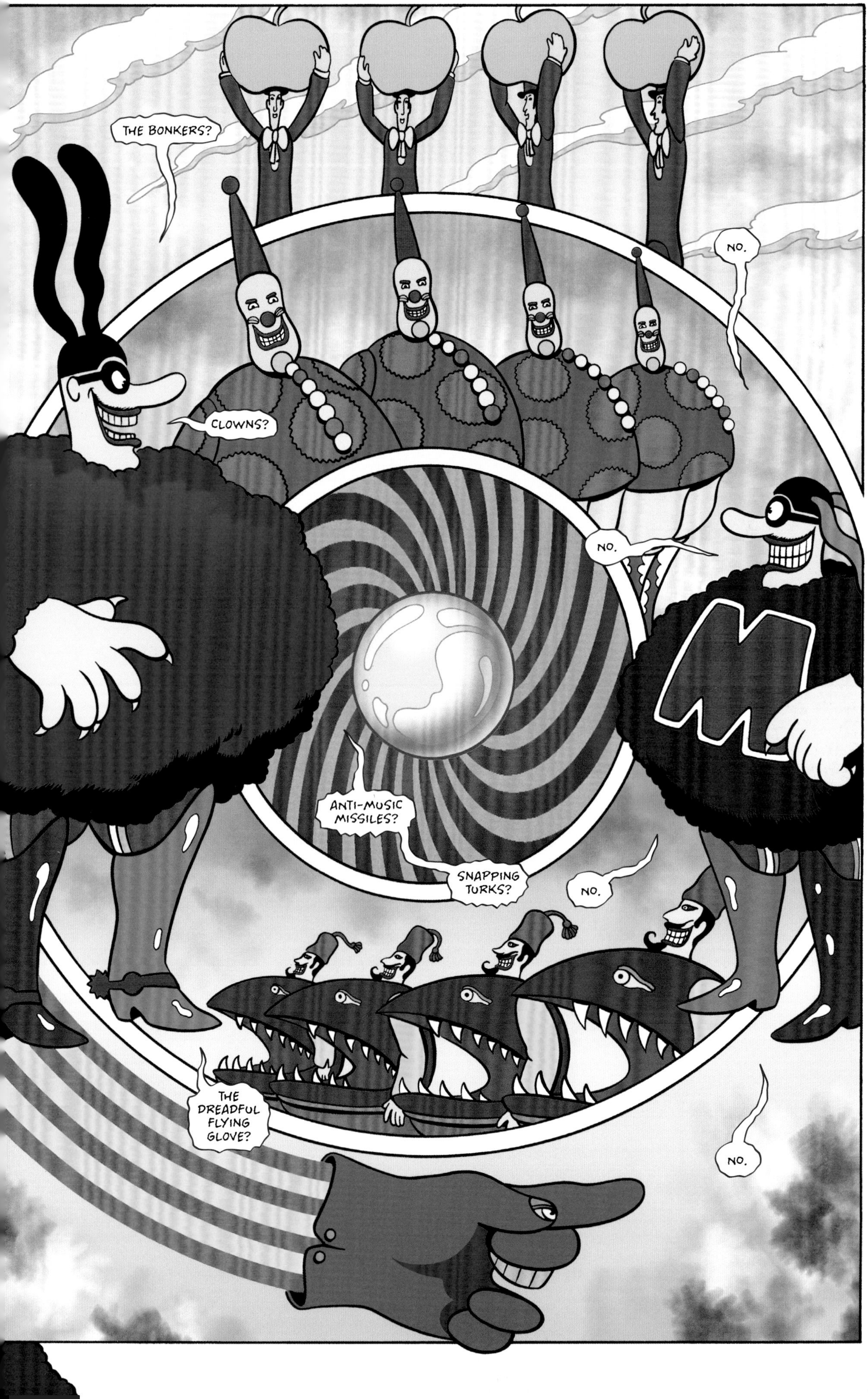
THE BONKERS?
NO.
CLOWNS?
NO.
ANTI-MUSIC MISSILES?
NO.
SNAPPING TURKS?
NO.
THE DREADFUL FLYING GLOVE?
NO.

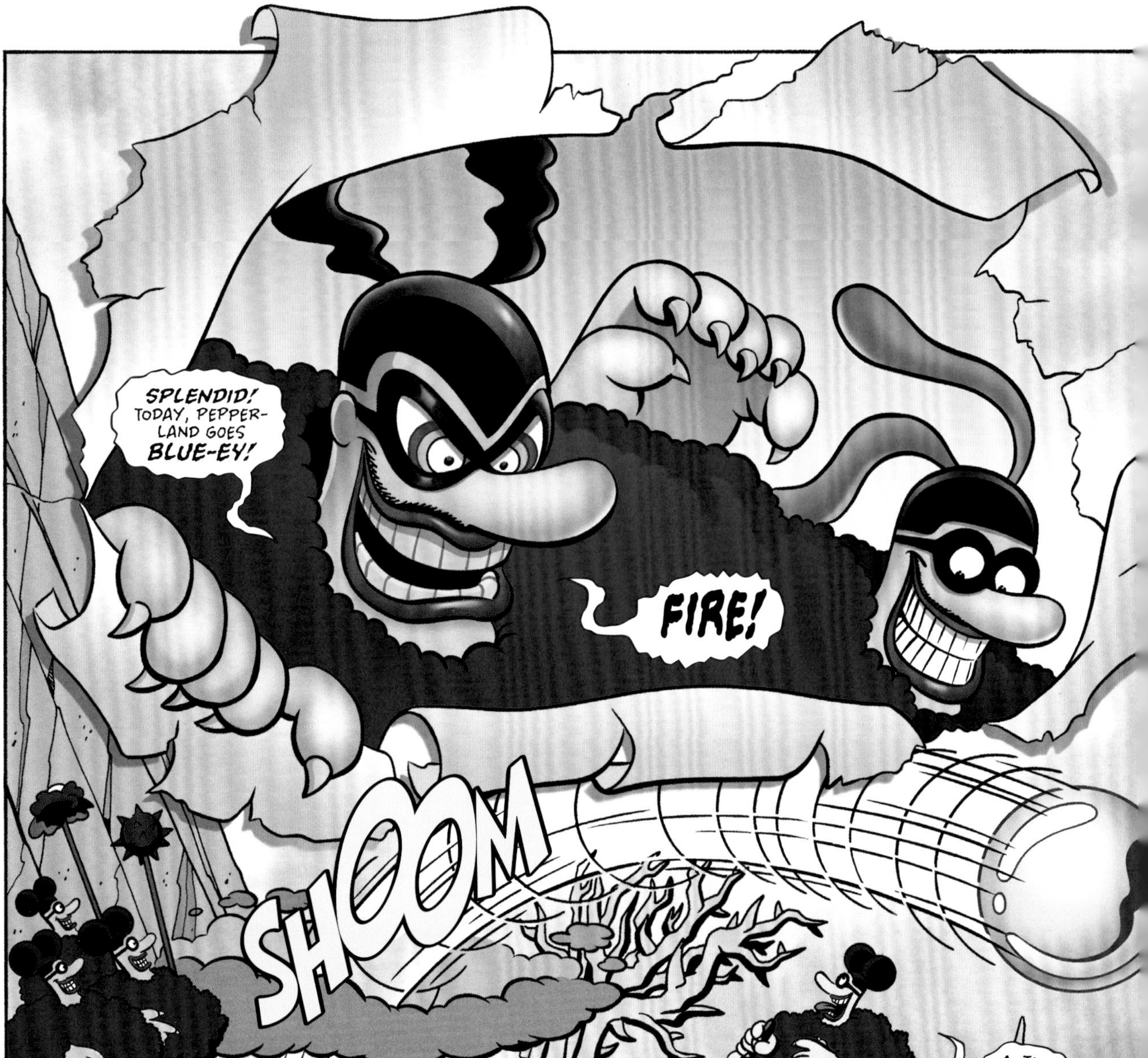
SPLENDID! TODAY, PEPPER-LAND GOES BLUE-EY!
FIRE!
SHOOM
ANTI-MUSIC MISSILE--AWAY!

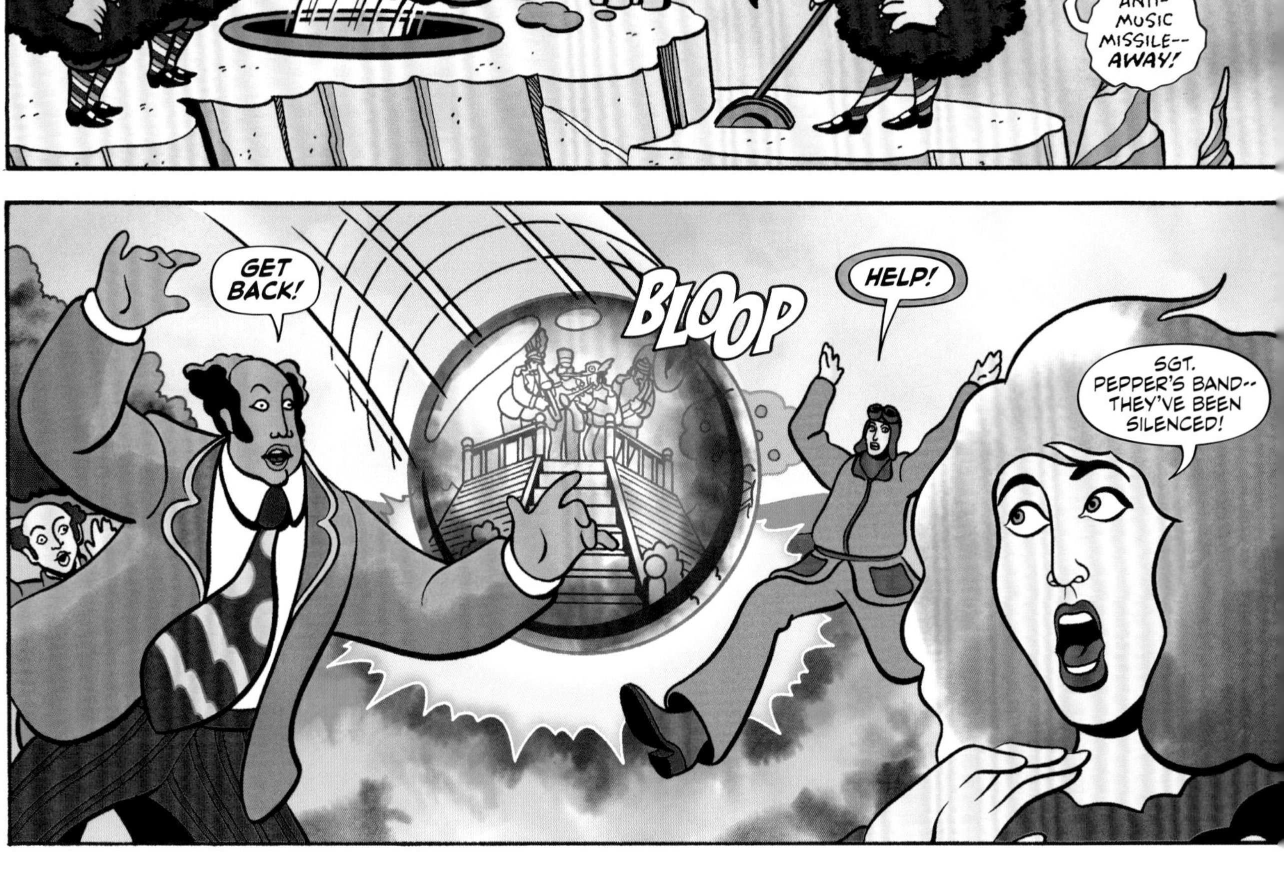
GET BACK!
BLOOP
HELP!
SGT. PEPPER'S BAND--THEY'VE BEEN SILENCED!

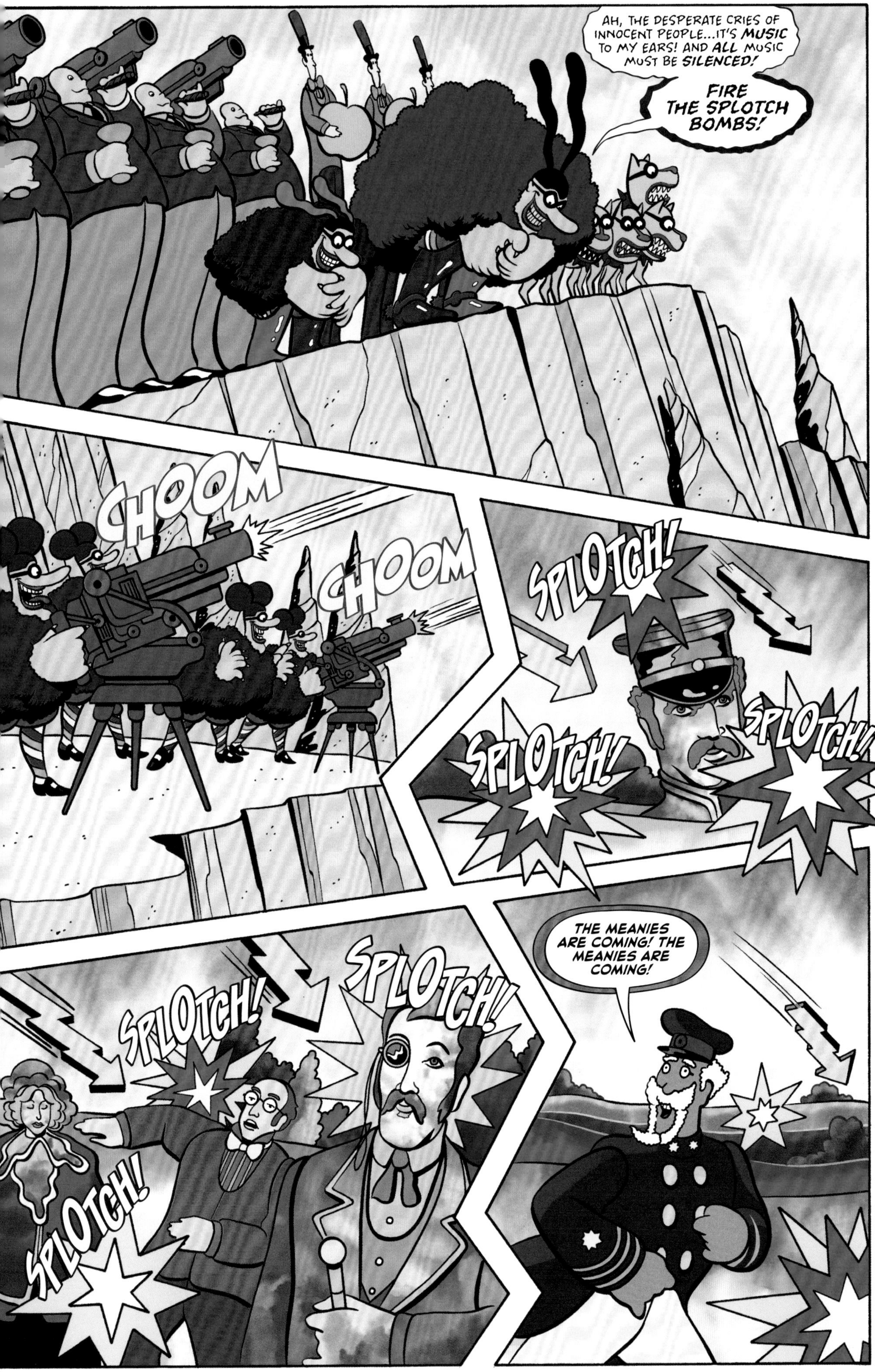

AH, THE DESPERATE CRIES OF INNOCENT PEOPLE...IT'S MUSIC TO MY EARS! AND ALL MUSIC MUST BE SILENCED!
FIRE THE SPLOTCH BOMBS!
CHOOM
CHOOM
SPLOTCH!
SPLOTCH!
SPLOTCH!
SPLOTCH!
SPLOTCH!
SPLOTCH!
THE MEANIES ARE COMING! THE MEANIES ARE COMING!

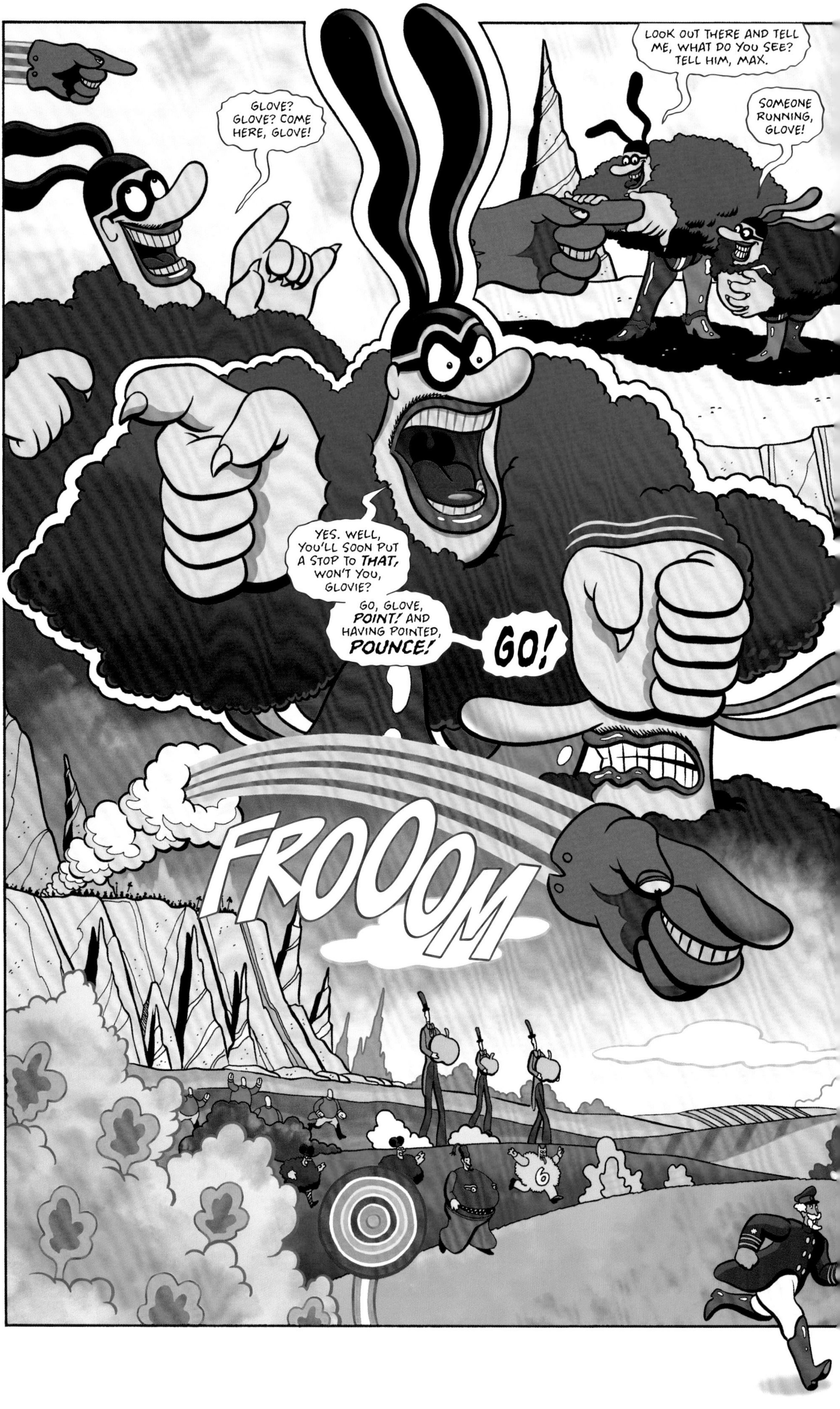
GLOVE? GLOVE? COME HERE, GLOVE!
LOOK OUT THERE AND TELL ME, WHAT DO YOU SEE? TELL HIM, MAX.
SOMEONE RUNNING, GLOVE!
YES. WELL, YOU'LL SOON PUT A STOP TO THAT, WON'T YOU, GLOVIE?
GO, GLOVE, POINT! AND HAVING POINTED, POUNCE!
GO!
FROOOM

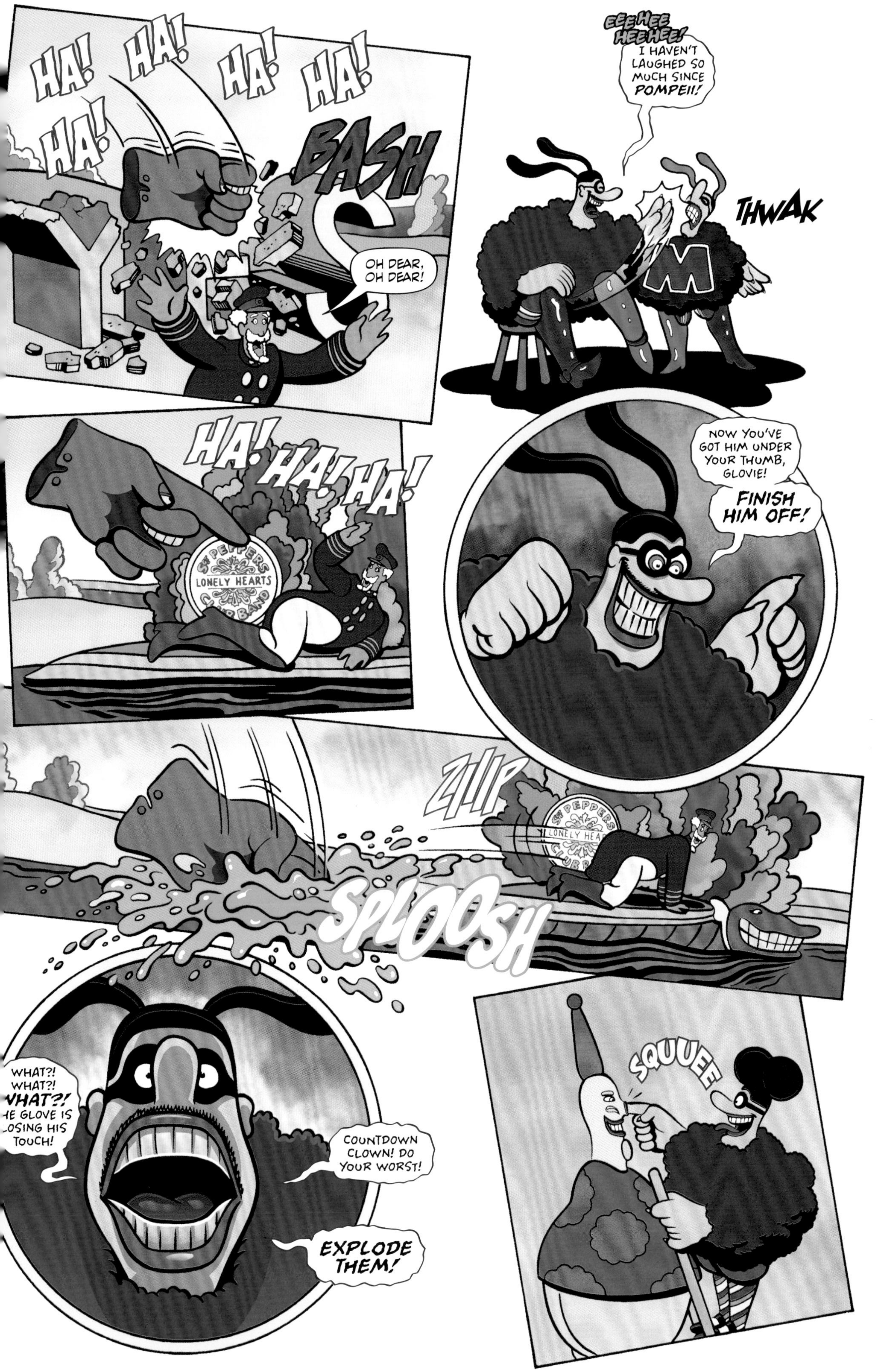
HA! HA! HA! HA! HA!
BASH
OH DEAR, OH DEAR!
EEEHEE HEEHEE! I HAVEN'T LAUGHED SO MUCH SINCE POMPEII!
THWAK
HA! HA! HA!
NOW YOU'VE GOT HIM UNDER YOUR THUMB, GLOVIE!
FINISH HIM OFF!
ZUIP
SPLOOSH
WHAT?! WHAT?! WHAT?! HE GLOVE IS OSING HIS TOUCH!
COUNTDOWN CLOWN! DO YOUR WORST!
EXPLODE THEM!
SQUUEE

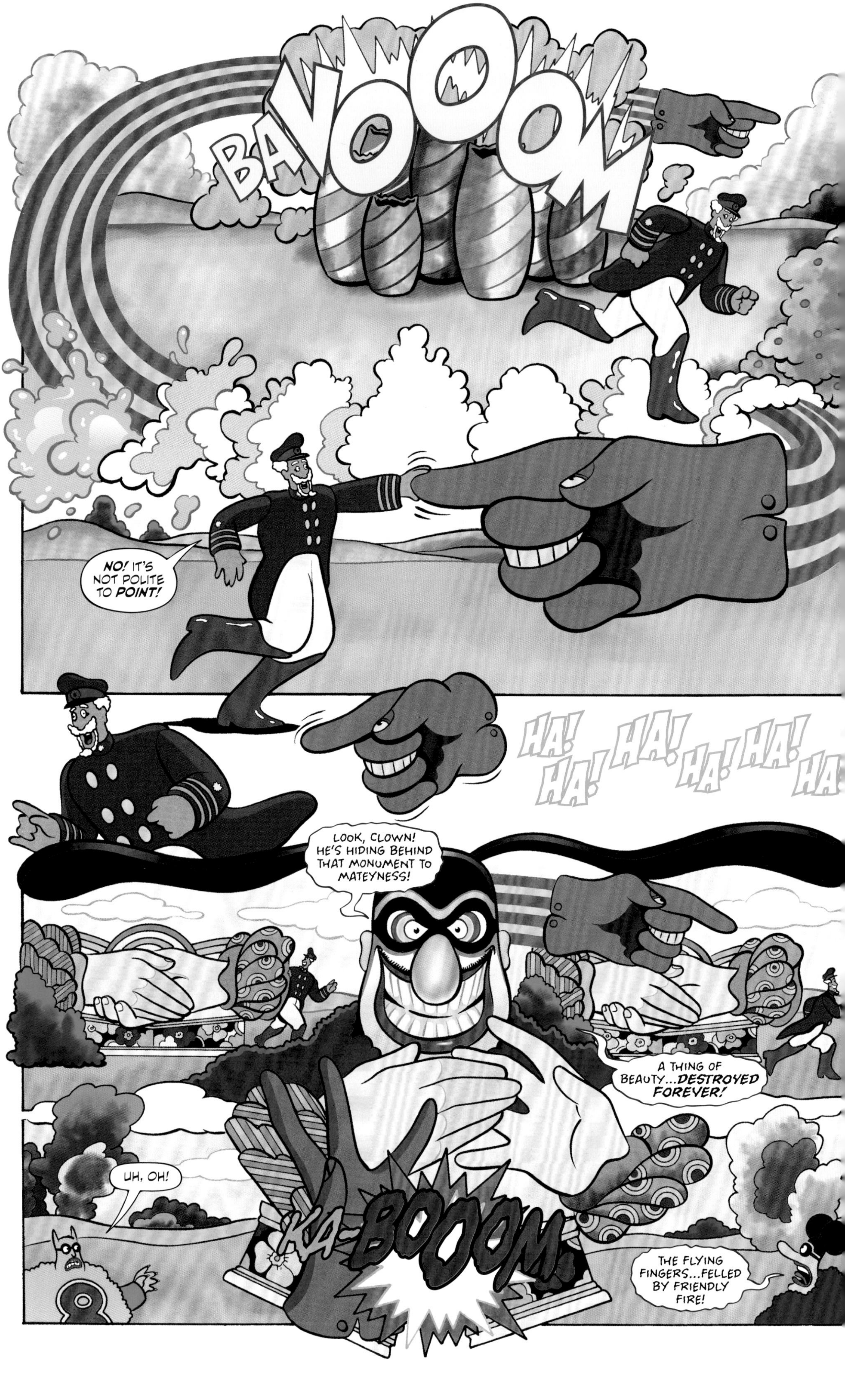
BAVOOOM
NO! IT'S NOT POLITE TO POINT!
HA! HA! HA! HA! HA! HA
LOOK, CLOWN! HE'S HIDING BEHIND THAT MONUMENT TO MATEYNESS!
A THING OF BEAUTY...DESTROYED FOREVER!
UH, OH!
KA-BOOOM!
THE FLYING FINGERS...FELLED BY FRIENDLY FIRE!

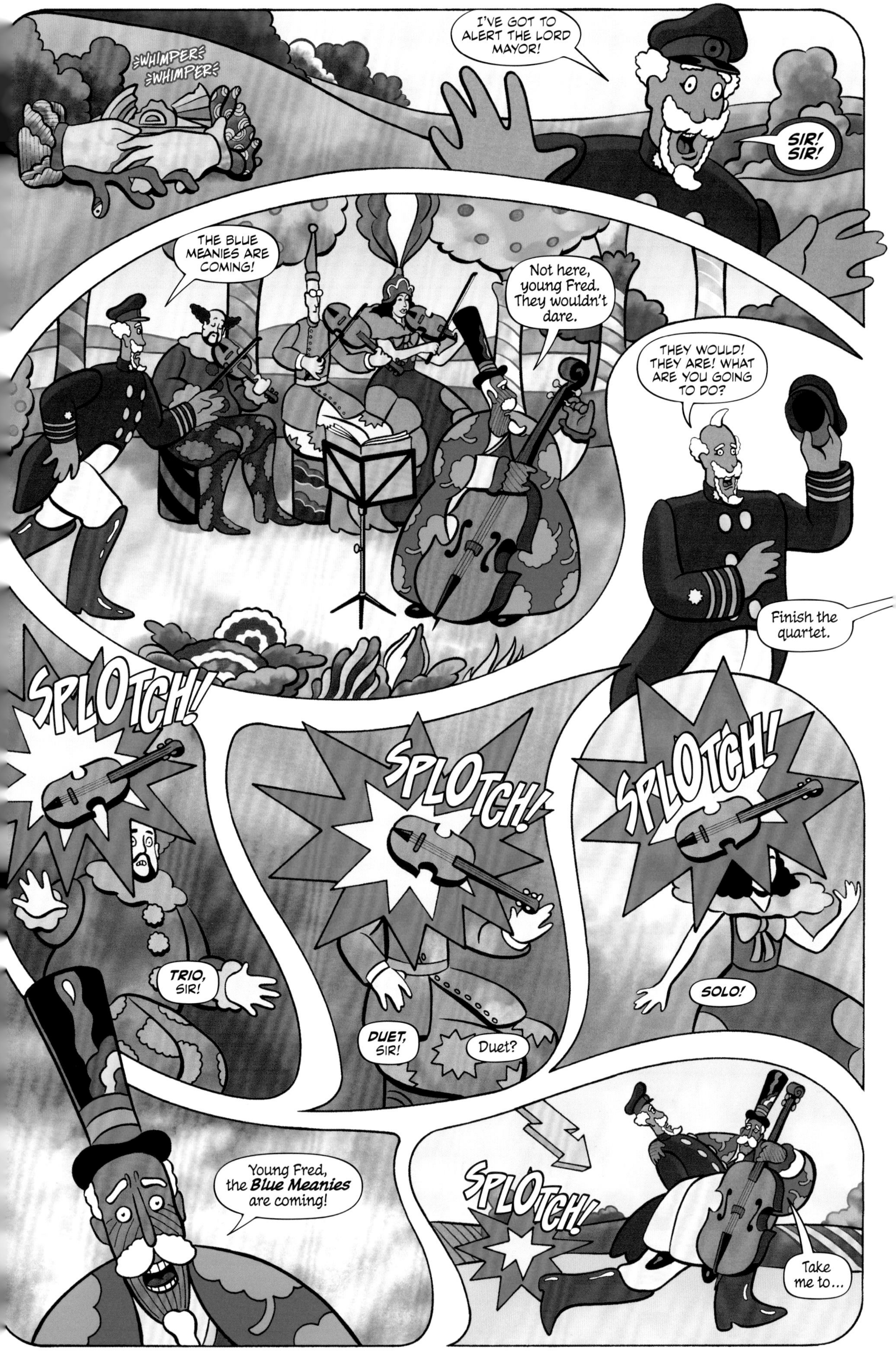

WHIMPER
WHIMPER
I'VE GOT TO ALERT THE LORD MAYOR!
SIR! SIR!
THE BLUE MEANIES ARE COMING!
Not here, young Fred. They wouldn't dare.
THEY WOULD! THEY ARE! WHAT ARE YOU GOING TO DO?
Finish the quartet.
SPLOTCH!
TRIO, SIR!
SPLOTCH!
DUET, SIR!
Duet?
SPLOTCH!
SOLO!
Young Fred, the Blue Meanies are coming!
SPLOTCH!
Take me to...

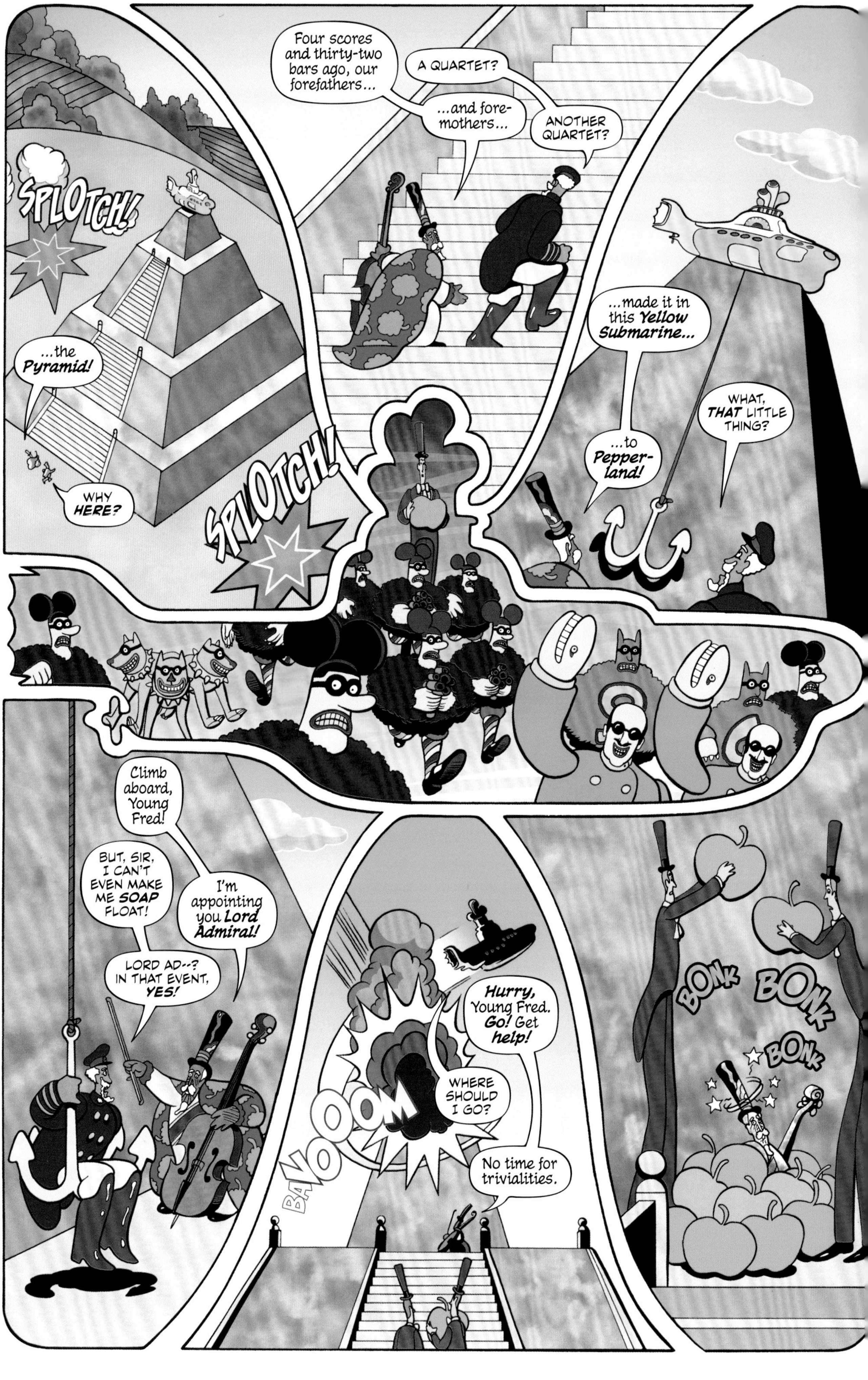
SPLOTCH!
...the Pyramid!
WHY HERE?
Four scores and thirty-two bars ago, our forefathers...
...and fore-mothers...
A QUARTET?
ANOTHER QUARTET?
...made it in this Yellow Submarine...
...to Pepper-land!
WHAT, THAT LITTLE THING?
SPLOTCH!
Climb aboard, Young Fred!
BUT, SIR, I CAN'T EVEN MAKE ME SOAP FLOAT!
I'm appointing you Lord Admiral!
LORD AD--? IN THAT EVENT, YES!
Hurry, Young Fred. Go! Get help!
WHERE SHOULD I GO?
No time for trivialities.
BAVOOOM
BONK
BONK
BONK

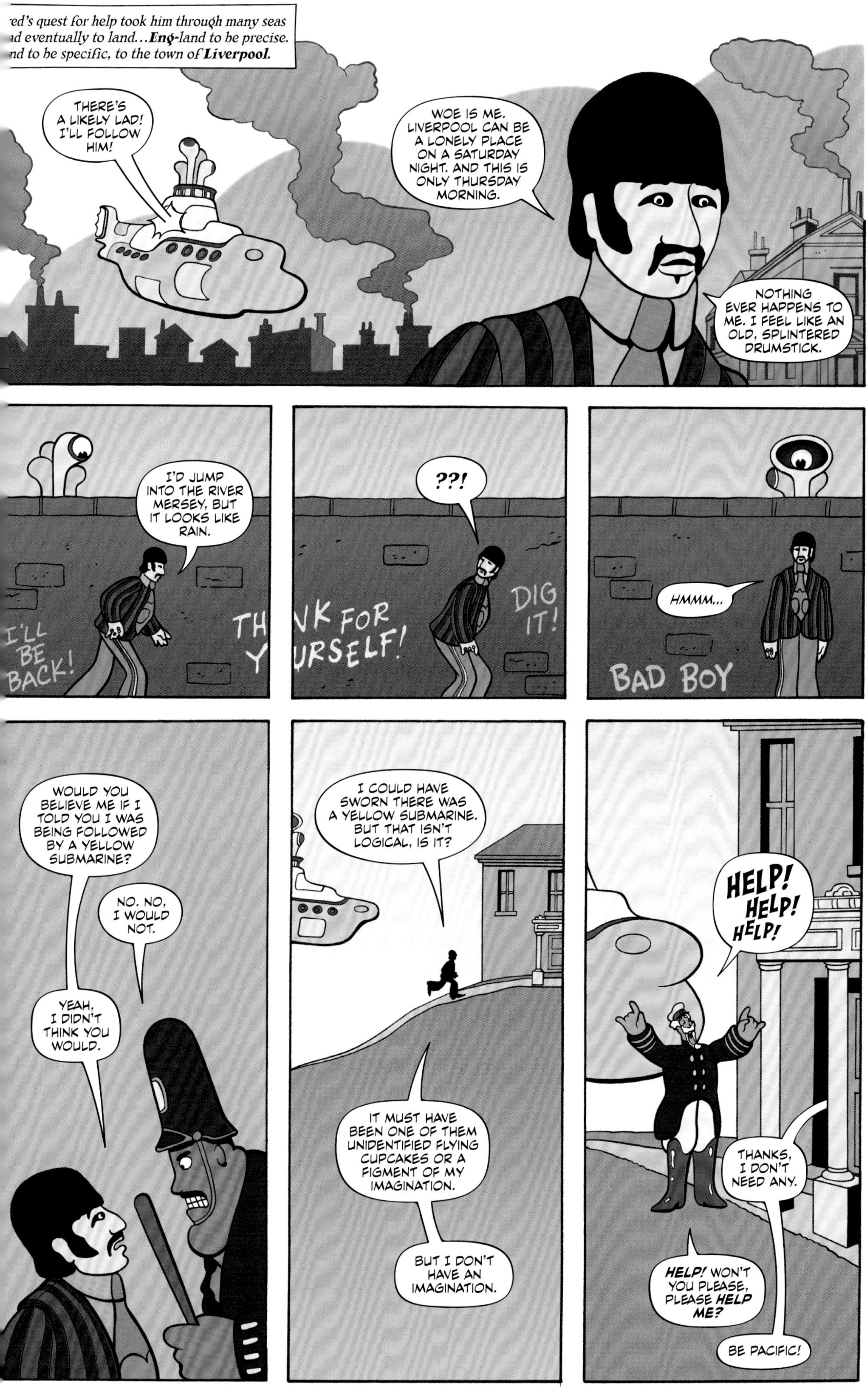
red's quest for help took him through many seas nd eventually to land…Eng-land to be precise. nd to be specific, to the town of Liverpool.
THERE'S A LIKELY LAD! I'LL FOLLOW HIM!
WOE IS ME. LIVERPOOL CAN BE A LONELY PLACE ON A SATURDAY NIGHT. AND THIS IS ONLY THURSDAY MORNING.
NOTHING EVER HAPPENS TO ME. I FEEL LIKE AN OLD, SPLINTERED DRUMSTICK.
I'D JUMP INTO THE RIVER MERSEY, BUT IT LOOKS LIKE RAIN.
I'LL BE BACK!
TH NK FOR Y URSELF!
??!
DIG IT!
HMMM...
BAD BOY
WOULD YOU BELIEVE ME IF I TOLD YOU I WAS BEING FOLLOWED BY A YELLOW SUBMARINE?
NO. NO, I WOULD NOT.
YEAH, I DIDN'T THINK YOU WOULD.
I COULD HAVE SWORN THERE WAS A YELLOW SUBMARINE. BUT THAT ISN'T LOGICAL, IS IT?
IT MUST HAVE BEEN ONE OF THEM UNIDENTIFIED FLYING CUPCAKES OR A FIGMENT OF MY IMAGINATION.
BUT I DON'T HAVE AN IMAGINATION.
HELP! HELP! HELP!
THANKS, I DON'T NEED ANY.
HELP! WON'T YOU PLEASE, PLEASE HELP ME?
BE PACIFIC!

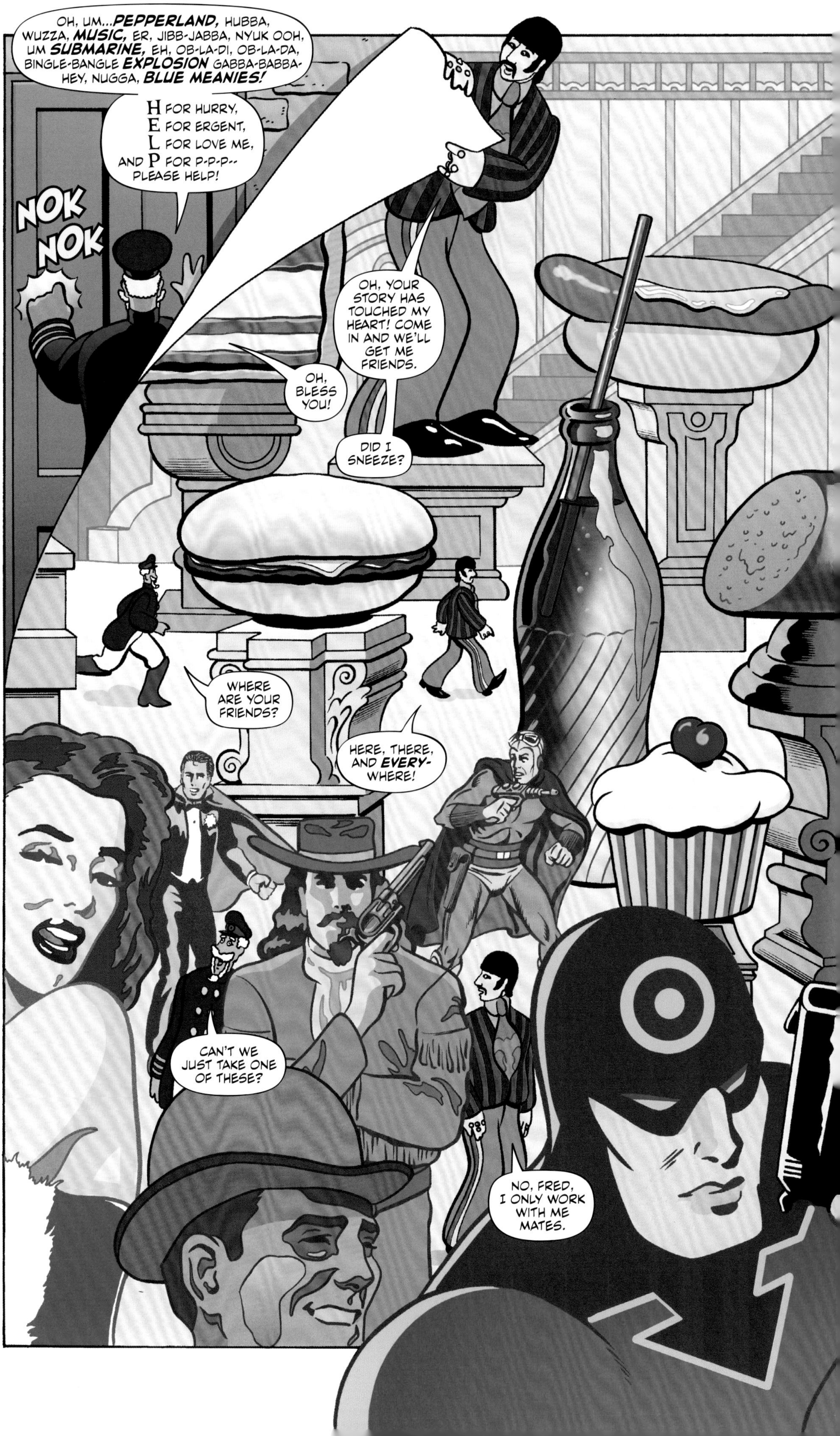
OH, UM...**PEPPERLAND,** HUBBA, WUZZA, **MUSIC,** ER, JIBB-JABBA, NYUK OOH, UM **SUBMARINE,** EH, OB-LA-DI, OB-LA-DA, BINGLE-BANGLE **EXPLOSION** GABBA-BABBA-HEY, NUGGA, **BLUE MEANIES!**
H FOR HURRY, E FOR ERGENT, L FOR LOVE ME, AND P FOR P-P-P-- PLEASE HELP!
NOK NOK
OH, YOUR STORY HAS TOUCHED MY HEART! COME IN AND WE'LL GET ME FRIENDS.
OH, BLESS YOU!
DID I SNEEZE?
WHERE ARE YOUR FRIENDS?
HERE, THERE, AND **EVERY-**WHERE!
CAN'T WE JUST TAKE ONE OF THESE?
NO, FRED, I ONLY WORK WITH ME MATES.

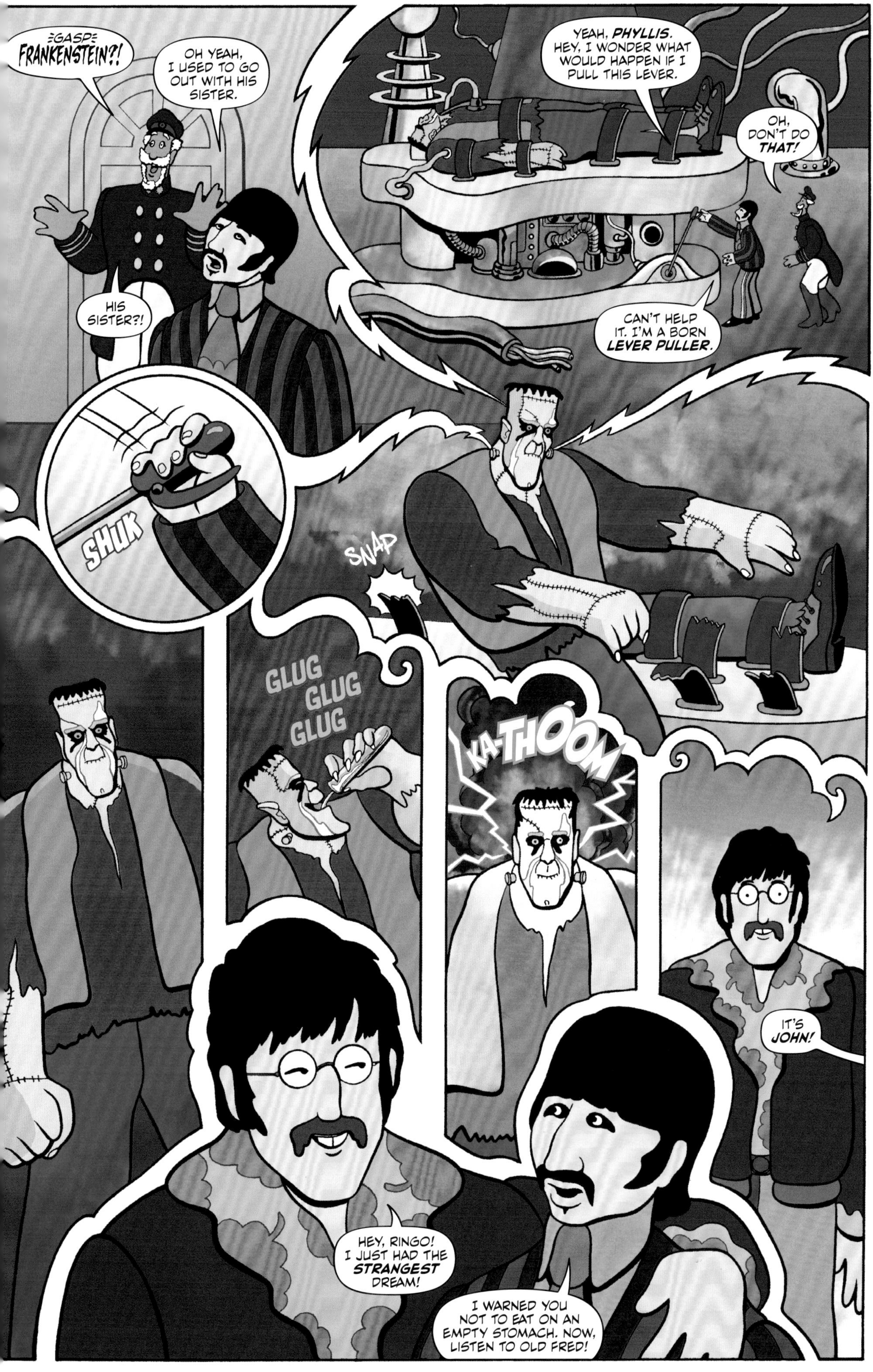

GASP
FRANKENSTEIN?!
OH YEAH, I USED TO GO OUT WITH HIS SISTER.
HIS SISTER?!
YEAH, PHYLLIS. HEY, I WONDER WHAT WOULD HAPPEN IF I PULL THIS LEVER.
OH, DON'T DO THAT!
CAN'T HELP IT. I'M A BORN LEVER PULLER.
SHUK
SNAP
GLUG GLUG GLUG
KA-THOOM
IT'S JOHN!
HEY, RINGO! I JUST HAD THE STRANGEST DREAM!
I WARNED YOU NOT TO EAT ON AN EMPTY STOMACH. NOW, LISTEN TO OLD FRED!

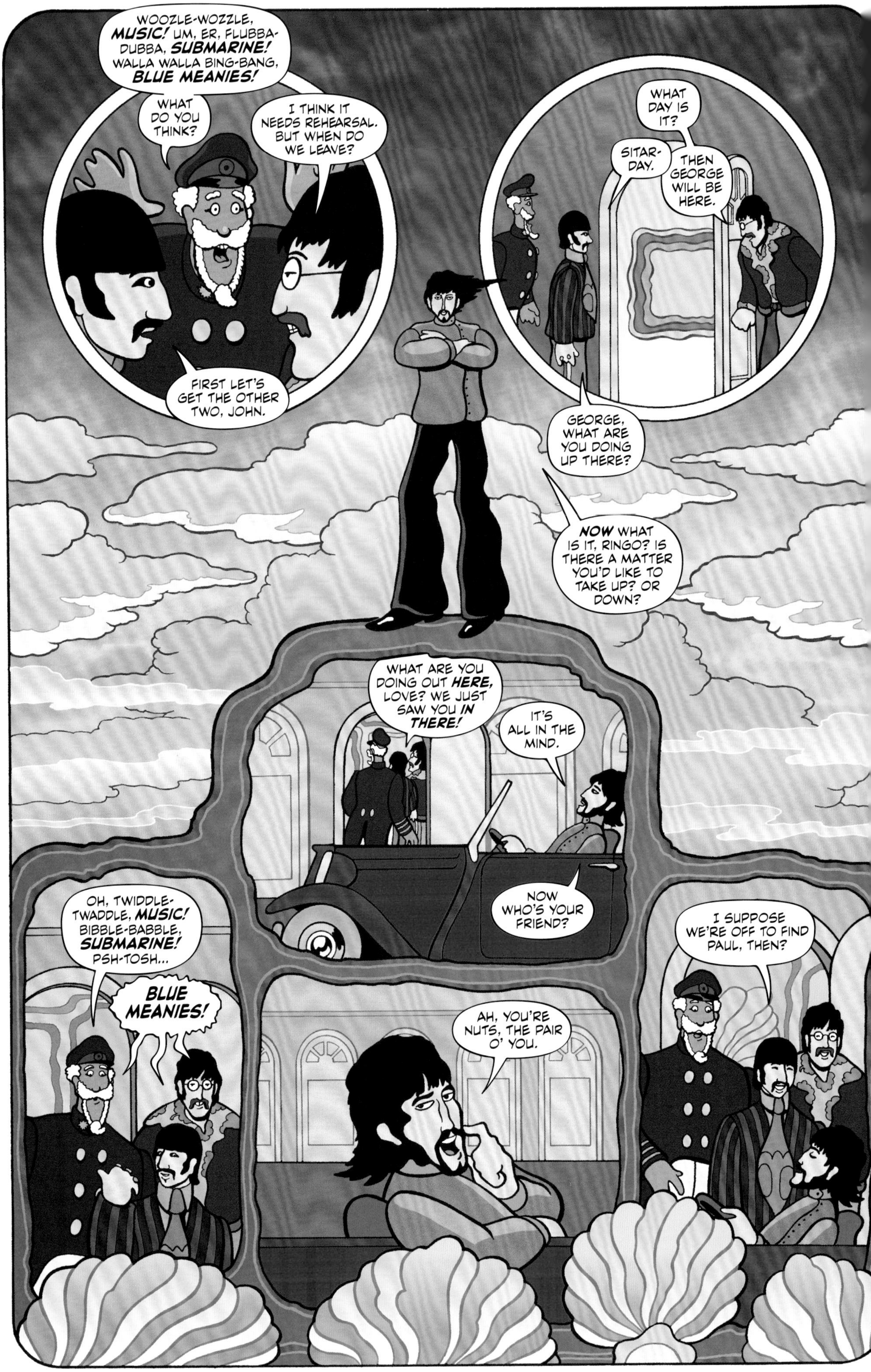
WOOZLE-WOZZLE, **MUSIC!** UM, ER, FLUBBA-DUBBA, **SUBMARINE!** WALLA WALLA BING-BANG, **BLUE MEANIES!**
WHAT DO YOU THINK?
I THINK IT NEEDS REHEARSAL. BUT WHEN DO WE LEAVE?
FIRST LET'S GET THE OTHER TWO, JOHN.
WHAT DAY IS IT?
SITAR-DAY.
THEN GEORGE WILL BE HERE.
GEORGE, WHAT ARE YOU DOING UP THERE?
NOW WHAT IS IT, RINGO? IS THERE A MATTER YOU'D LIKE TO TAKE UP? OR DOWN?
WHAT ARE YOU DOING OUT ***HERE,*** LOVE? WE JUST SAW YOU ***IN THERE!***
IT'S ALL IN THE MIND.
NOW WHO'S YOUR FRIEND?
OH, TWIDDLE-TWADDLE, **MUSIC!** BIBBLE-BABBLE, **SUBMARINE!** PSH-TOSH...
BLUE MEANIES!
AH, YOU'RE NUTS, THE PAIR O' YOU.
I SUPPOSE WE'RE OFF TO FIND PAUL, THEN?

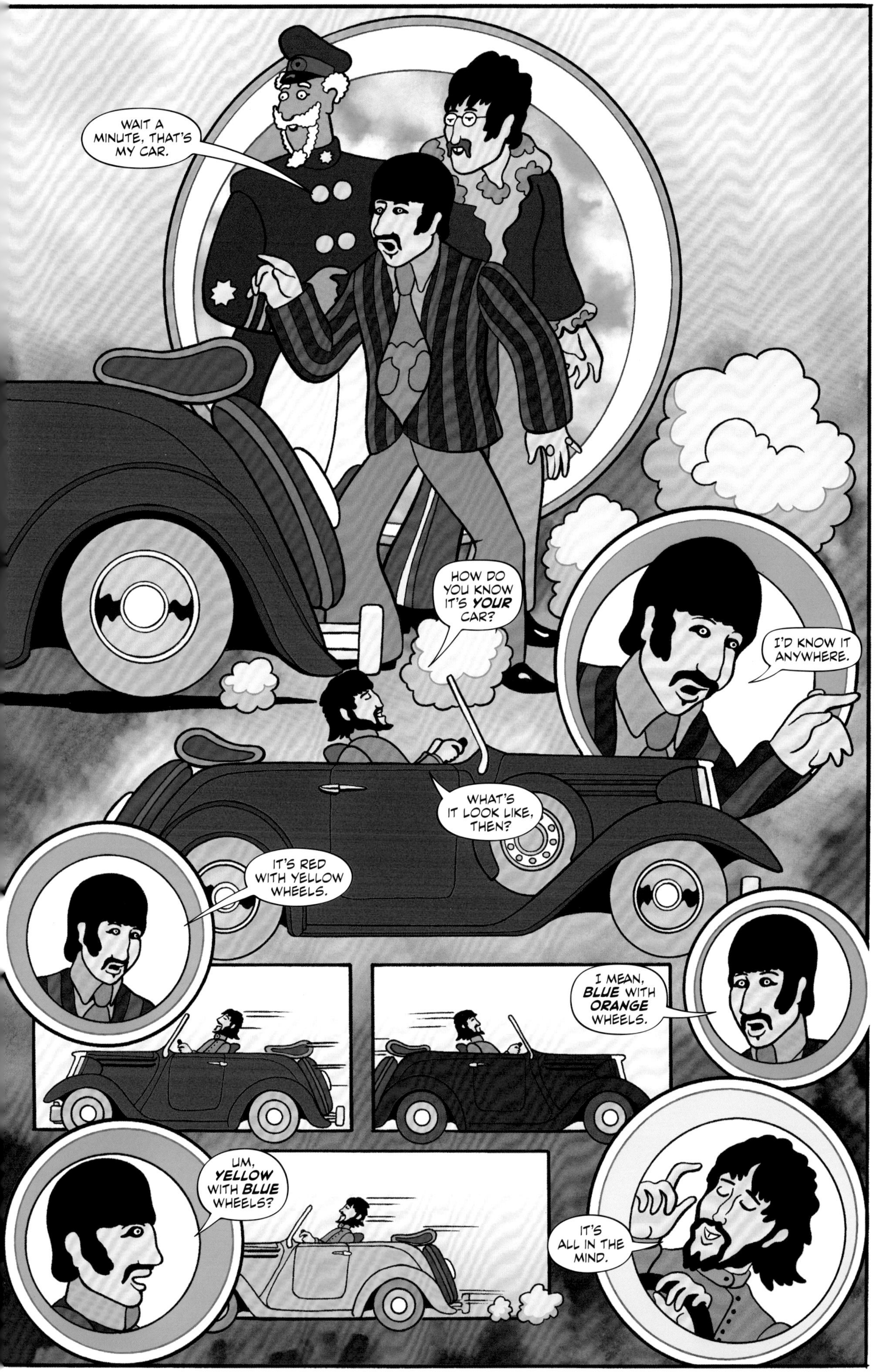

WAIT A MINUTE, THAT'S MY CAR.
HOW DO YOU KNOW IT'S **YOUR** CAR?
I'D KNOW IT ANYWHERE.
WHAT'S IT LOOK LIKE, THEN?
IT'S RED WITH YELLOW WHEELS.
I MEAN, **BLUE** WITH **ORANGE** WHEELS.
UM, **YELLOW** WITH **BLUE** WHEELS?
IT'S ALL IN THE MIND.

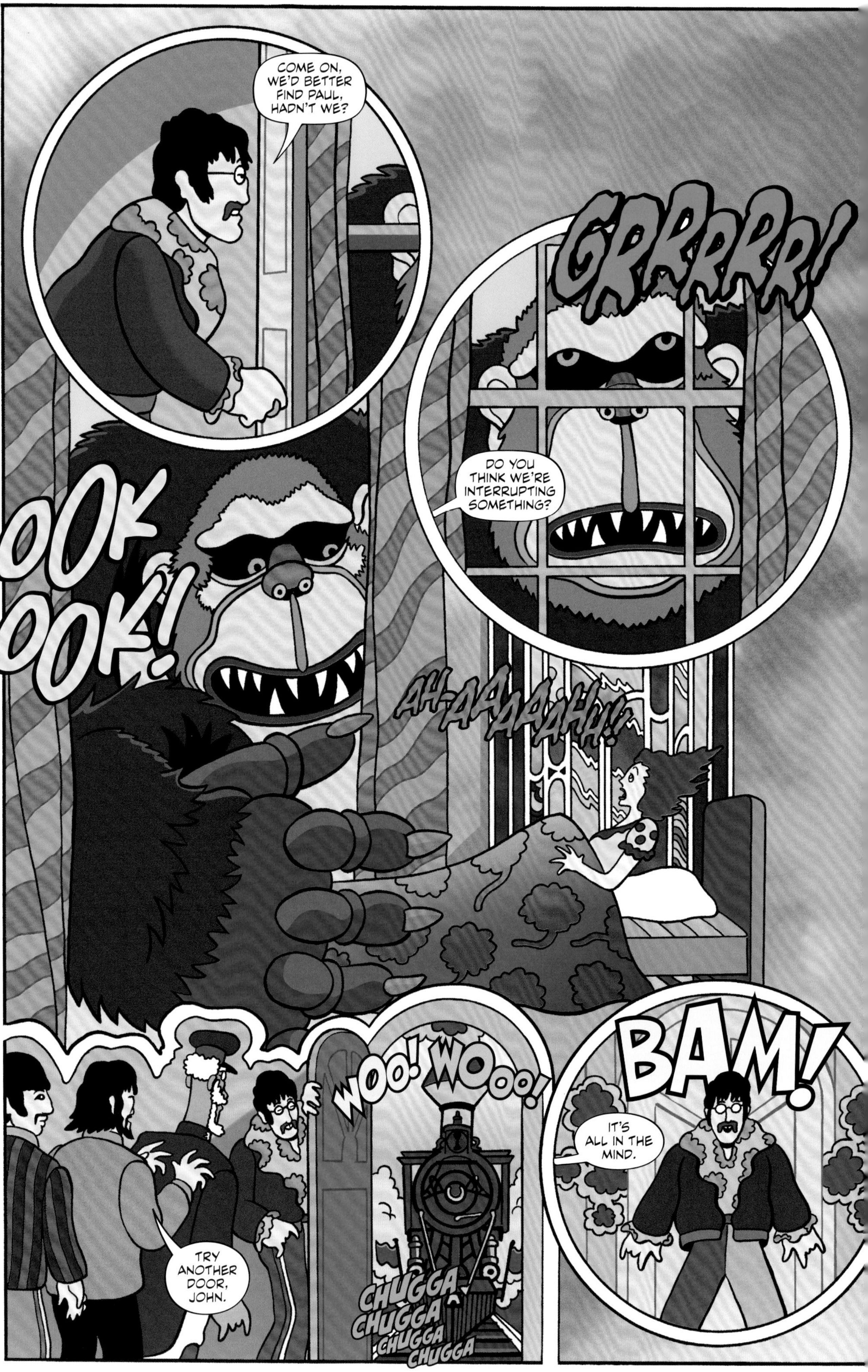
COME ON, WE'D BETTER FIND PAUL, HADN'T WE?
GRRRRR!
DO YOU THINK WE'RE INTERRUPTING SOMETHING?
OOK OOK!
AH-AAAAAHH!
TRY ANOTHER DOOR, JOHN.
WOO! WOOO!
CHUGGA CHUGGA CHUGGA CHUGGA
BAM!
IT'S ALL IN THE MIND.

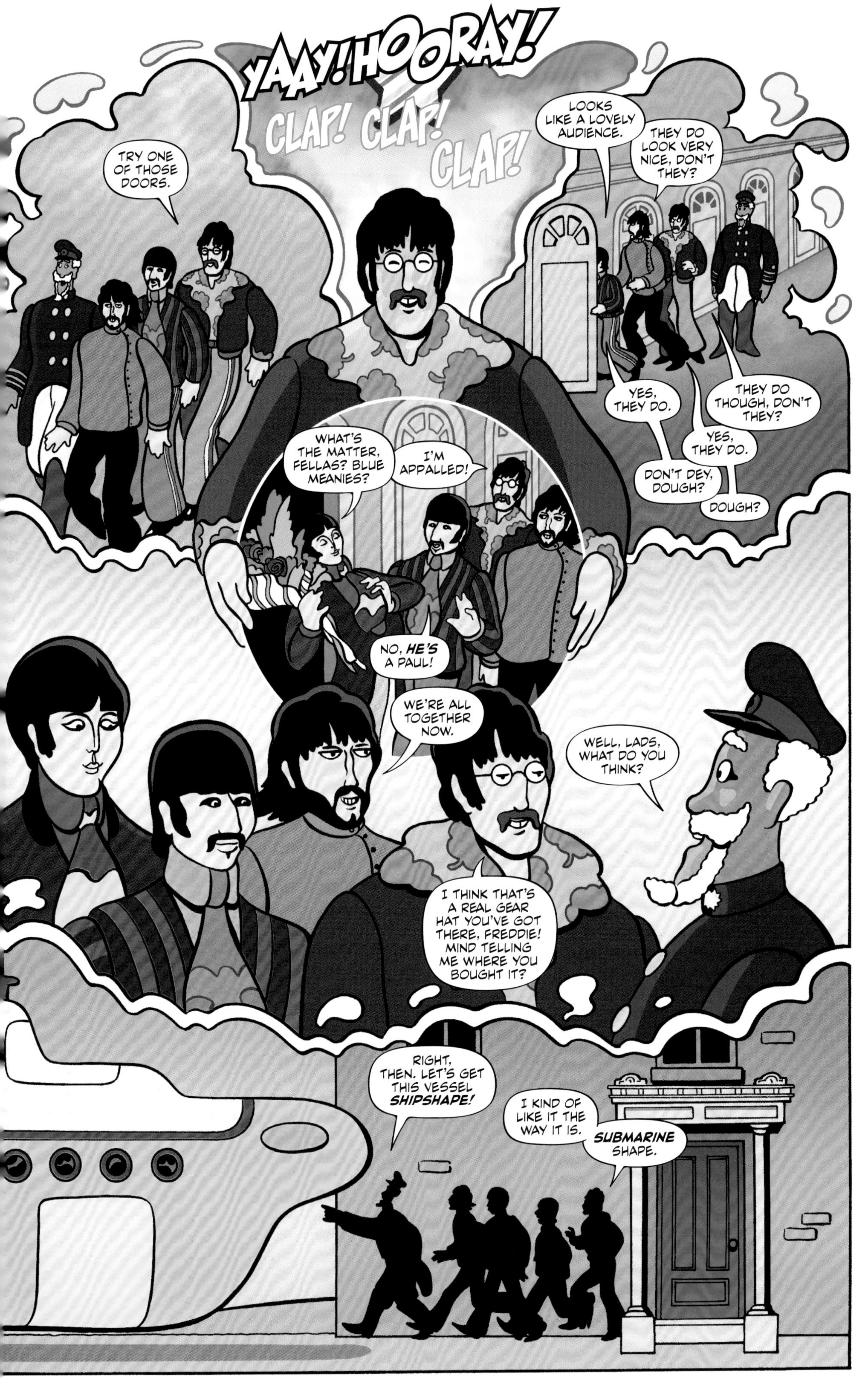
YAAY! HOORAY!
CLAP! CLAP! CLAP!
TRY ONE OF THOSE DOORS.
LOOKS LIKE A LOVELY AUDIENCE.
THEY DO LOOK VERY NICE, DON'T THEY?
YES, THEY DO.
THEY DO THOUGH, DON'T THEY?
YES, THEY DO.
DON'T DEY, DOUGH?
DOUGH?
WHAT'S THE MATTER, FELLAS? BLUE MEANIES?
I'M APPALLED!
NO, HE'S A PAUL!
WE'RE ALL TOGETHER NOW.
WELL, LADS, WHAT DO YOU THINK?
I THINK THAT'S A REAL GEAR HAT YOU'VE GOT THERE, FREDDIE! MIND TELLING ME WHERE YOU BOUGHT IT?
RIGHT, THEN. LET'S GET THIS VESSEL SHIPSHAPE!
I KIND OF LIKE IT THE WAY IT IS.
SUBMARINE SHAPE.

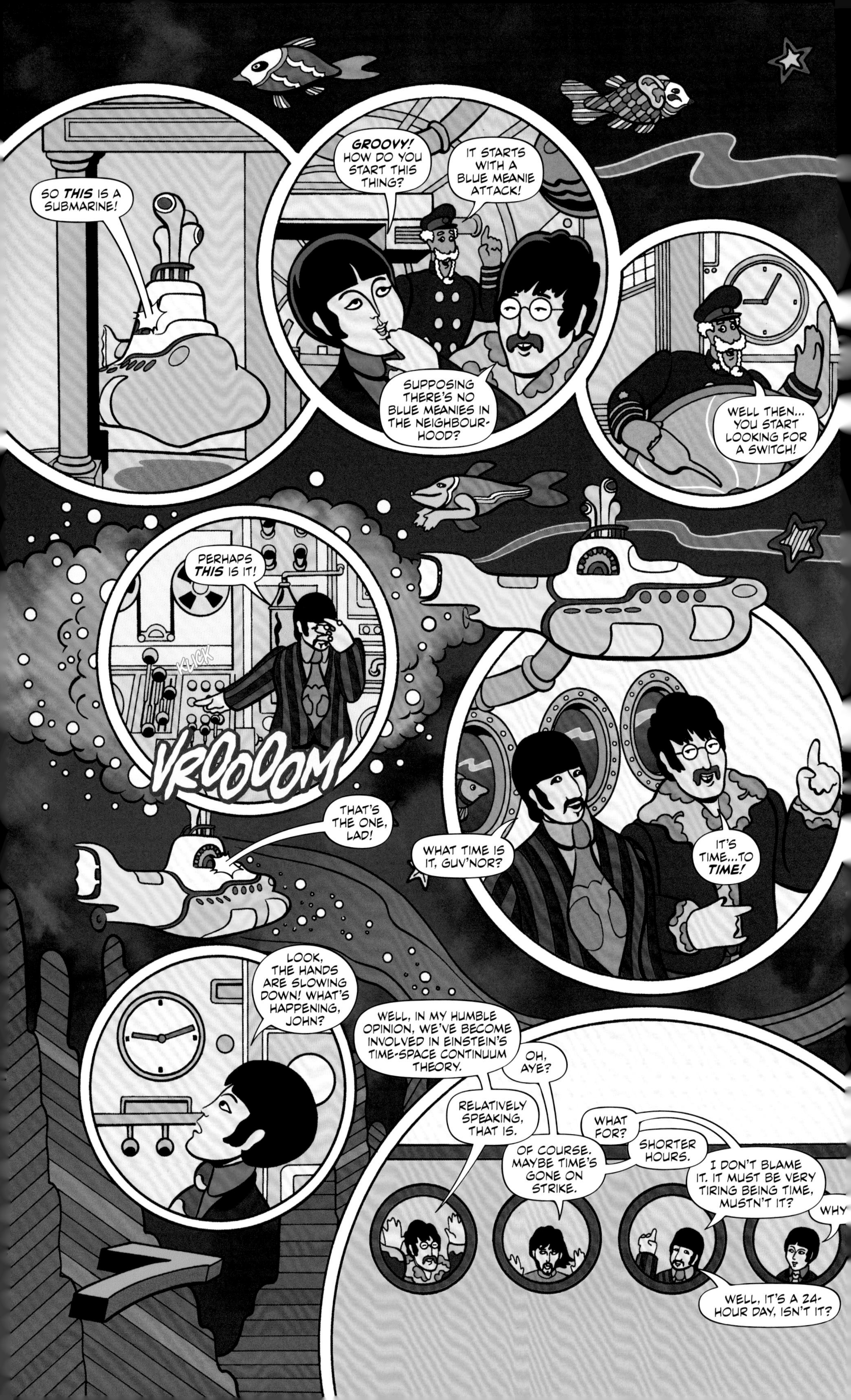
SO THIS IS A SUBMARINE!
GROOVY! HOW DO YOU START THIS THING?
IT STARTS WITH A BLUE MEANIE ATTACK!
SUPPOSING THERE'S NO BLUE MEANIES IN THE NEIGHBOURHOOD?
WELL THEN... YOU START LOOKING FOR A SWITCH!
PERHAPS THIS IS IT!
KLICK
VROOOOM
THAT'S THE ONE, LAD!
WHAT TIME IS IT, GUV'NOR?
IT'S TIME...TO TIME!
LOOK, THE HANDS ARE SLOWING DOWN! WHAT'S HAPPENING, JOHN?
WELL, IN MY HUMBLE OPINION, WE'VE BECOME INVOLVED IN EINSTEIN'S TIME-SPACE CONTINUUM THEORY.
OH, AYE?
RELATIVELY SPEAKING, THAT IS.
OF COURSE. MAYBE TIME'S GONE ON STRIKE.
WHAT FOR?
SHORTER HOURS.
I DON'T BLAME IT. IT MUST BE VERY TIRING BEING TIME, MUSTN'T IT?
WHY
WELL, IT'S A 24-HOUR DAY, ISN'T IT?

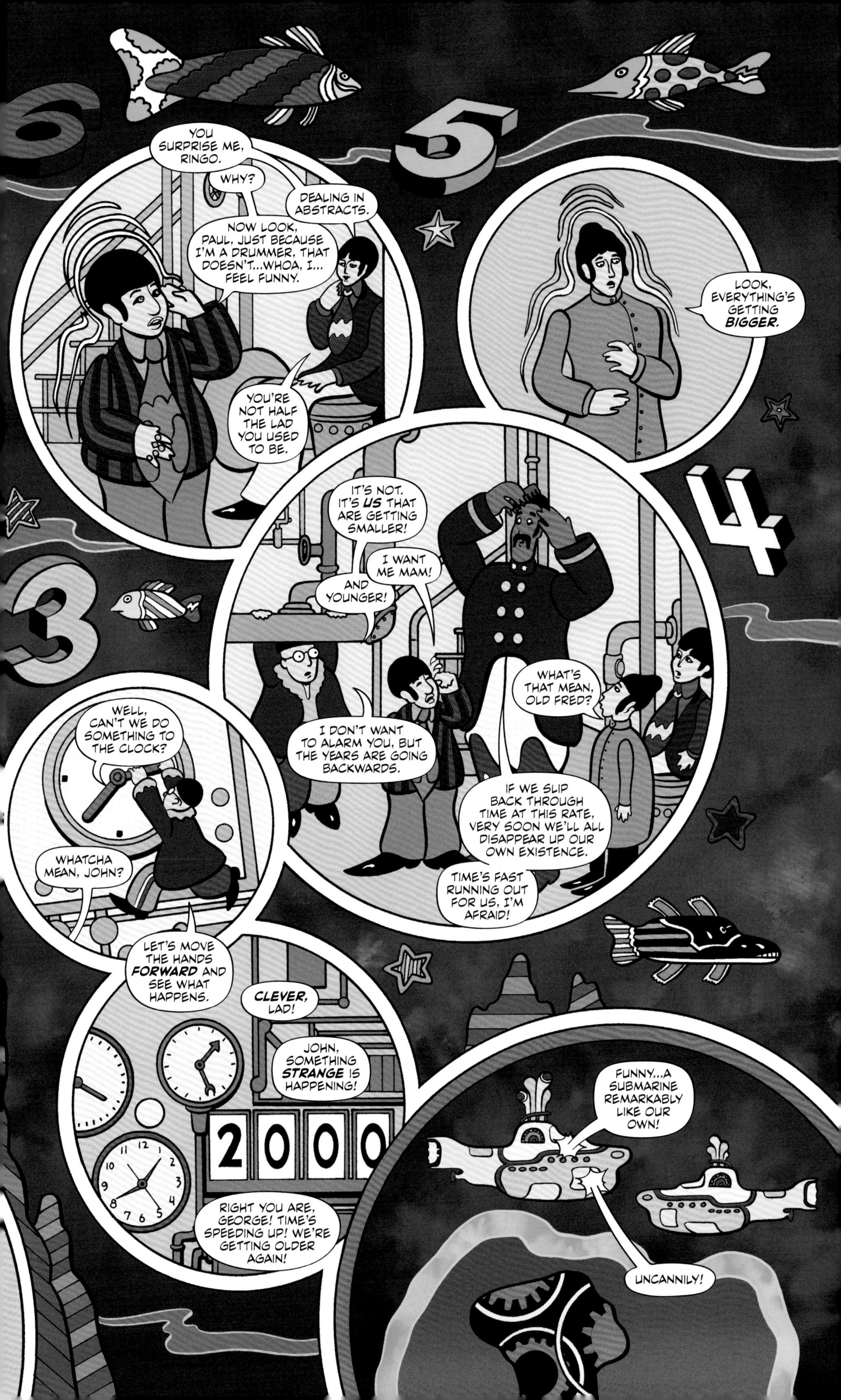
YOU SURPRISE ME, RINGO.
WHY?
DEALING IN ABSTRACTS.
NOW LOOK, PAUL, JUST BECAUSE I'M A DRUMMER, THAT DOESN'T...WHOA, I... FEEL FUNNY.
YOU'RE NOT HALF THE LAD YOU USED TO BE.
LOOK, EVERYTHING'S GETTING **BIGGER.**
IT'S NOT. IT'S ***US*** THAT ARE GETTING SMALLER!
I WANT ME MAM!
AND YOUNGER!
WHAT'S THAT MEAN, OLD FRED?
I DON'T WANT TO ALARM YOU, BUT THE YEARS ARE GOING BACKWARDS.
IF WE SLIP BACK THROUGH TIME AT THIS RATE, VERY SOON WE'LL ALL DISAPPEAR UP OUR OWN EXISTENCE.
TIME'S FAST RUNNING OUT FOR US, I'M AFRAID!
WELL, CAN'T WE DO SOMETHING TO THE CLOCK?
WHATCHA MEAN, JOHN?
LET'S MOVE THE HANDS ***FORWARD*** AND SEE WHAT HAPPENS.
CLEVER, LAD!
JOHN, SOMETHING ***STRANGE*** IS HAPPENING!
2000
RIGHT YOU ARE, GEORGE! TIME'S SPEEDING UP! WE'RE GETTING OLDER AGAIN!
FUNNY...A SUBMARINE REMARKABLY LIKE OUR OWN!
UNCANNILY!

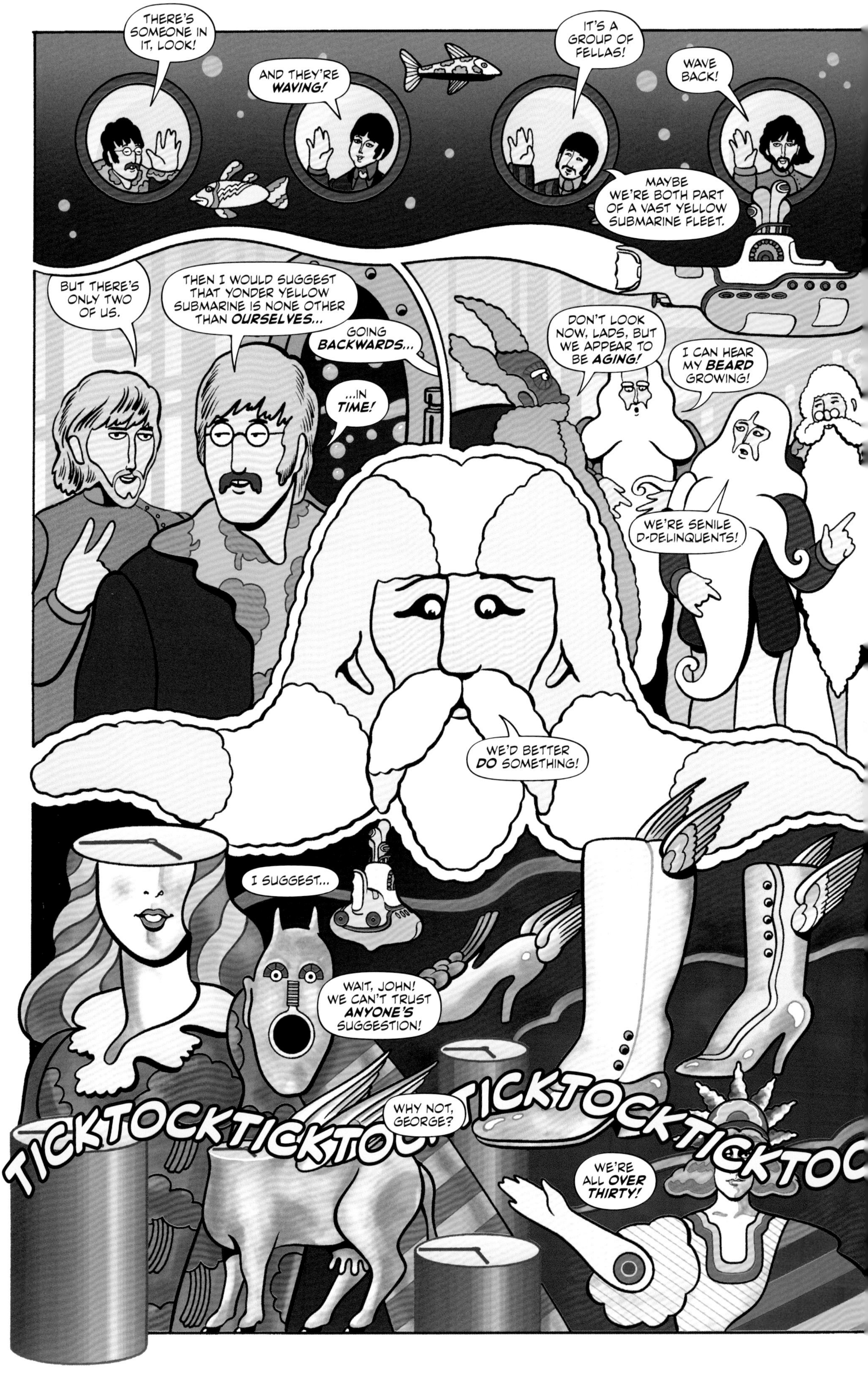
THERE'S SOMEONE IN IT, LOOK!
AND THEY'RE WAVING!
IT'S A GROUP OF FELLAS!
WAVE BACK!
MAYBE WE'RE BOTH PART OF A VAST YELLOW SUBMARINE FLEET.
BUT THERE'S ONLY TWO OF US.
THEN I WOULD SUGGEST THAT YONDER YELLOW SUBMARINE IS NONE OTHER THAN OURSELVES...
GOING BACKWARDS...
...IN TIME!
DON'T LOOK NOW, LADS, BUT WE APPEAR TO BE AGING!
I CAN HEAR MY BEARD GROWING!
WE'RE SENILE D-DELINQUENTS!
WE'D BETTER DO SOMETHING!
I SUGGEST...
WAIT, JOHN! WE CAN'T TRUST ANYONE'S SUGGESTION!
WHY NOT, GEORGE?
WE'RE ALL OVER THIRTY!
TICKTOCKTICKTOCKTICKTOCKTICKTOC

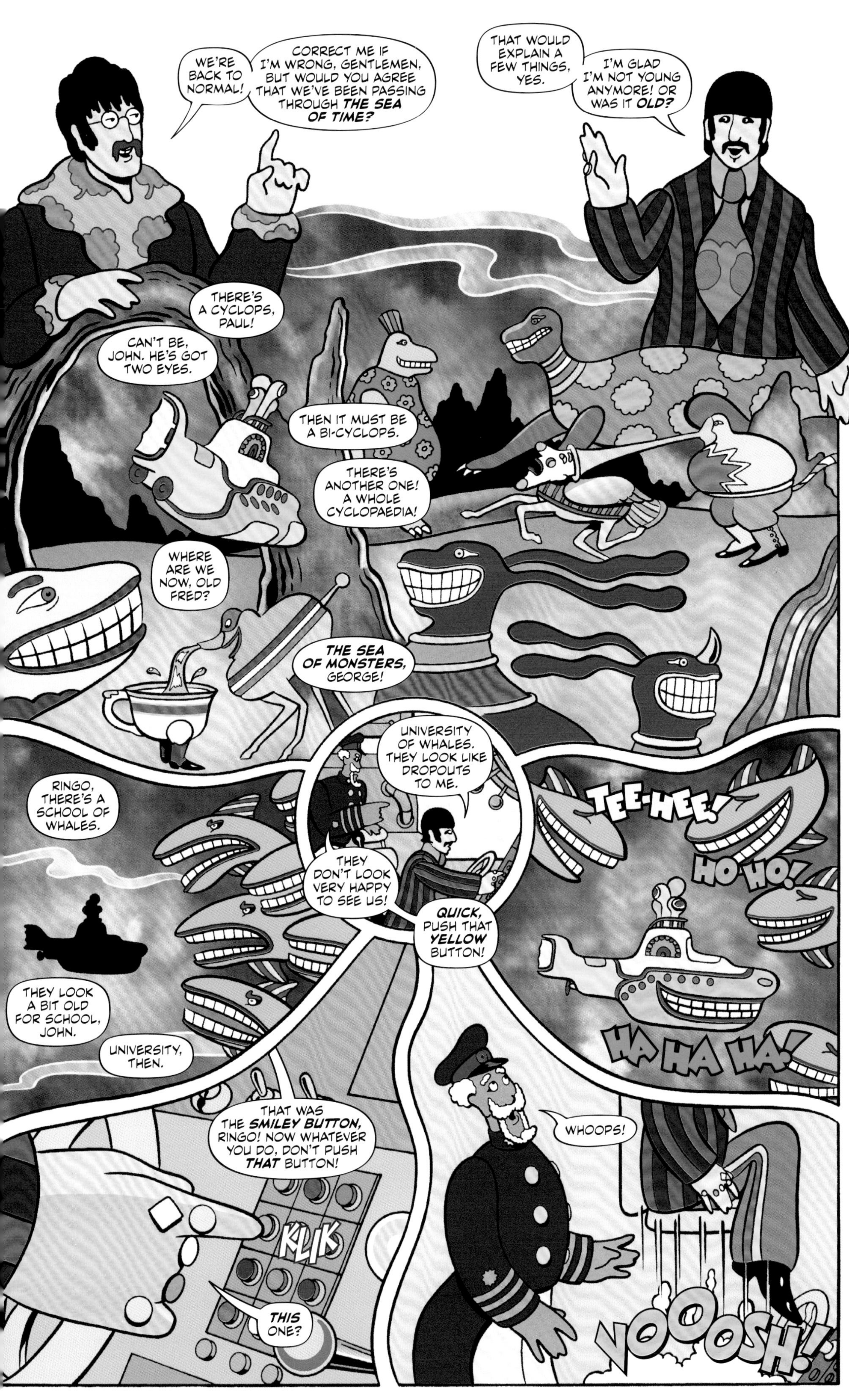
WE'RE BACK TO NORMAL!
CORRECT ME IF I'M WRONG, GENTLEMEN, BUT WOULD YOU AGREE THAT WE'VE BEEN PASSING THROUGH THE SEA OF TIME?
THAT WOULD EXPLAIN A FEW THINGS, YES.
I'M GLAD I'M NOT YOUNG ANYMORE! OR WAS IT OLD?
THERE'S A CYCLOPS, PAUL!
CAN'T BE, JOHN. HE'S GOT TWO EYES.
THEN IT MUST BE A BI-CYCLOPS.
THERE'S ANOTHER ONE! A WHOLE CYCLOPAEDIA!
WHERE ARE WE NOW, OLD FRED?
THE SEA OF MONSTERS, GEORGE!
RINGO, THERE'S A SCHOOL OF WHALES.
THEY LOOK A BIT OLD FOR SCHOOL, JOHN.
UNIVERSITY, THEN.
UNIVERSITY OF WHALES. THEY LOOK LIKE DROPOUTS TO ME.
THEY DON'T LOOK VERY HAPPY TO SEE US!
QUICK, PUSH THAT YELLOW BUTTON!
TEE-HEE!
HO HO!
HA HA HA!
THAT WAS THE SMILEY BUTTON, RINGO! NOW WHATEVER YOU DO, DON'T PUSH THAT BUTTON!
KLIK
THIS ONE?
WHOOPS!
VOOOOSH!!

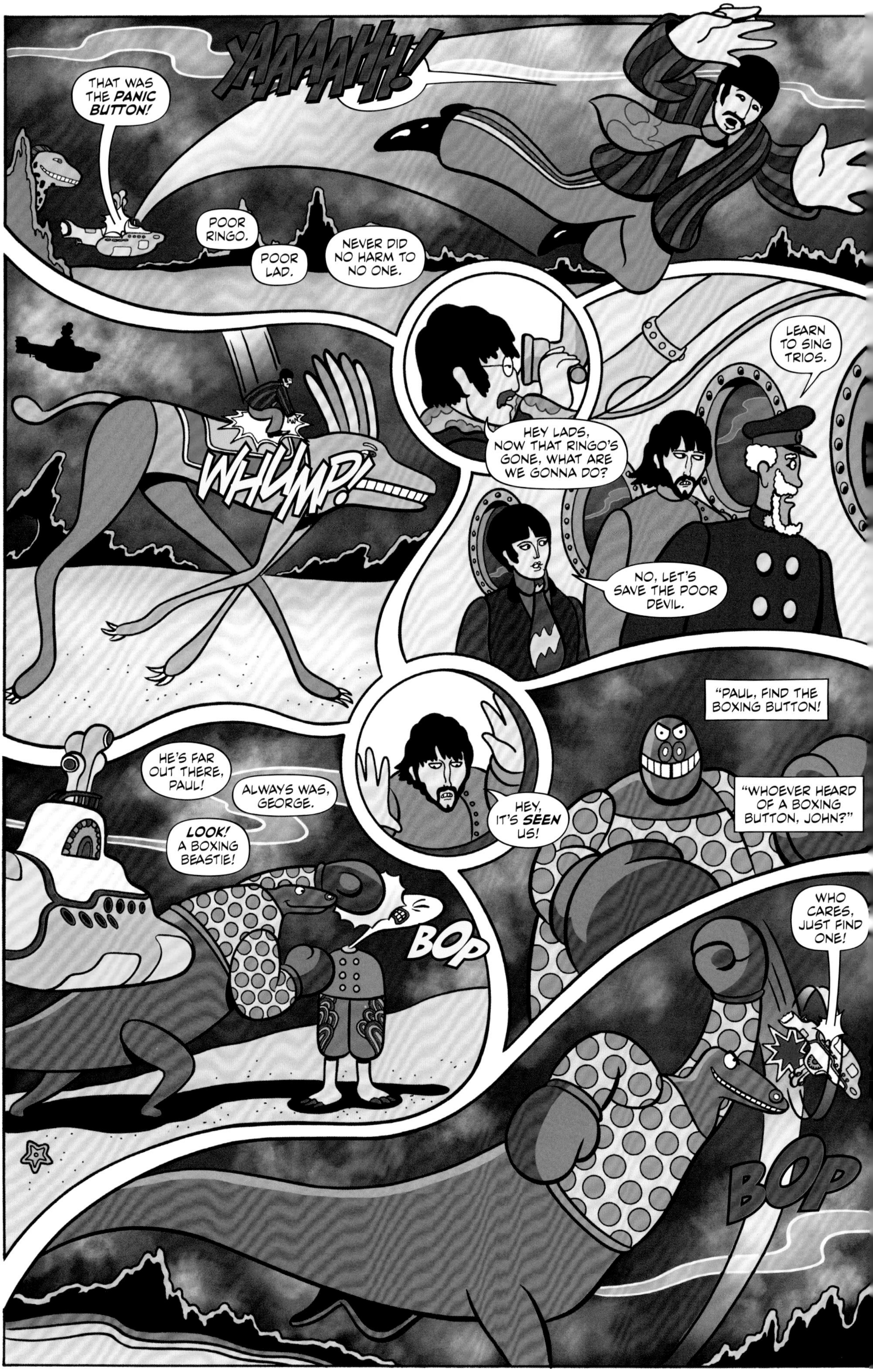
YAAAAHH!
THAT WAS THE PANIC BUTTON!
POOR RINGO.
POOR LAD.
NEVER DID NO HARM TO NO ONE.
WHUMP!
LEARN TO SING TRIOS.
HEY LADS, NOW THAT RINGO'S GONE, WHAT ARE WE GONNA DO?
NO, LET'S SAVE THE POOR DEVIL.
HE'S FAR OUT THERE, PAUL!
ALWAYS WAS, GEORGE.
LOOK! A BOXING BEASTIE!
HEY, IT'S SEEN US!
"PAUL, FIND THE BOXING BUTTON!
"WHOEVER HEARD OF A BOXING BUTTON, JOHN?"
BOP
WHO CARES, JUST FIND ONE!
BOP

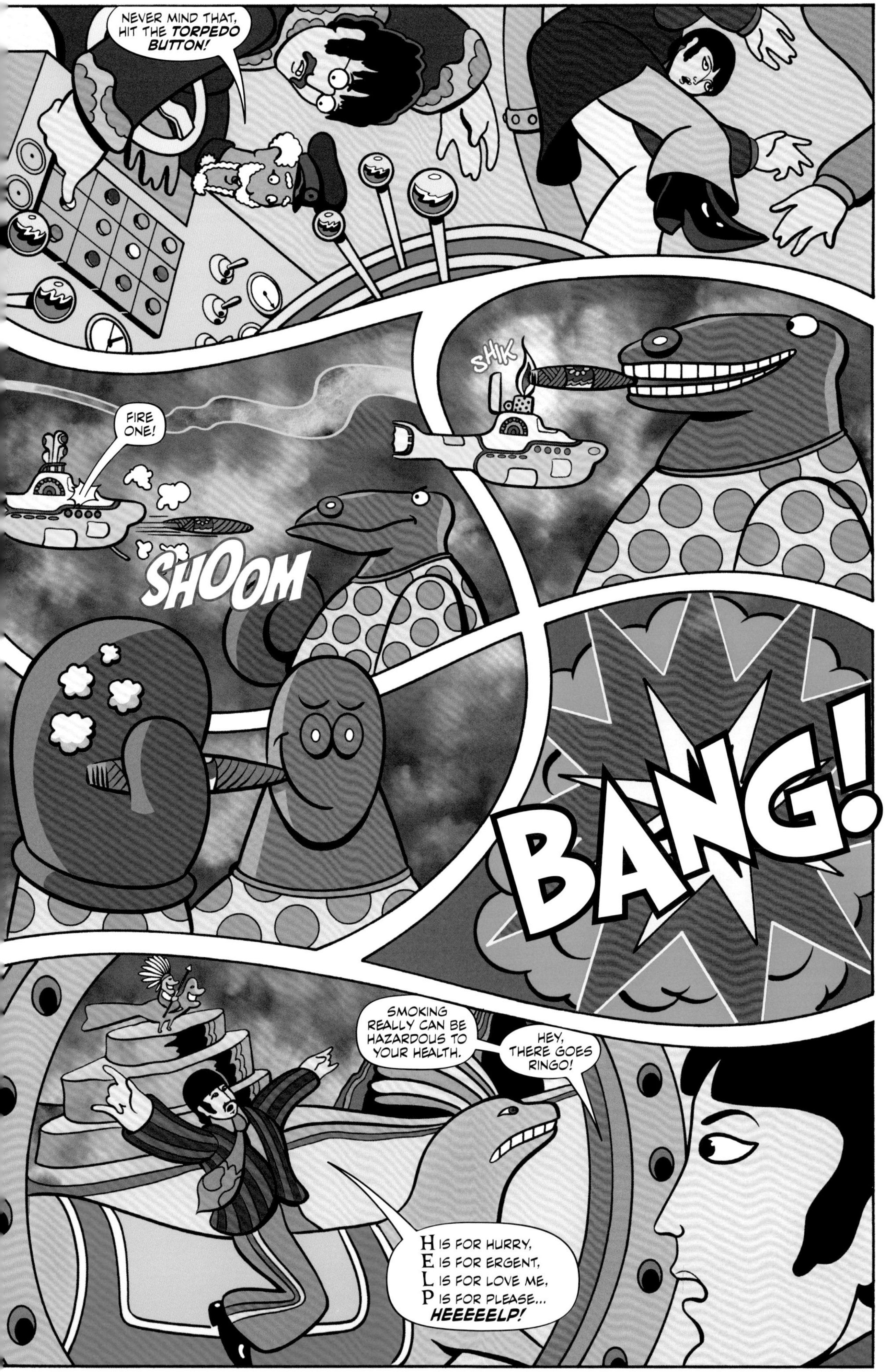
NEVER MIND THAT, HIT THE TORPEDO BUTTON!
FIRE ONE!
SHOOM
SHIK
BANG!
SMOKING REALLY CAN BE HAZARDOUS TO YOUR HEALTH.
HEY, THERE GOES RINGO!
H IS FOR HURRY,
E IS FOR ERGENT,
L IS FOR LOVE ME,
P IS FOR PLEASE...
HEEEEELP!

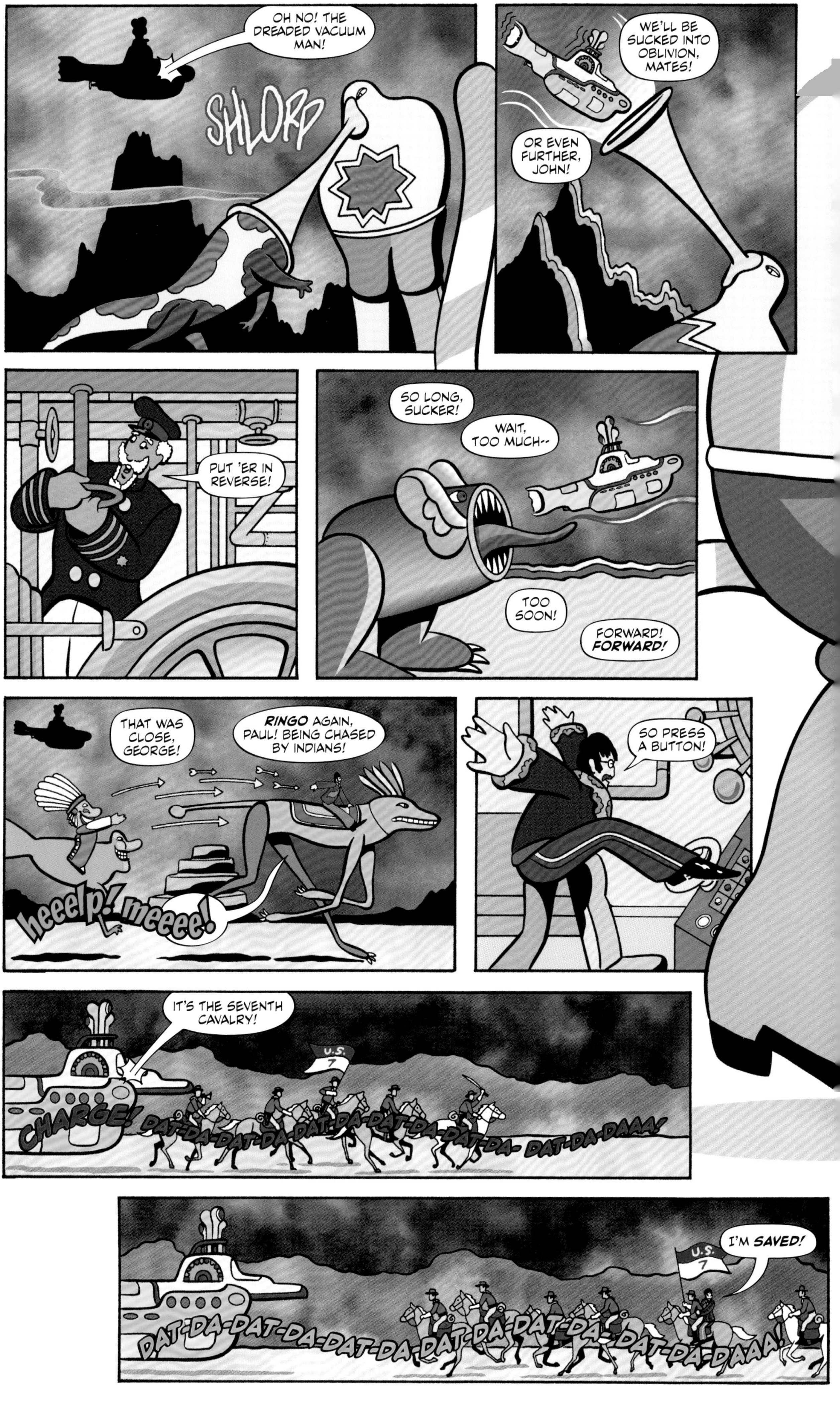
OH NO! THE DREADED VACUUM MAN!
SHLORP
WE'LL BE SUCKED INTO OBLIVION, MATES!
OR EVEN FURTHER, JOHN!
PUT 'ER IN REVERSE!
SO LONG, SUCKER!
WAIT, TOO MUCH--
TOO SOON!
FORWARD! FORWARD!
THAT WAS CLOSE, GEORGE!
RINGO AGAIN, PAUL! BEING CHASED BY INDIANS!
heeelp! meeee!
SO PRESS A BUTTON!
IT'S THE SEVENTH CAVALRY!
U.S. 7
CHARGE! DAT-DA-DAT-DA-DAT-DA-DAT-DA-DAT-DA- DAT-DA-DAAA!
I'M SAVED!
U.S. 7
DAT-DA-DAT-DA-DAT-DA-DAT-DA-DAT-DA-DAT-DA-DAAA!

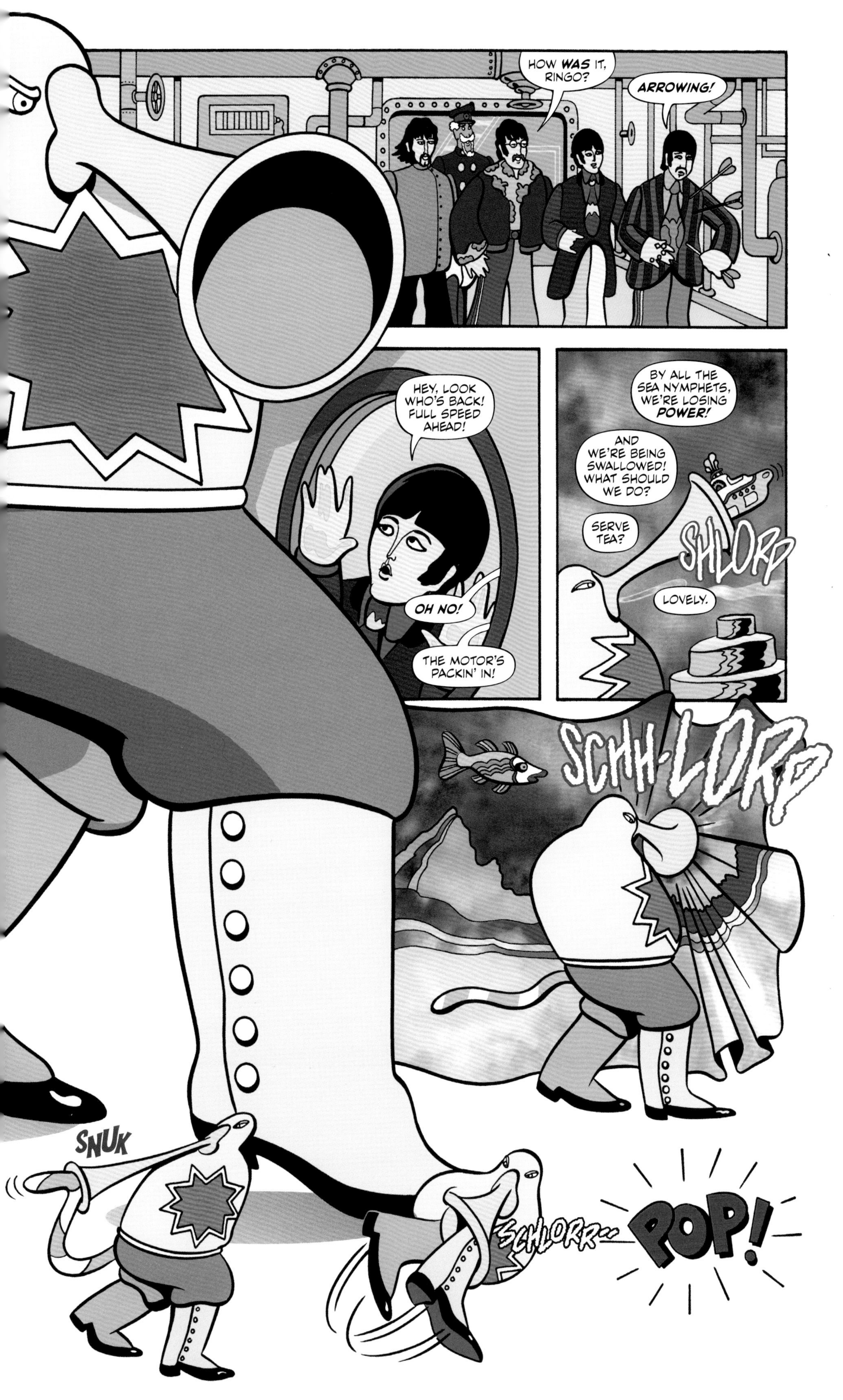

HOW WAS IT, RINGO?
ARROWING!
HEY, LOOK WHO'S BACK! FULL SPEED AHEAD!
OH NO!
THE MOTOR'S PACKIN' IN!
BY ALL THE SEA NYMPHETS, WE'RE LOSING POWER!
AND WE'RE BEING SWALLOWED! WHAT SHOULD WE DO?
SERVE TEA?
SHLORP
LOVELY.
SCHH-LORP
SNUK
SCHLORRR--
POP!

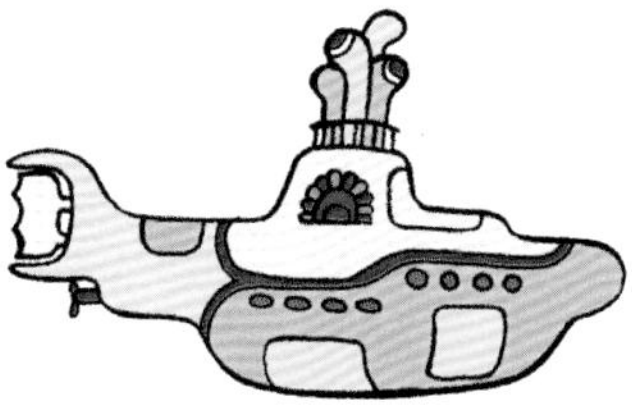

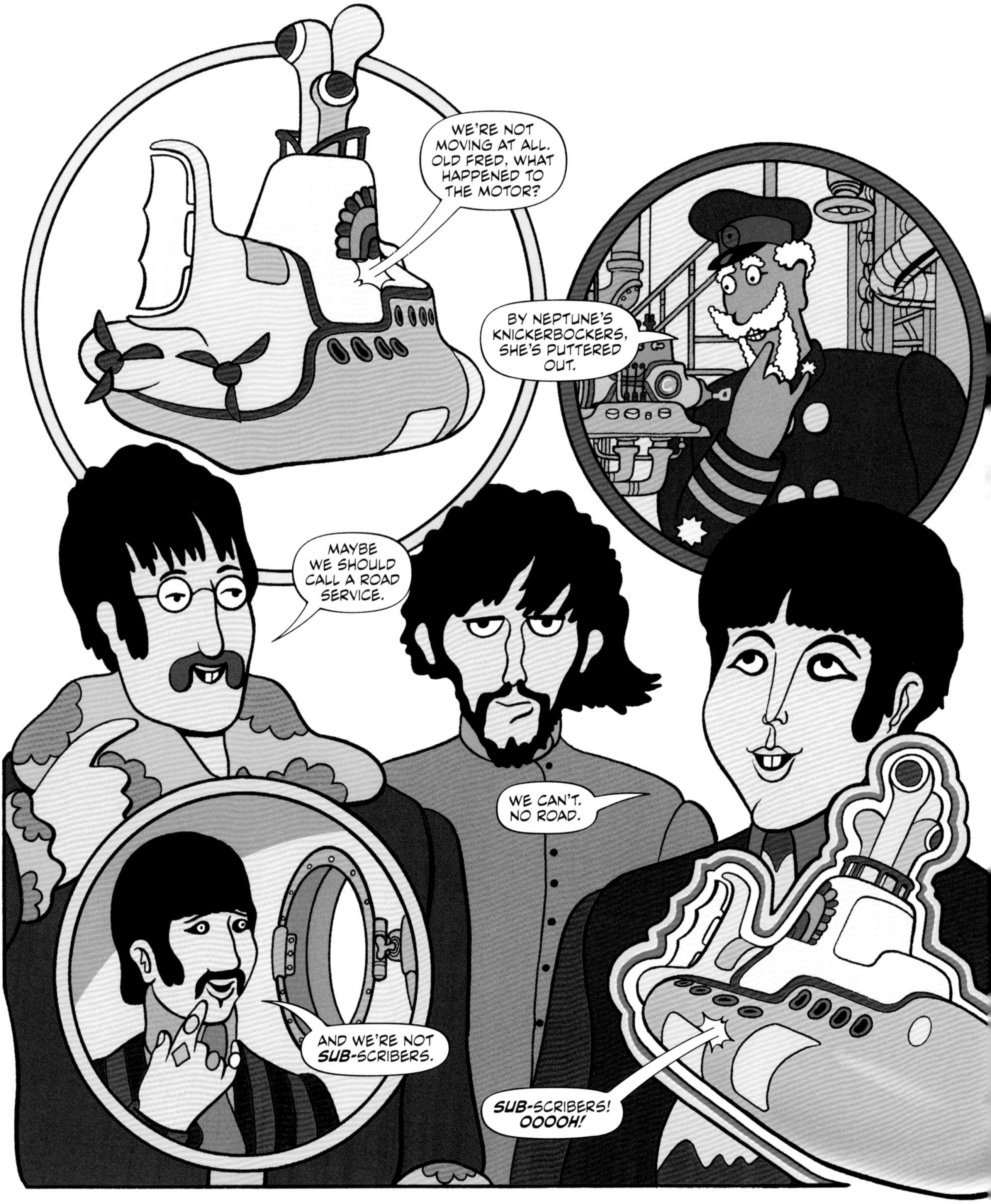
WE'RE NOT MOVING AT ALL. OLD FRED, WHAT HAPPENED TO THE MOTOR?
BY NEPTUNE'S KNICKERBOCKERS, SHE'S PUTTERED OUT.
MAYBE WE SHOULD CALL A ROAD SERVICE.
WE CAN'T. NO ROAD.
AND WE'RE NOT *SUB*-SCRIBERS.
SUB-SCRIBERS! *OOOOH!*

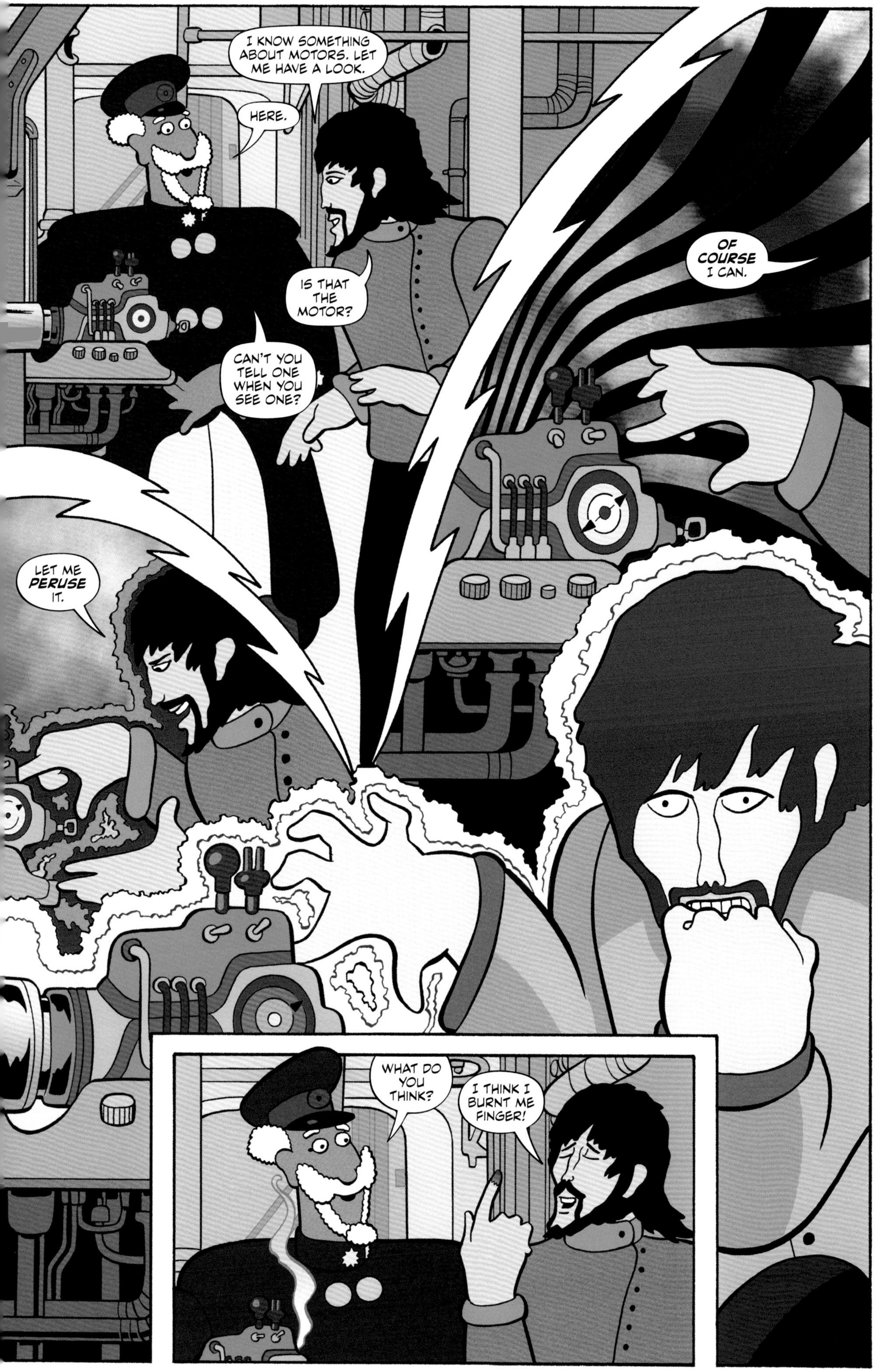
I KNOW SOMETHING ABOUT MOTORS. LET ME HAVE A LOOK.
HERE.
IS THAT THE MOTOR?
CAN'T YOU TELL ONE WHEN YOU SEE ONE?
OF COURSE I CAN.
LET ME PERUSE IT.
WHAT DO YOU THINK?
I THINK I BURNT ME FINGER!

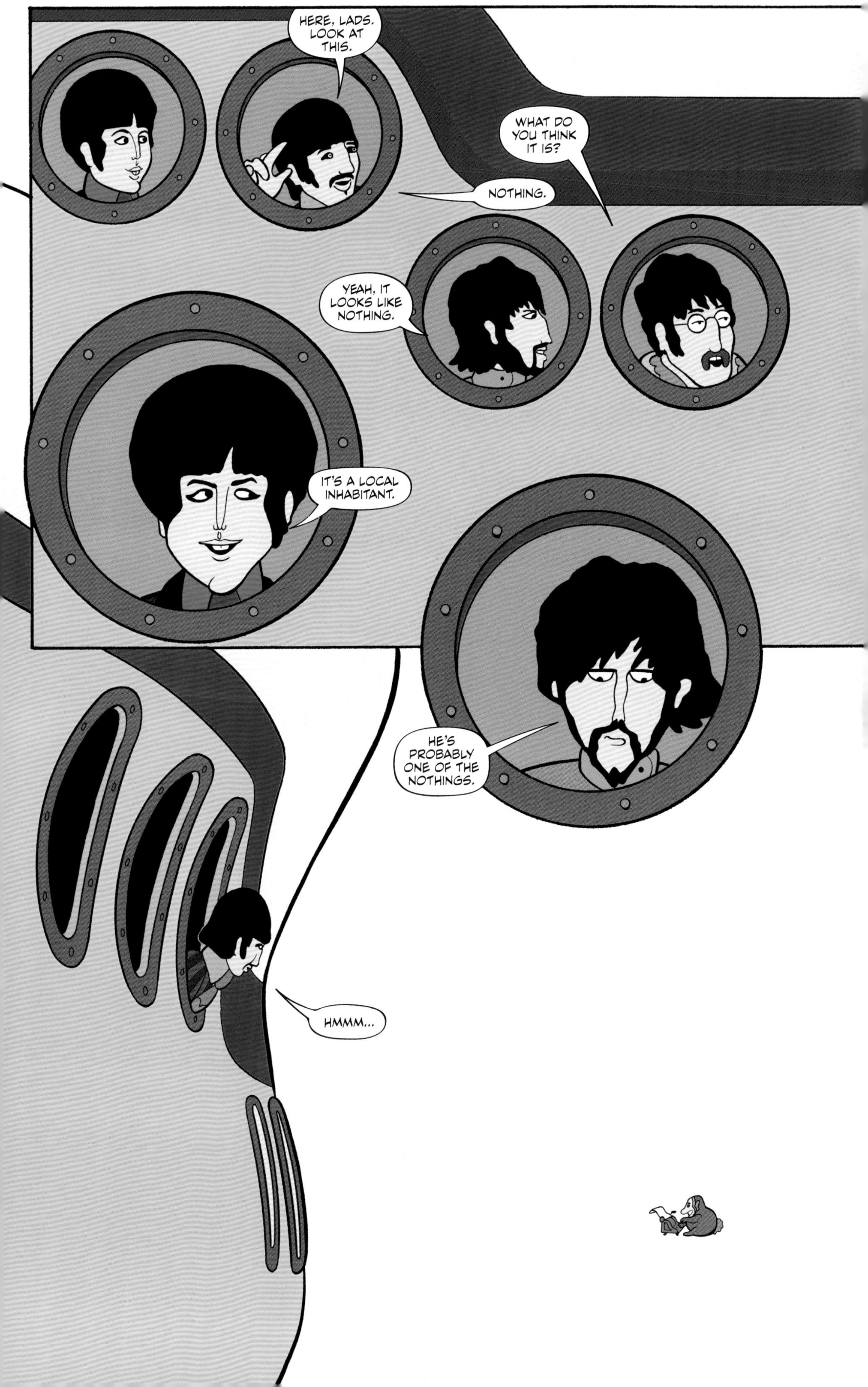
HERE, LADS. LOOK AT THIS.
WHAT DO YOU THINK IT IS?
NOTHING.
YEAH, IT LOOKS LIKE NOTHING.
IT'S A LOCAL INHABITANT.
HE'S PROBABLY ONE OF THE NOTHINGS.
HMMM...

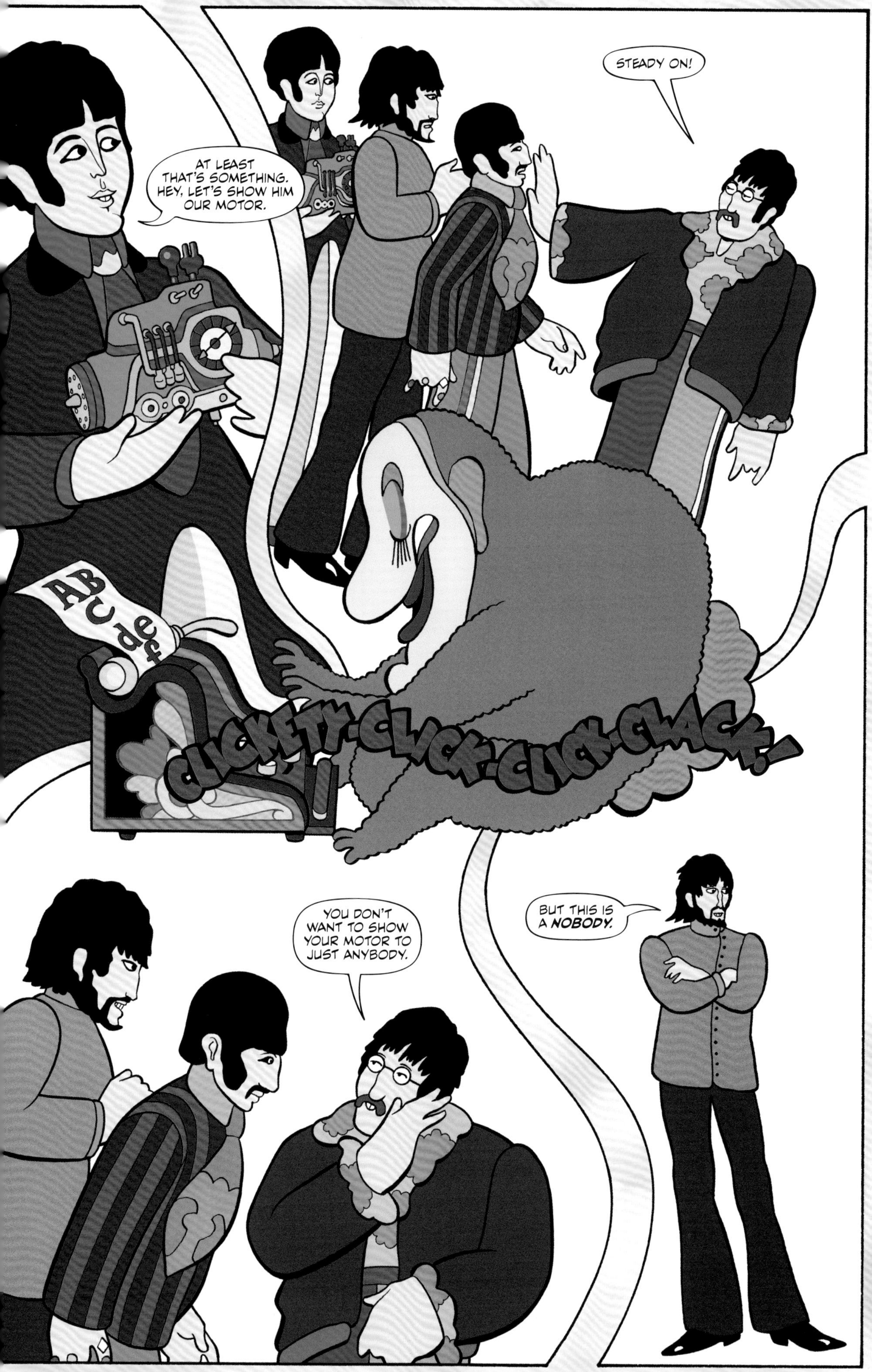
AT LEAST THAT'S SOMETHING. HEY, LET'S SHOW HIM OUR MOTOR.
STEADY ON!
ABCdef
CLICKETY-CLICK-CLICK-CLACK!
YOU DON'T WANT TO SHOW YOUR MOTOR TO JUST ANYBODY.
BUT THIS IS A **NOBODY**.

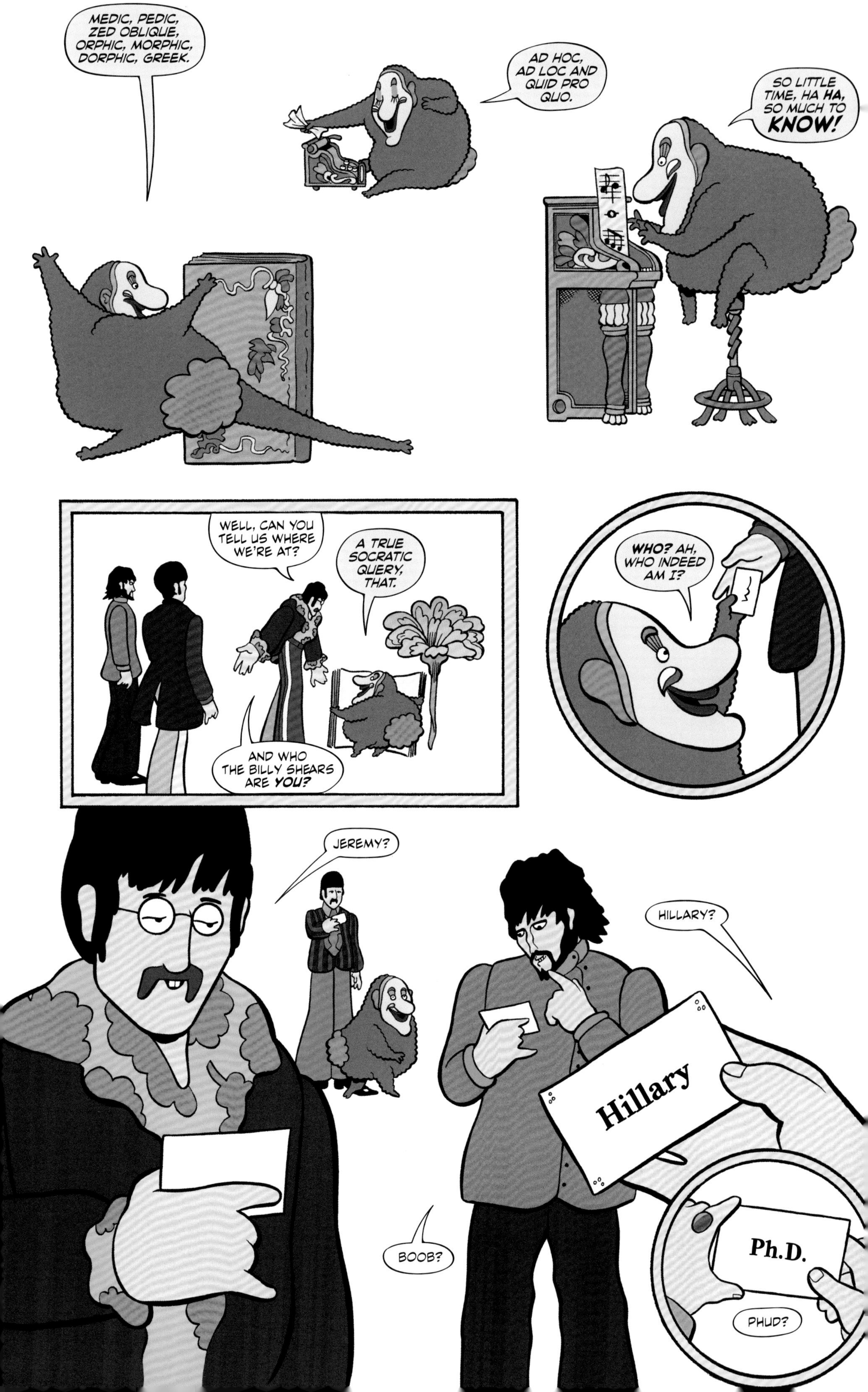

MEDIC, PEDIC, ZED OBLIQUE, ORPHIC, MORPHIC, DORPHIC, GREEK.
AD HOC, AD LOC AND QUID PRO QUO.
SO LITTLE TIME, HA **HA**, SO MUCH TO **KNOW!**
WELL, CAN YOU TELL US WHERE WE'RE AT?
A TRUE SOCRATIC QUERY, THAT.
AND WHO THE BILLY SHEARS ARE **YOU?**
WHO? AH, WHO INDEED AM I?
JEREMY?
HILLARY?
Hillary
BOOB?
Ph.D.
PHUD?

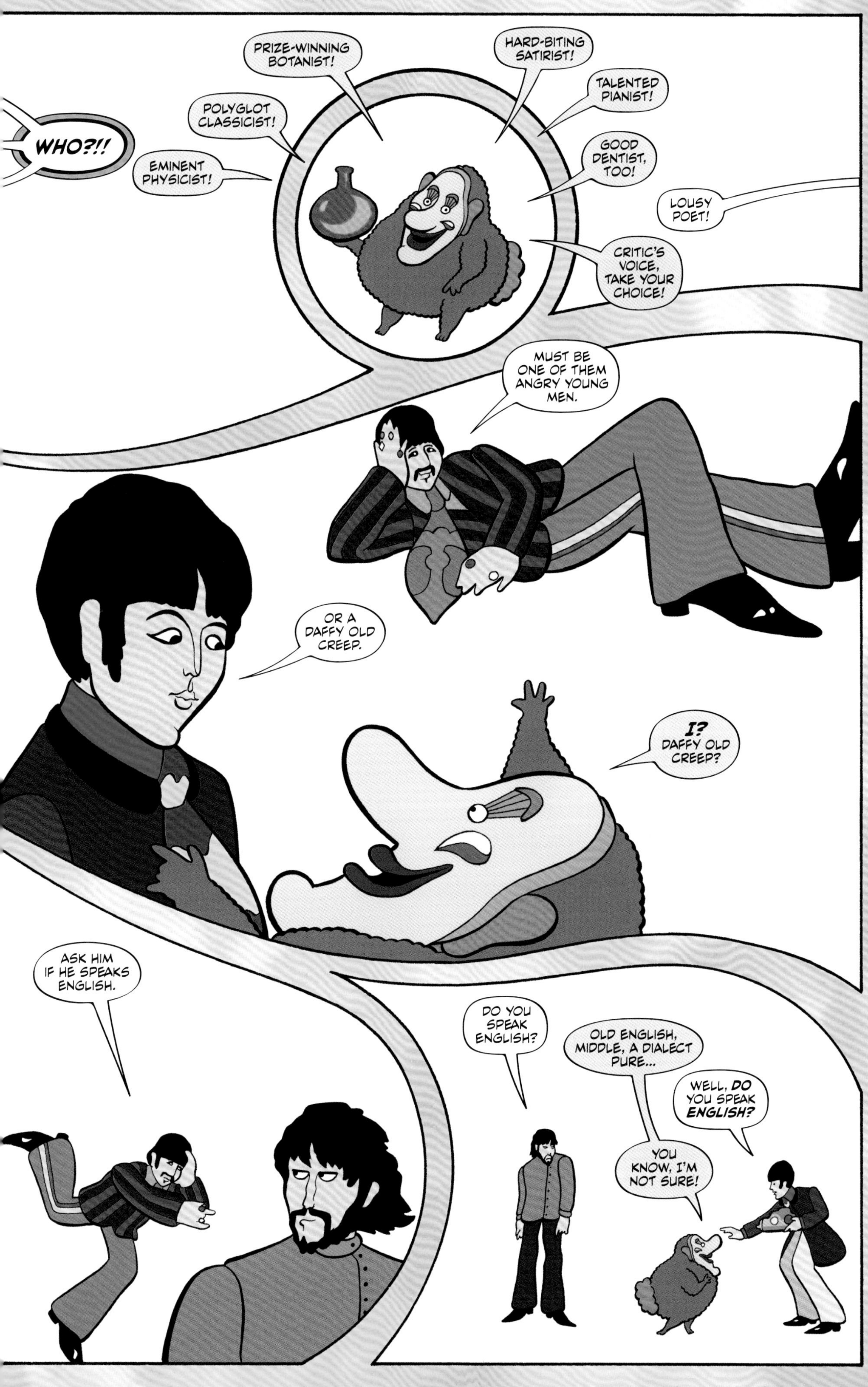
WHO?!!
EMINENT PHYSICIST!
POLYGLOT CLASSICIST!
PRIZE-WINNING BOTANIST!
HARD-BITING SATIRIST!
TALENTED PIANIST!
GOOD DENTIST, TOO!
LOUSY POET!
CRITIC'S VOICE, TAKE YOUR CHOICE!
MUST BE ONE OF THEM ANGRY YOUNG MEN.
OR A DAFFY OLD CREEP.
I? DAFFY OLD CREEP?
ASK HIM IF HE SPEAKS ENGLISH.
DO YOU SPEAK ENGLISH?
OLD ENGLISH, MIDDLE, A DIALECT PURE...
YOU KNOW, I'M NOT SURE!
WELL, DO YOU SPEAK ENGLISH?

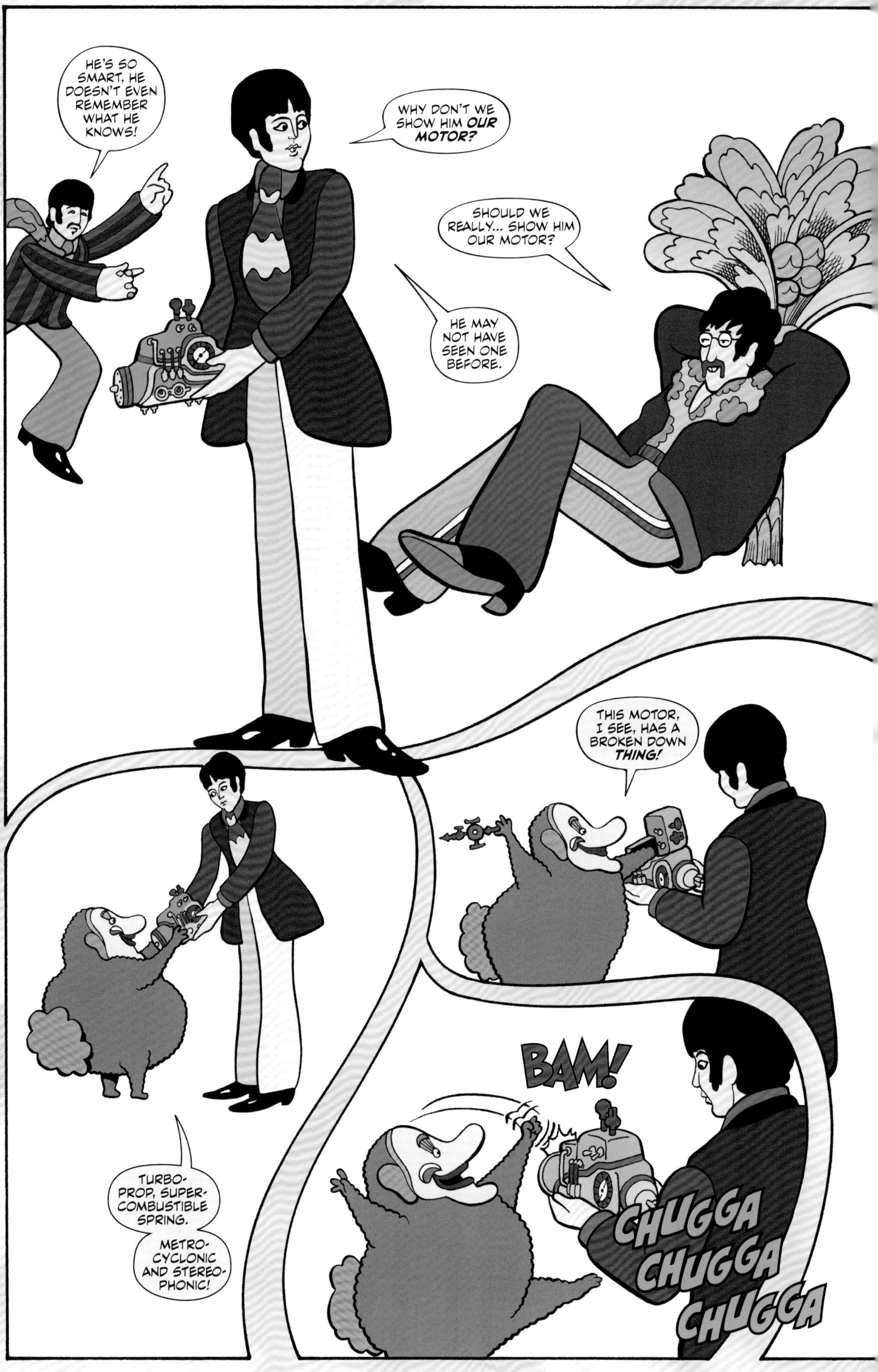
HE'S SO SMART, HE DOESN'T EVEN REMEMBER WHAT HE KNOWS!
WHY DON'T WE SHOW HIM *OUR MOTOR?*
SHOULD WE REALLY... SHOW HIM OUR MOTOR?
HE MAY NOT HAVE SEEN ONE BEFORE.
THIS MOTOR, I SEE, HAS A BROKEN DOWN *THING!*
TURBO-PROP, SUPER-COMBUSTIBLE SPRING.
METRO-CYCLONIC AND STEREO-PHONIC!
BAM!
CHUGGA CHUGGA CHUGGA

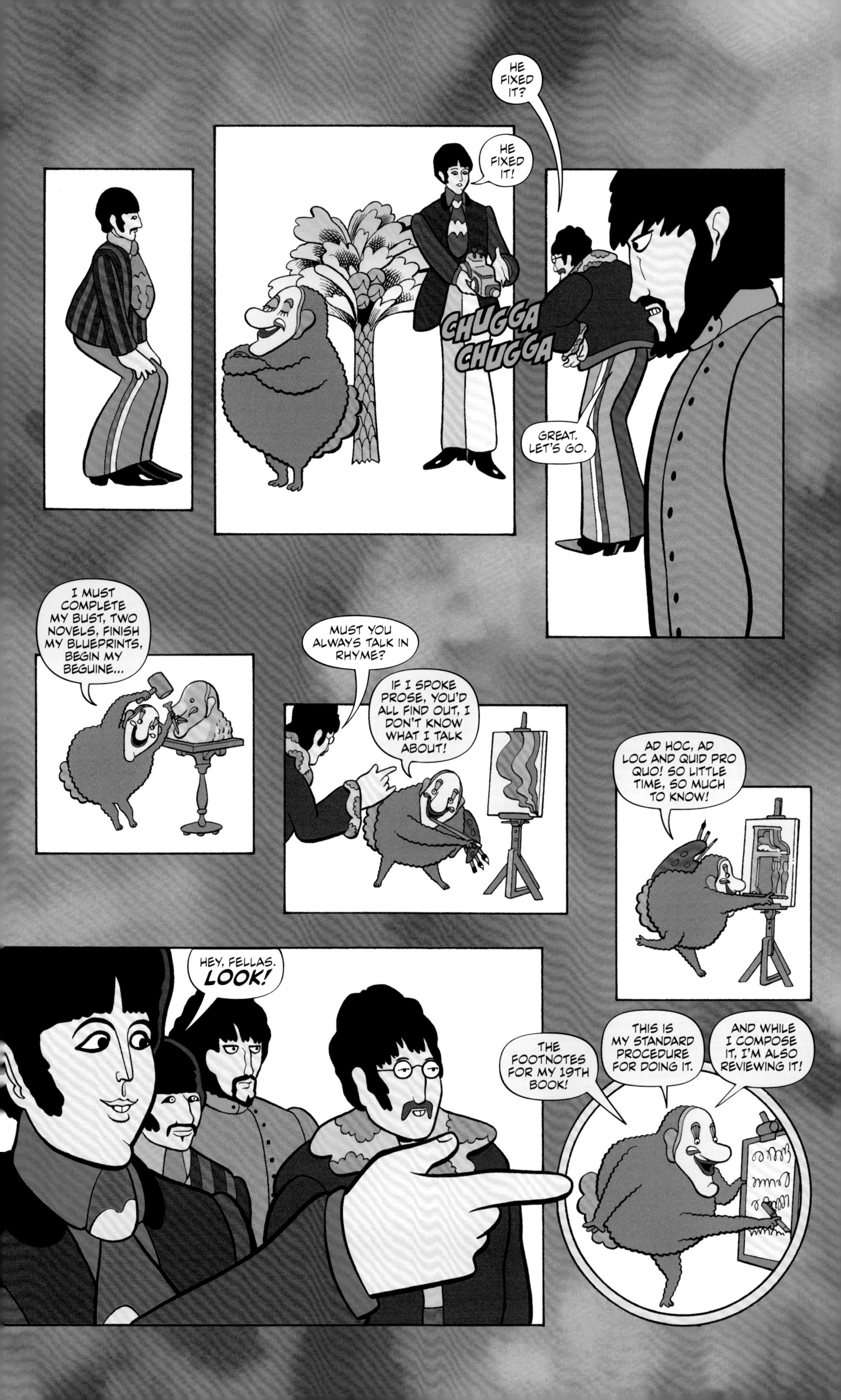
HE FIXED IT!
HE FIXED IT?
CHUGGA CHUGGA
GREAT. LET'S GO.
I MUST COMPLETE MY BUST, TWO NOVELS, FINISH MY BLUEPRINTS, BEGIN MY BEGUINE...
MUST YOU ALWAYS TALK IN RHYME?
IF I SPOKE PROSE, YOU'D ALL FIND OUT, I DON'T KNOW WHAT I TALK ABOUT!
AD HOC, AD LOC AND QUID PRO QUO! SO LITTLE TIME, SO MUCH TO KNOW!
HEY, FELLAS. LOOK!
THE FOOTNOTES FOR MY 19TH BOOK!
THIS IS MY STANDARD PROCEDURE FOR DOING IT.
AND WHILE I COMPOSE IT, I'M ALSO REVIEWING IT!

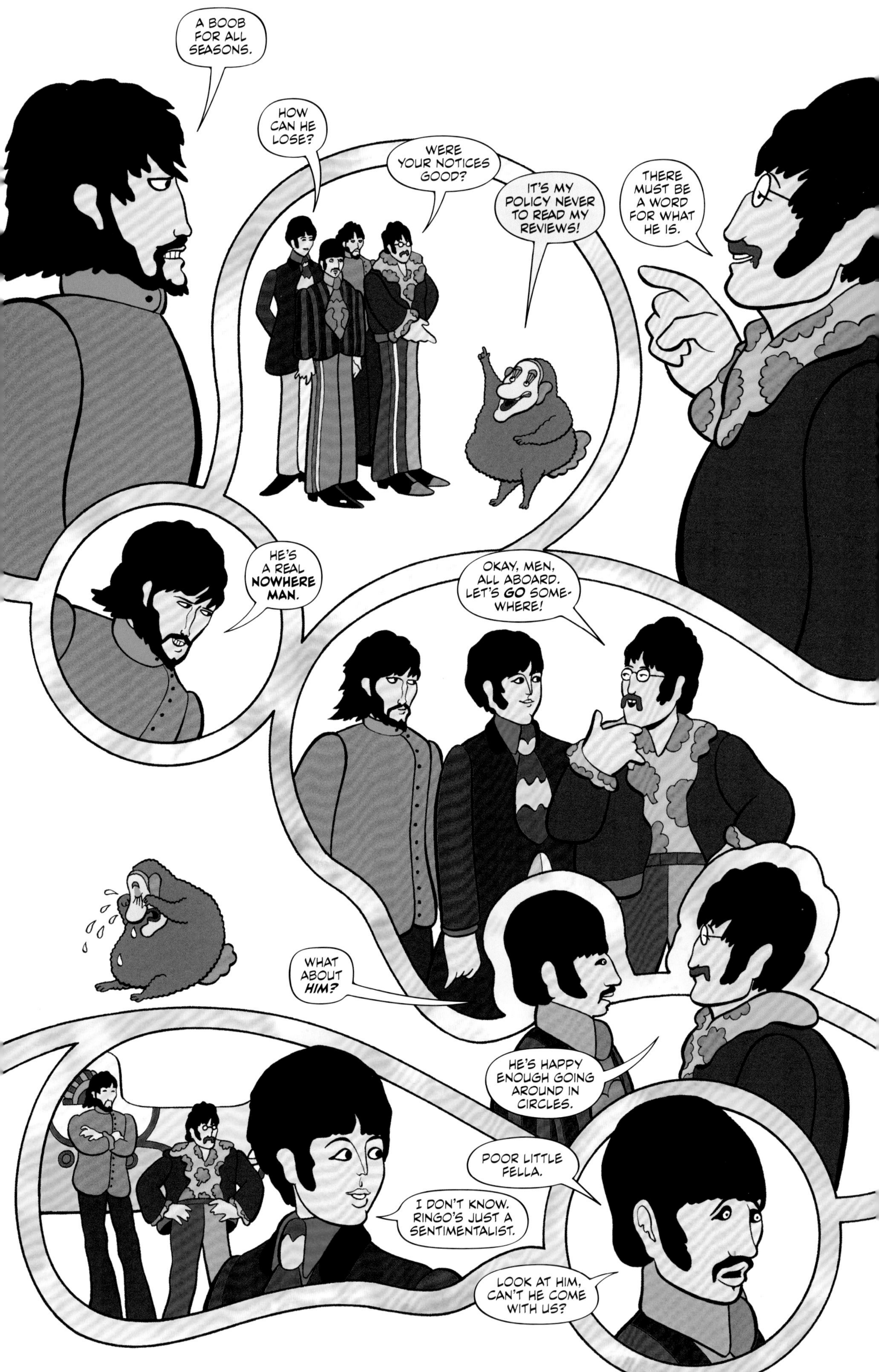
A BOOB FOR ALL SEASONS.
HOW CAN HE LOSE?
WERE YOUR NOTICES GOOD?
IT'S MY POLICY NEVER TO READ MY REVIEWS!
THERE MUST BE A WORD FOR WHAT HE IS.
HE'S A REAL **NOWHERE MAN**.
OKAY, MEN, ALL ABOARD. LET'S **GO** SOME-WHERE!
WHAT ABOUT ***HIM?***
HE'S HAPPY ENOUGH GOING AROUND IN CIRCLES.
POOR LITTLE FELLA.
I DON'T KNOW. RINGO'S JUST A SENTIMENTALIST.
LOOK AT HIM, CAN'T HE COME WITH US?

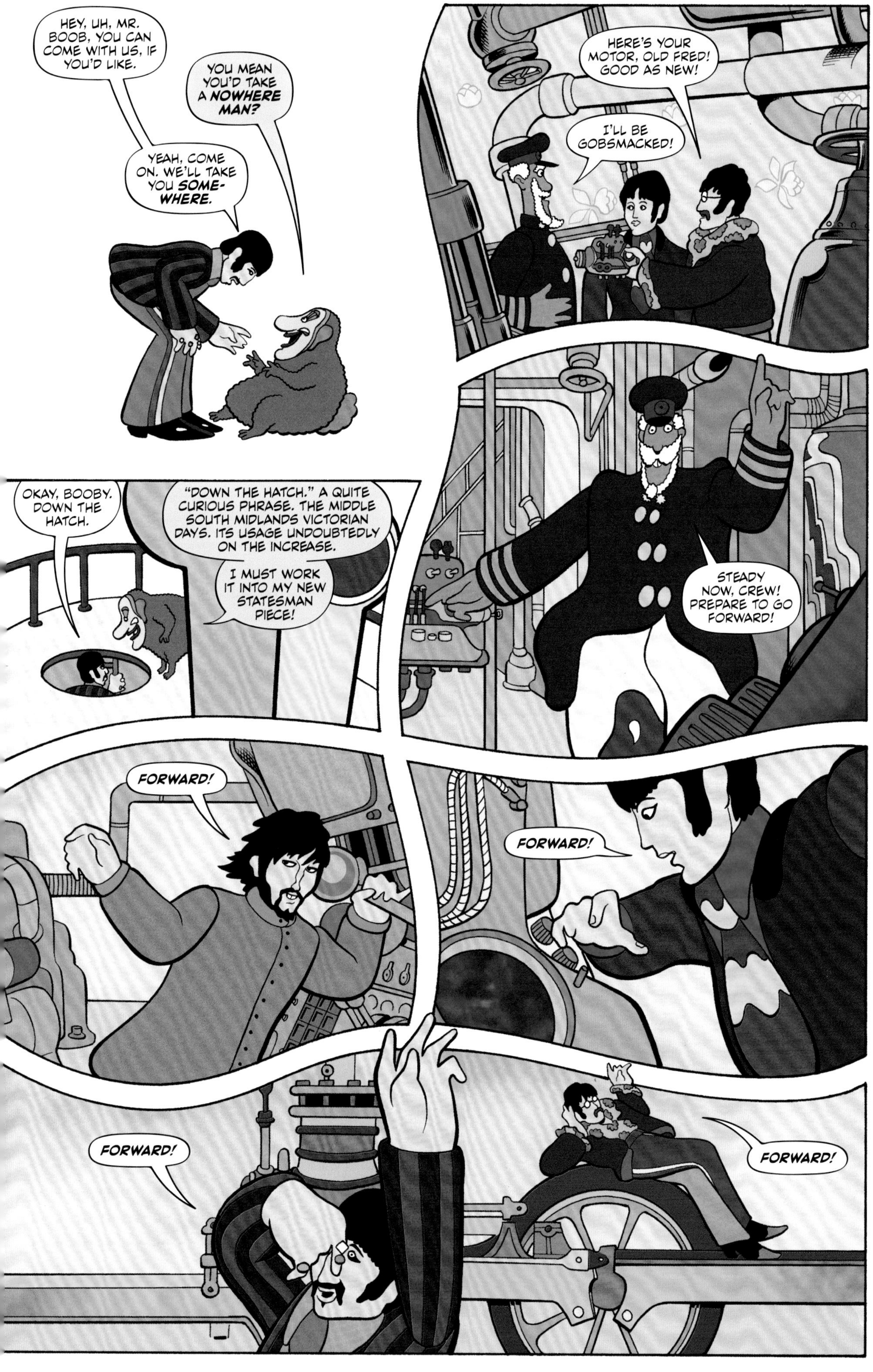
HEY, UH, MR. BOOB, YOU CAN COME WITH US, IF YOU'D LIKE.
YOU MEAN YOU'D TAKE A **NOWHERE MAN?**
YEAH, COME ON. WE'LL TAKE YOU **SOME-WHERE.**
HERE'S YOUR MOTOR, OLD FRED! GOOD AS NEW!
I'LL BE GOBSMACKED!
OKAY, BOOBY. DOWN THE HATCH.
"DOWN THE HATCH." A QUITE CURIOUS PHRASE. THE MIDDLE SOUTH MIDLANDS VICTORIAN DAYS. ITS USAGE UNDOUBTEDLY ON THE INCREASE.
I MUST WORK IT INTO MY NEW STATESMAN PIECE!
STEADY NOW, CREW! PREPARE TO GO FORWARD!
FORWARD!
FORWARD!
FORWARD!
FORWARD!

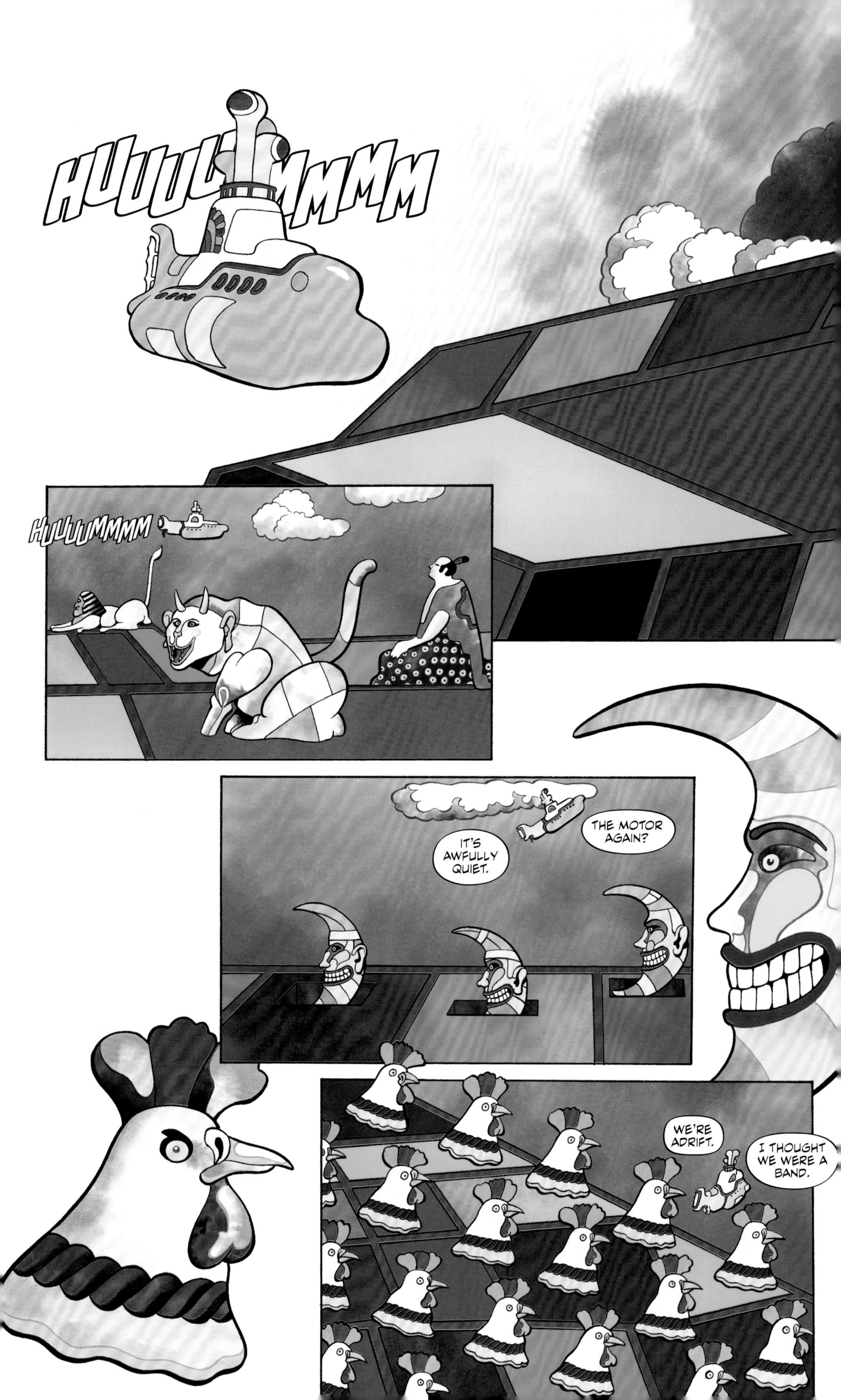
HUUUUMMMM
HUUUUMMMM
IT'S AWFULLY QUIET.
THE MOTOR AGAIN?
WE'RE ADRIFT.
I THOUGHT WE WERE A BAND.

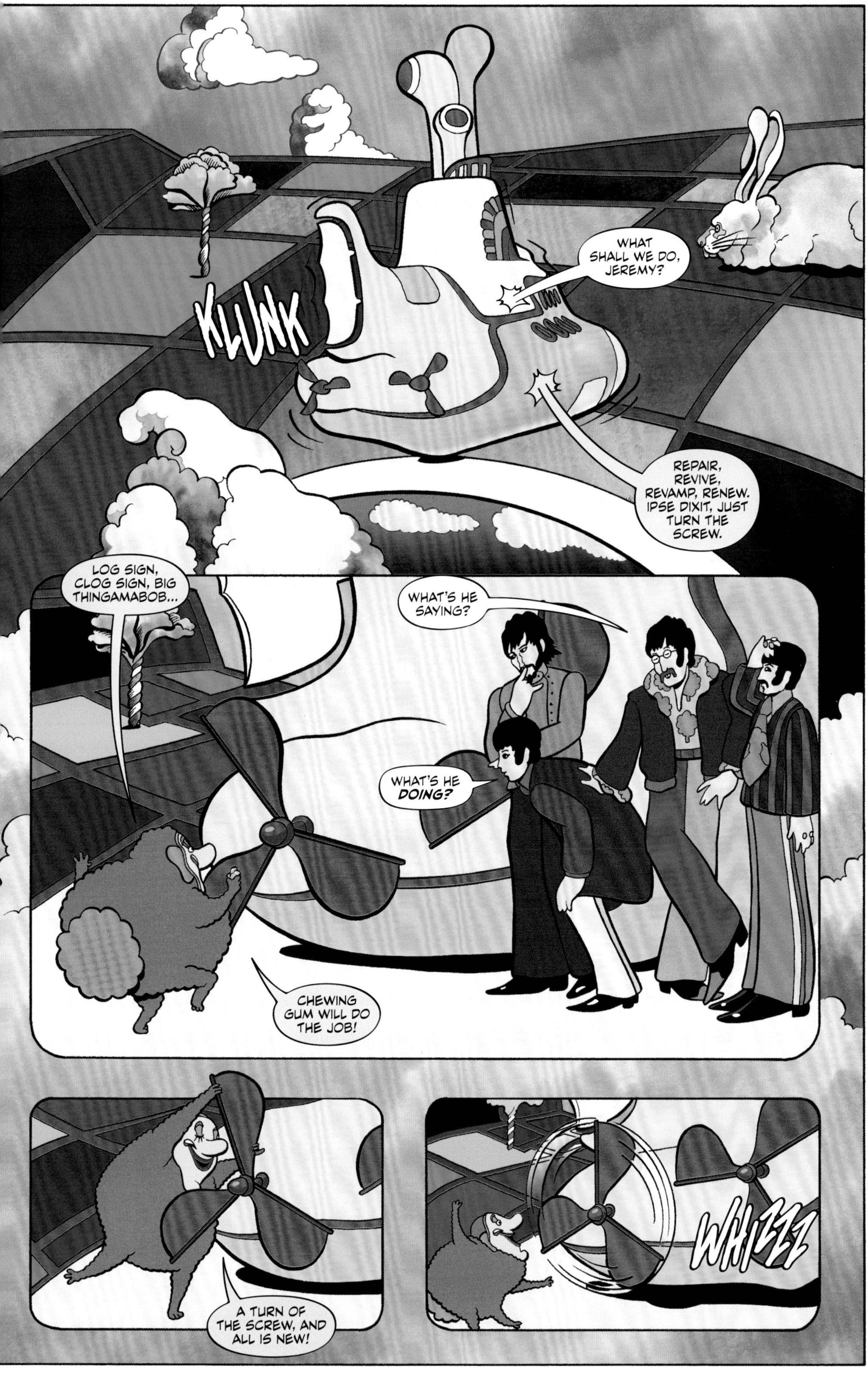
KLUNK
WHAT SHALL WE DO, JEREMY?
REPAIR, REVIVE, REVAMP, RENEW. IPSE DIXIT, JUST TURN THE SCREW.
LOG SIGN, CLOG SIGN, BIG THINGAMABOB...
WHAT'S HE SAYING?
WHAT'S HE *DOING?*
CHEWING GUM WILL DO THE JOB!
A TURN OF THE SCREW, AND ALL IS NEW!
WHIZZZ

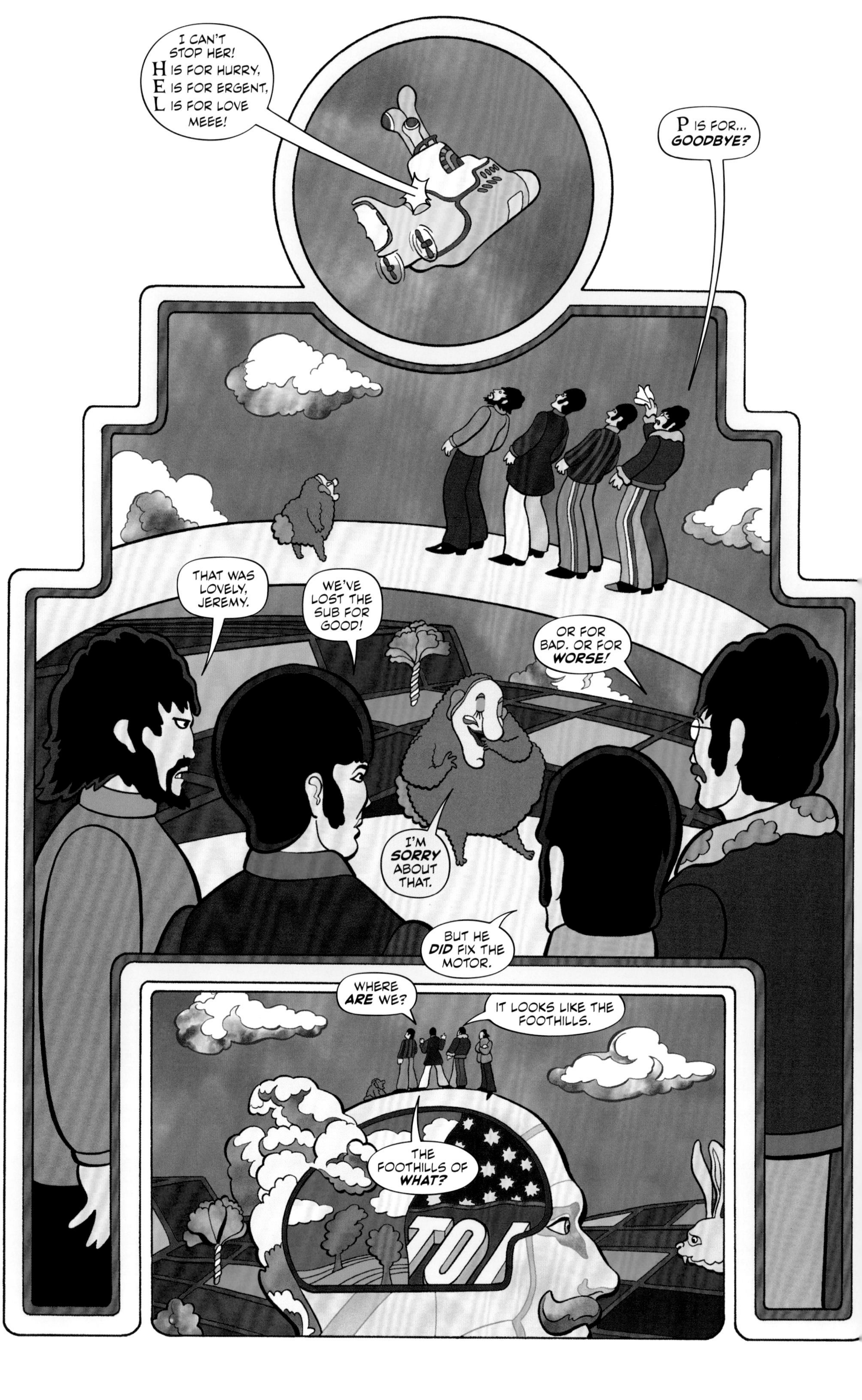
I CAN'T STOP HER! H IS FOR HURRY, E IS FOR ERGENT, L IS FOR LOVE MEEE!
P IS FOR... GOODBYE?
THAT WAS LOVELY, JEREMY.
WE'VE LOST THE SUB FOR GOOD!
OR FOR BAD. OR FOR WORSE!
I'M SORRY ABOUT THAT.
BUT HE DID FIX THE MOTOR.
WHERE ARE WE?
IT LOOKS LIKE THE FOOTHILLS.
THE FOOTHILLS OF WHAT?
TO

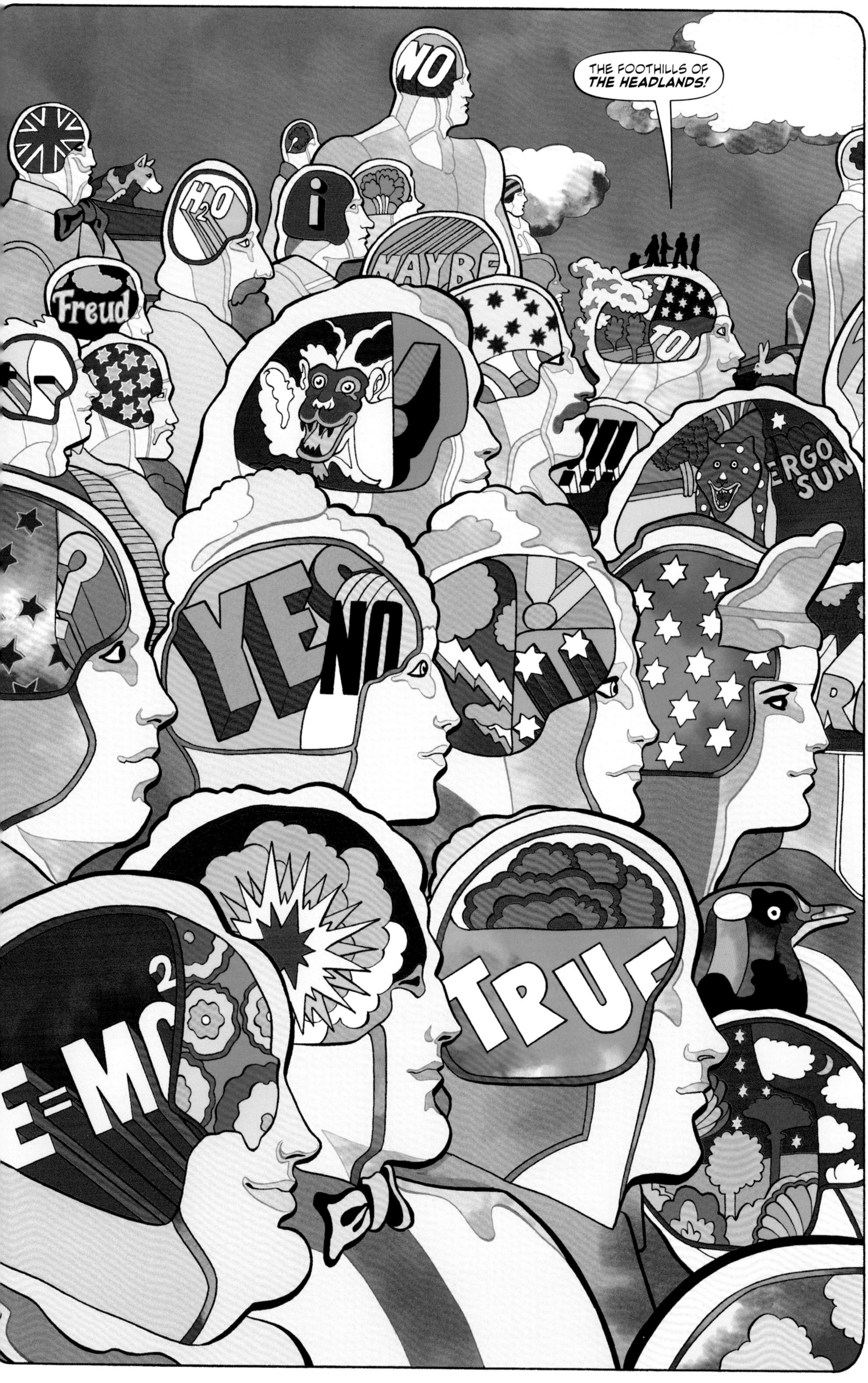
THE FOOTHILLS OF
THE HEADLANDS!
NO
Freud
MAYBE
YES
NO
ERGO
SUM
TRUE

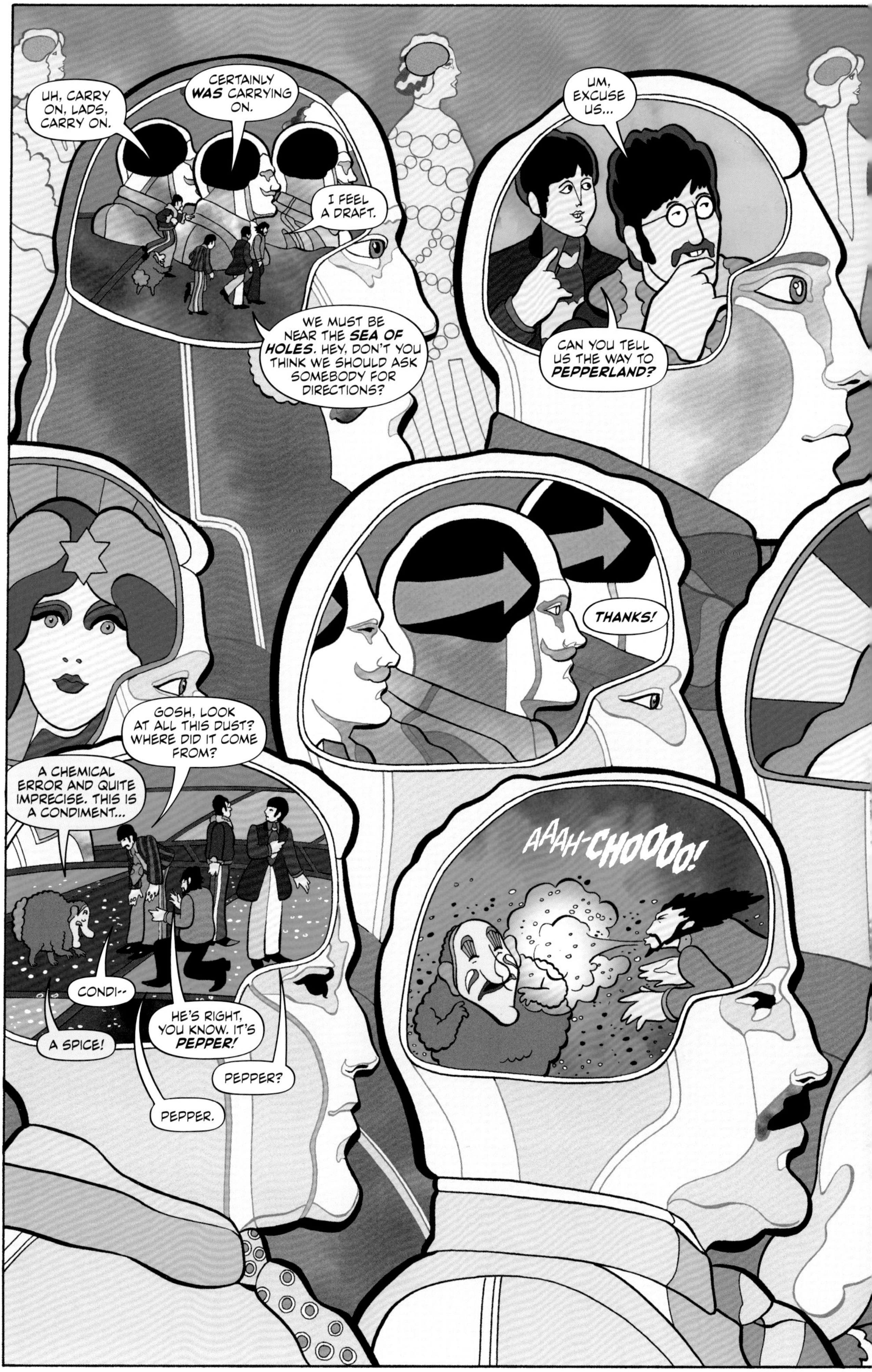
UH, CARRY ON, LADS, CARRY ON.
CERTAINLY **WAS** CARRYING ON.
I FEEL A DRAFT.
WE MUST BE NEAR THE **SEA OF HOLES**. HEY, DON'T YOU THINK WE SHOULD ASK SOMEBODY FOR DIRECTIONS?
UM, EXCUSE US...
CAN YOU TELL US THE WAY TO **PEPPERLAND?**
THANKS!
GOSH, LOOK AT ALL THIS DUST? WHERE DID IT COME FROM?
A CHEMICAL ERROR AND QUITE IMPRECISE. THIS IS A CONDIMENT...
CONDI--
A SPICE!
HE'S RIGHT, YOU KNOW. IT'S **PEPPER!**
PEPPER?
PEPPER.
AAAH-CHOOOO!

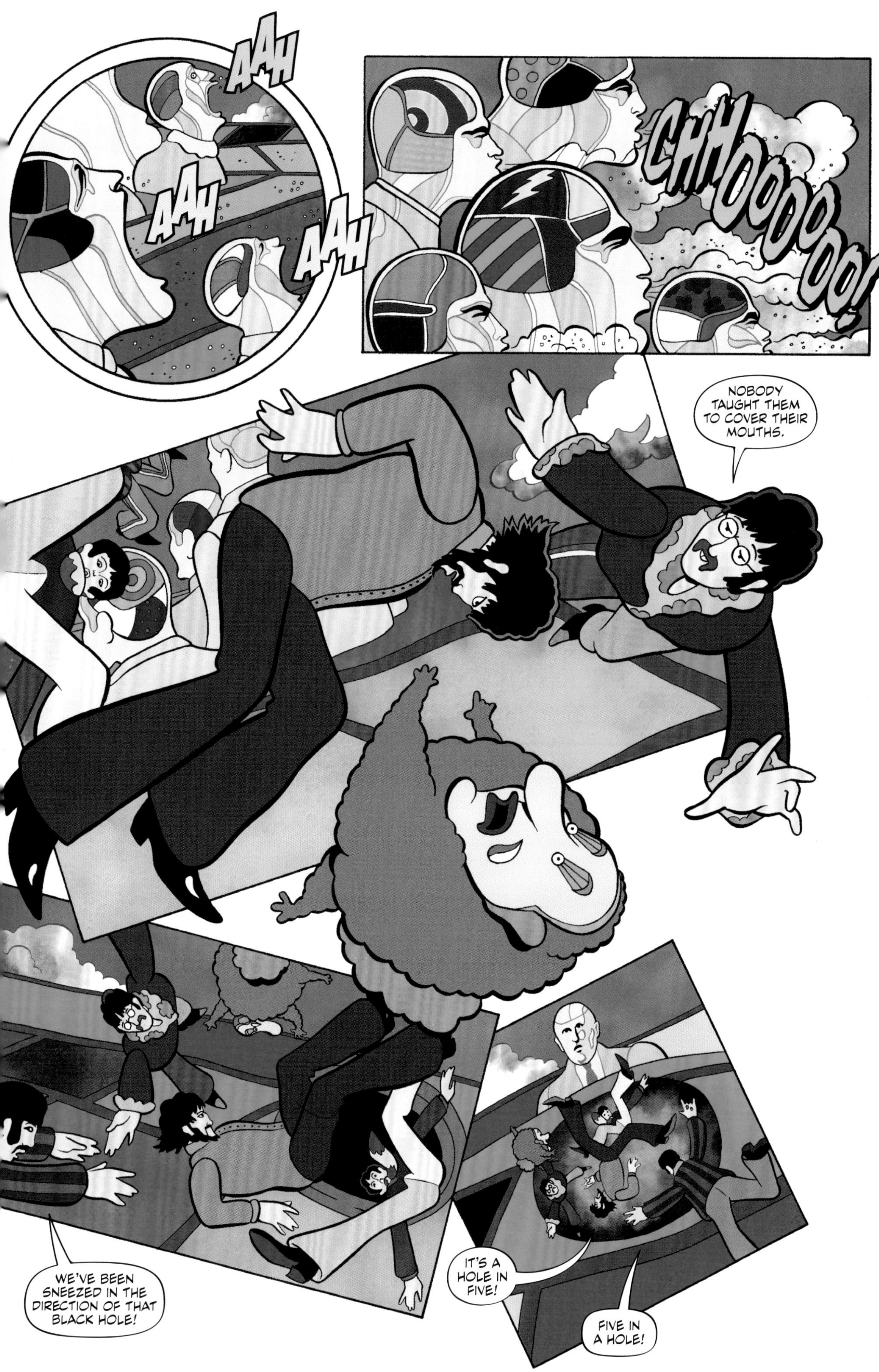
AAH
AAH
AAH
CHOOOOOOO!
NOBODY TAUGHT THEM TO COVER THEIR MOUTHS.
WE'VE BEEN SNEEZED IN THE DIRECTION OF THAT BLACK HOLE!
IT'S A HOLE IN FIVE!
FIVE IN A HOLE!

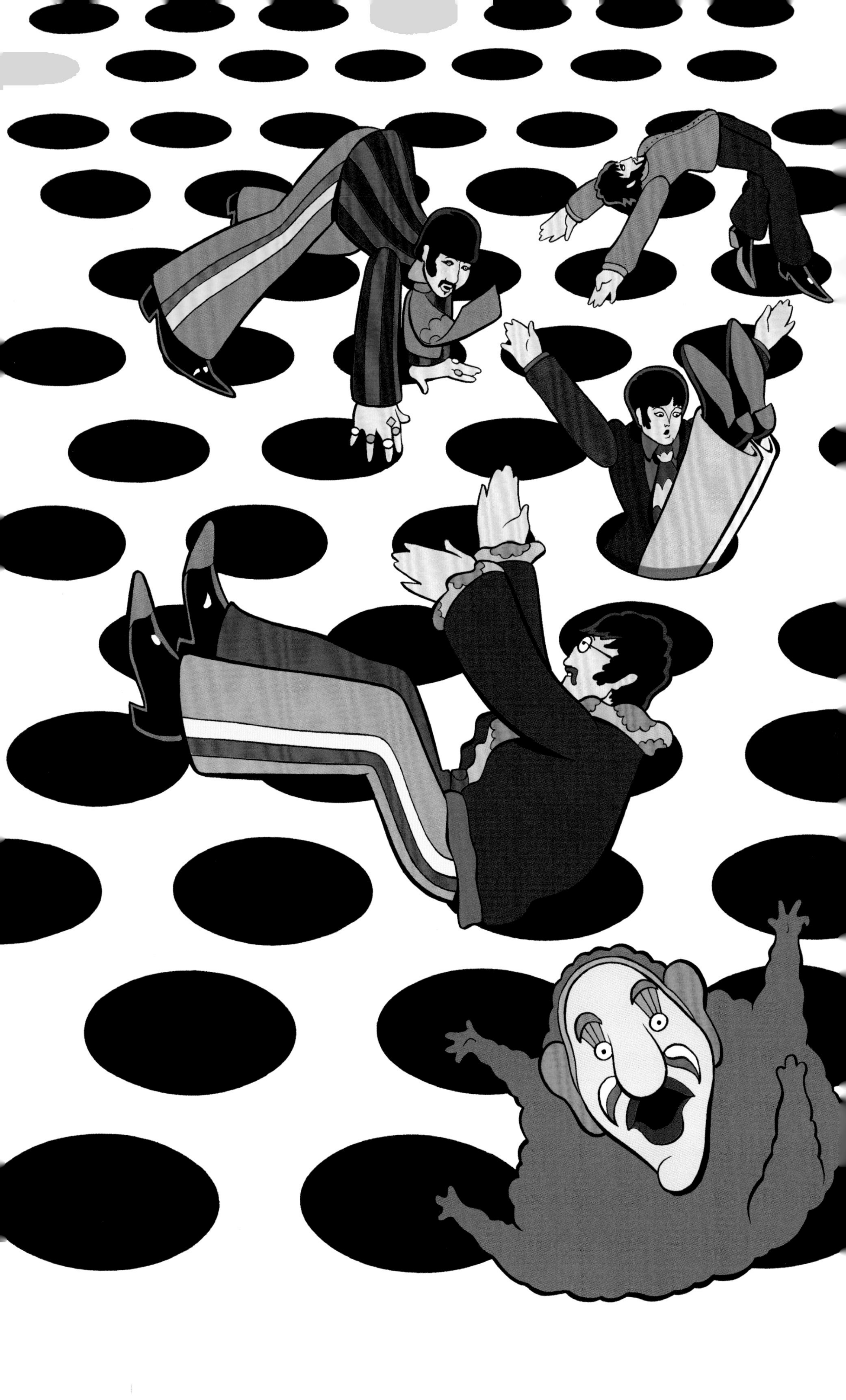

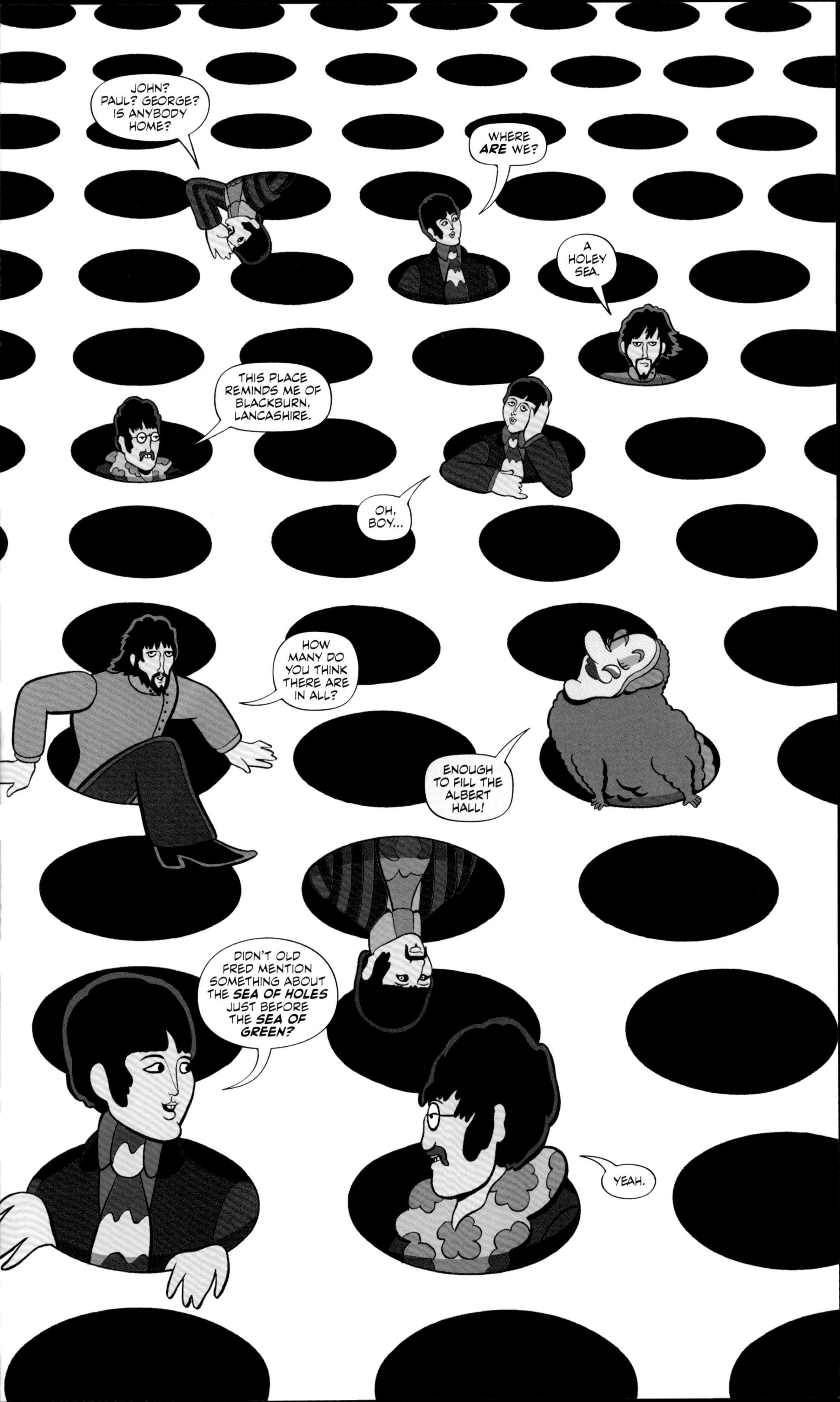
JOHN? PAUL? GEORGE? IS ANYBODY HOME?
WHERE **ARE** WE?
A HOLEY SEA.
THIS PLACE REMINDS ME OF BLACKBURN, LANCASHIRE.
OH, BOY...
HOW MANY DO YOU THINK THERE ARE IN ALL?
ENOUGH TO FILL THE ALBERT HALL!
DIDN'T OLD FRED MENTION SOMETHING ABOUT THE **SEA OF HOLES** JUST BEFORE THE **SEA OF GREEN?**
YEAH.

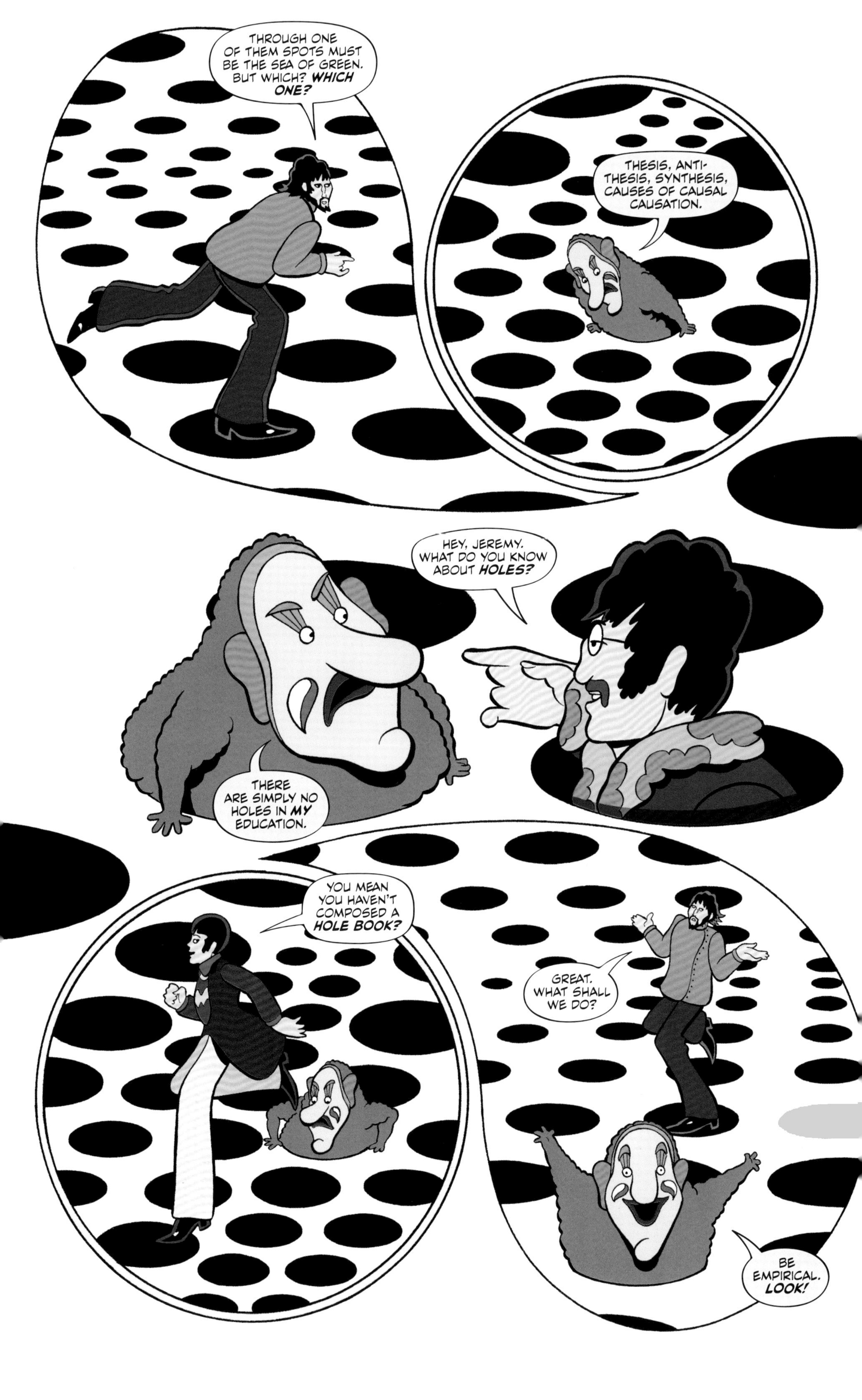

THROUGH ONE OF THEM SPOTS MUST BE THE SEA OF GREEN. BUT WHICH? *WHICH ONE?*
THESIS, ANTI-THESIS, SYNTHESIS, CAUSES OF CAUSAL CAUSATION.
HEY, JEREMY. WHAT DO YOU KNOW ABOUT *HOLES?*
THERE ARE SIMPLY NO HOLES IN *MY* EDUCATION.
YOU MEAN YOU HAVEN'T COMPOSED A *HOLE BOOK?*
GREAT. WHAT SHALL WE DO?
BE EMPIRICAL. *LOOK!*

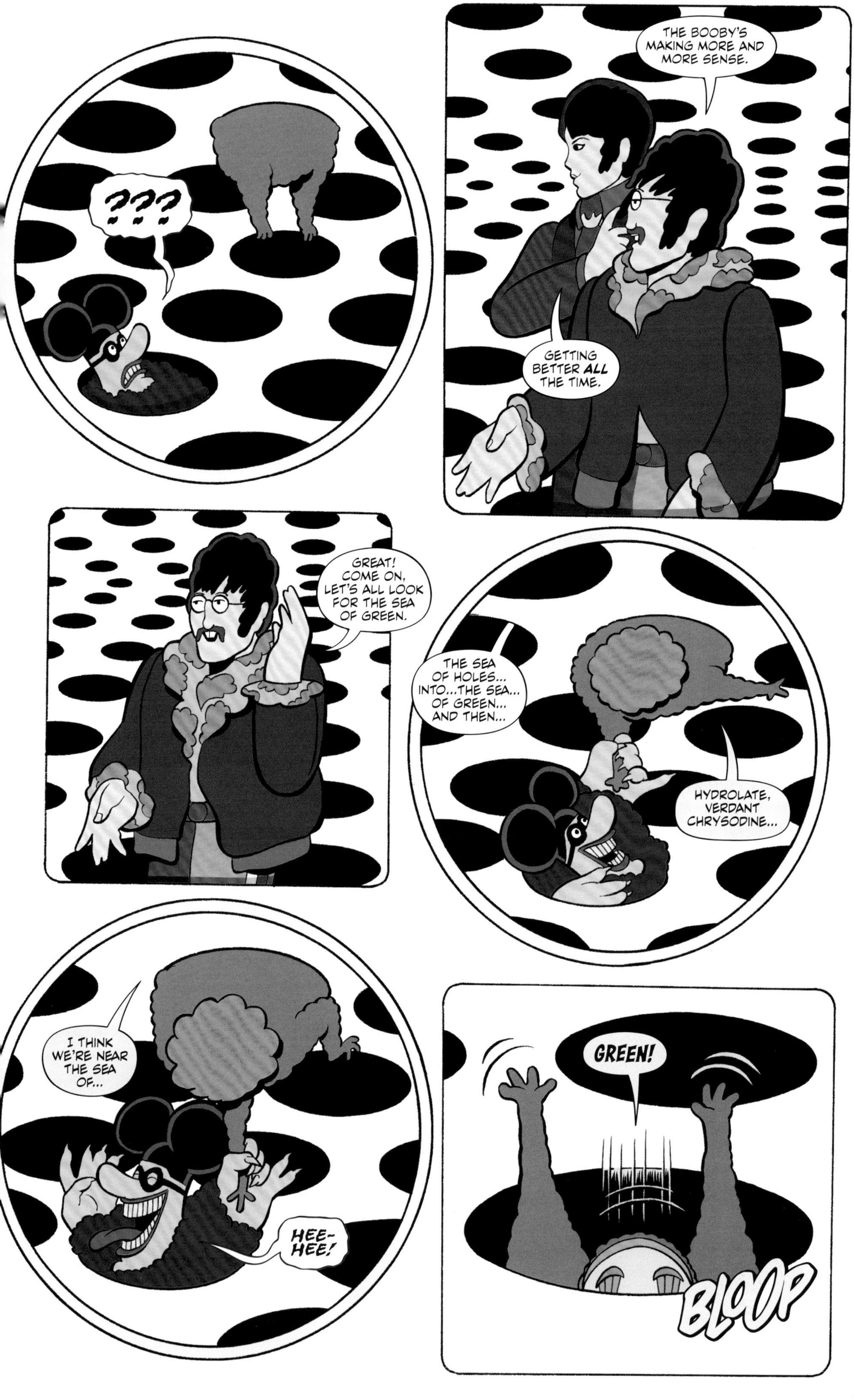
???
THE BOOBY'S MAKING MORE AND MORE SENSE.
GETTING BETTER ALL THE TIME.
GREAT! COME ON, LET'S ALL LOOK FOR THE SEA OF GREEN.
THE SEA OF HOLES... INTO...THE SEA... OF GREEN... AND THEN...
HYDROLATE, VERDANT CHRYSODINE...
I THINK WE'RE NEAR THE SEA OF...
HEE-HEE!
GREEN!
BLOOP

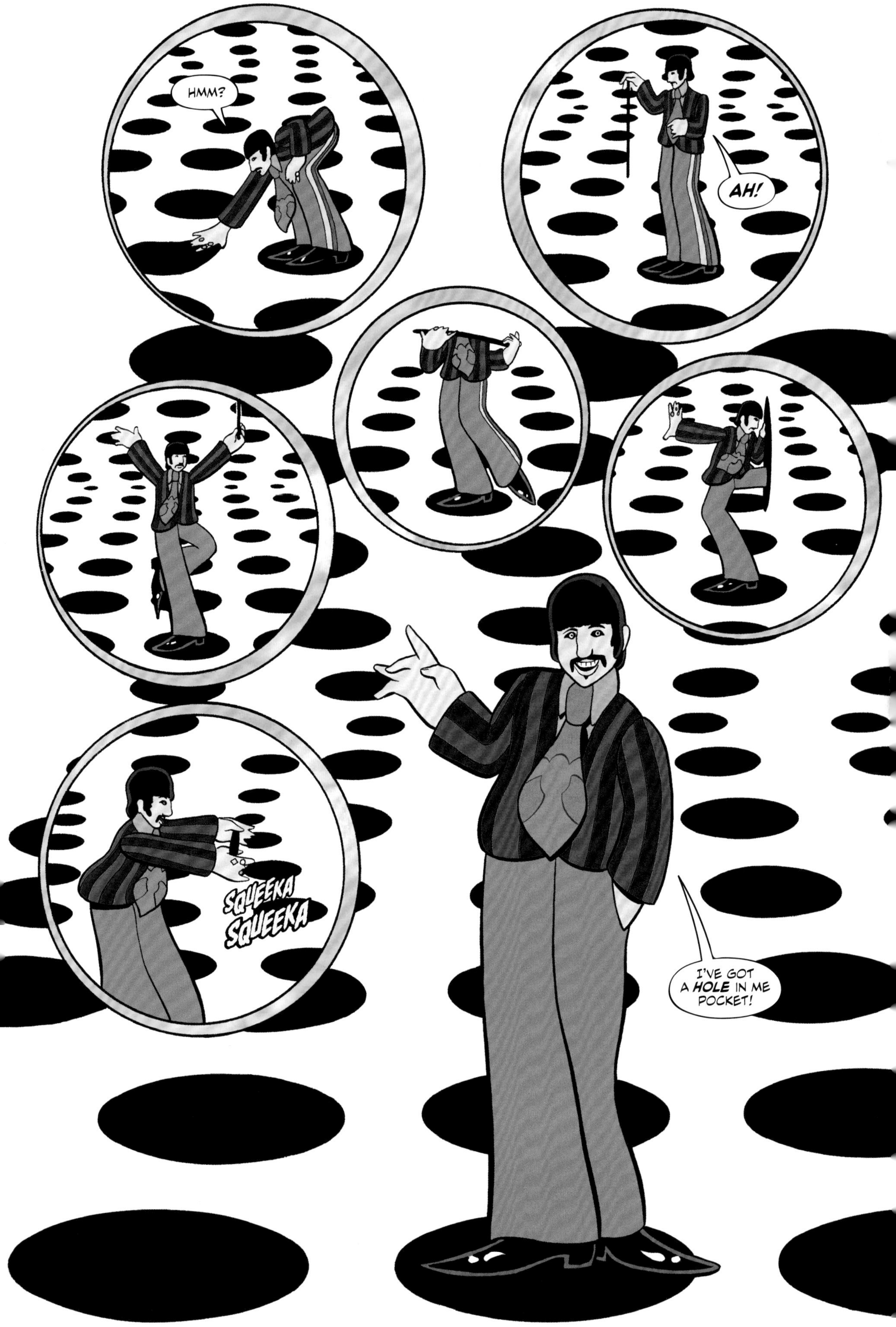
HMM?
AH!
SQUEEKA SQUEEKA
I'VE GOT A HOLE IN ME POCKET!

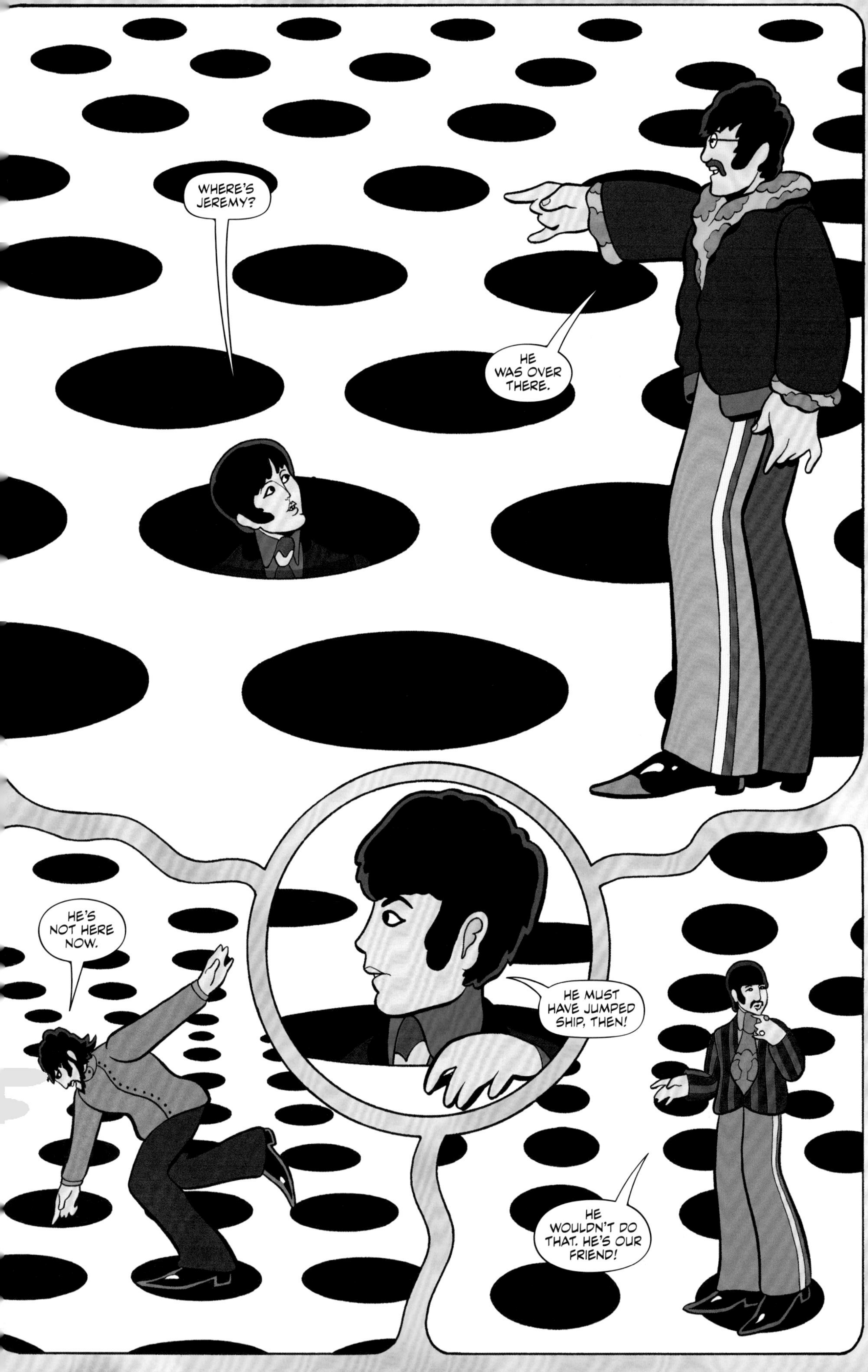
WHERE'S JEREMY?
HE WAS OVER THERE.
HE'S NOT HERE NOW.
HE MUST HAVE JUMPED SHIP, THEN!
HE WOULDN'T DO THAT. HE'S OUR FRIEND!

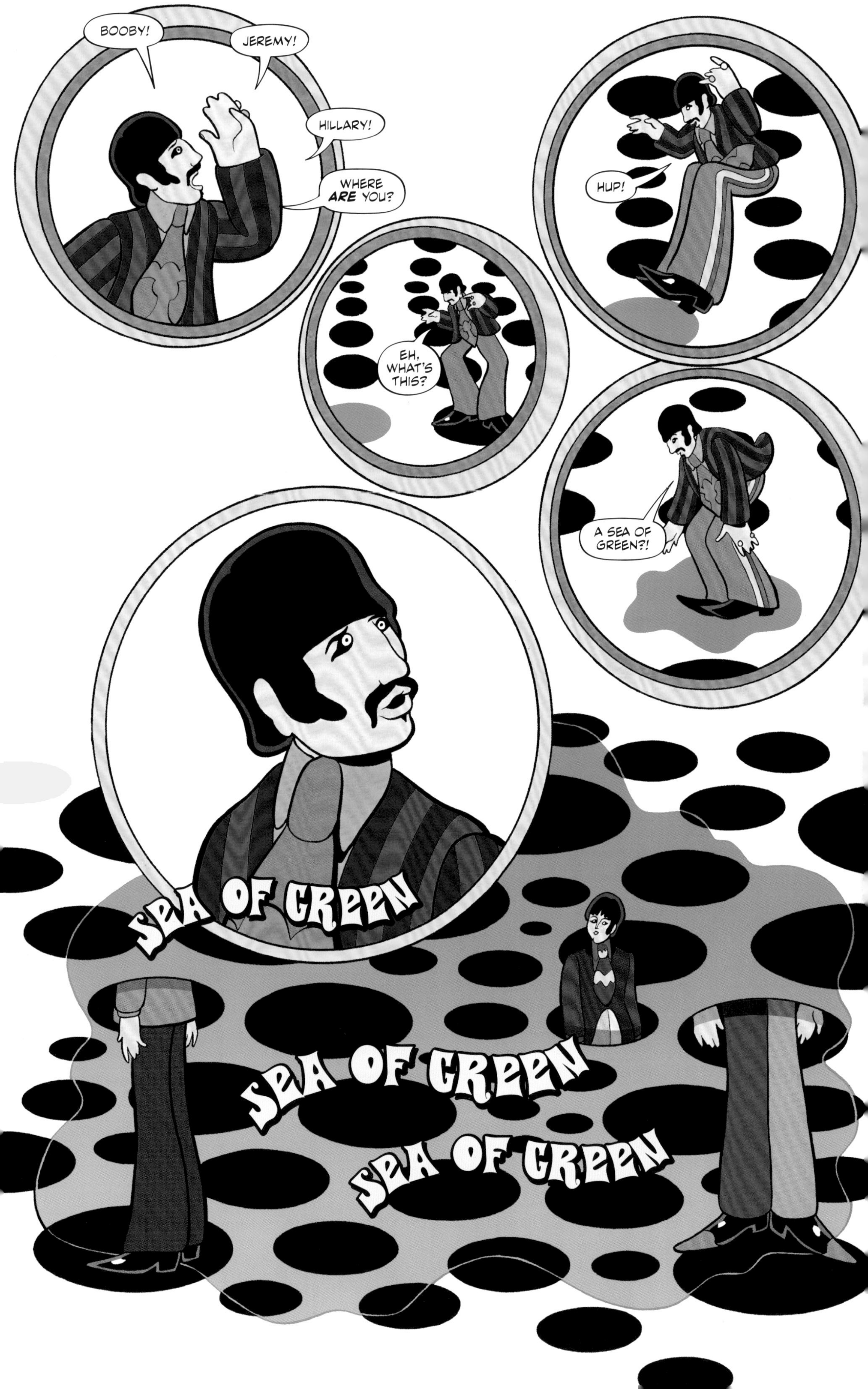
BOOBY!
JEREMY!
HILLARY!
WHERE ARE YOU?
EH, WHAT'S THIS?
HUP!
A SEA OF GREEN?!
SEA OF GREEN
SEA OF GREEN
SEA OF GREEN

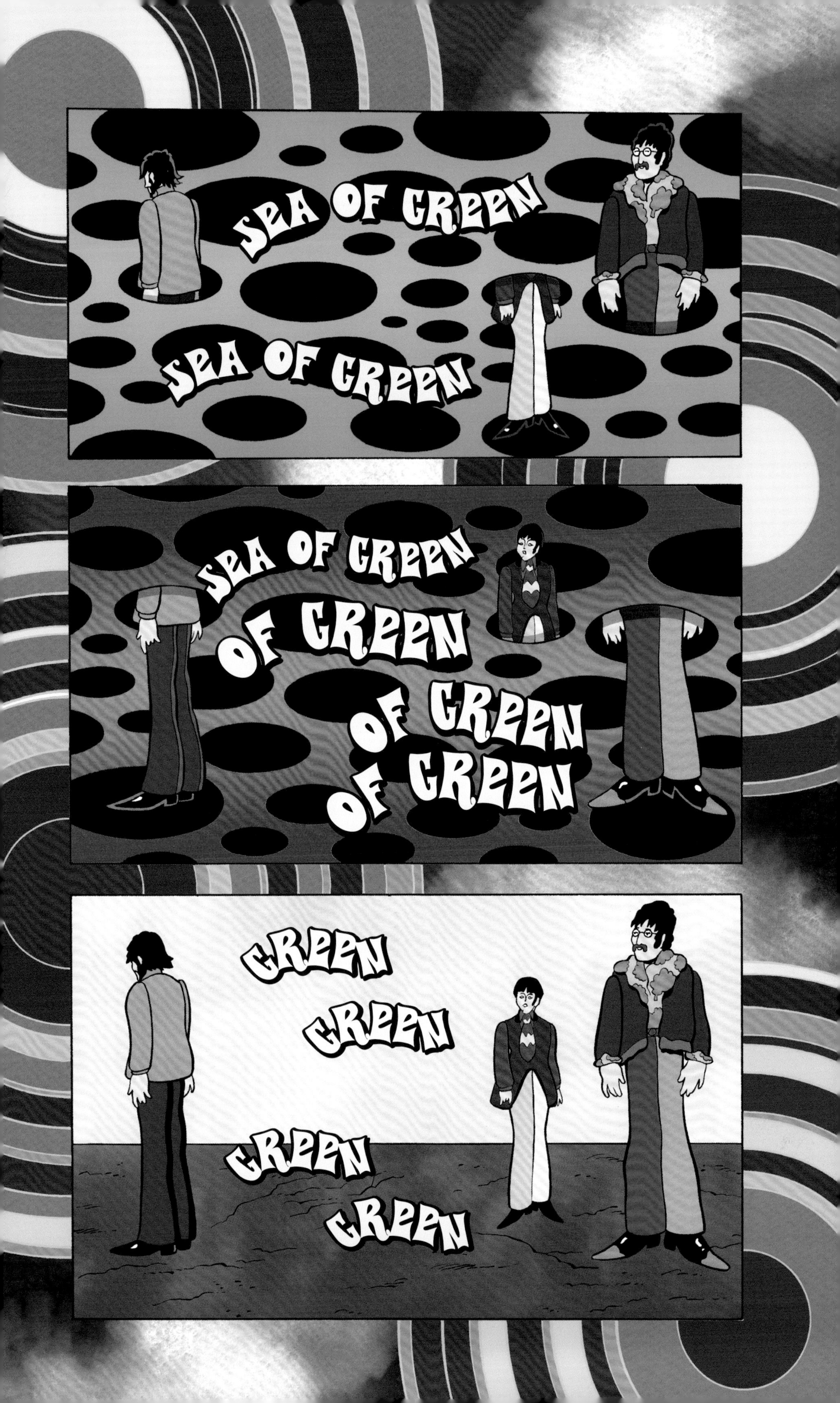

SEA OF GREEN
SEA OF GREEN
SEA OF GREEN
OF GREEN
OF GREEN
OF GREEN
GREEN
GREEN
GREEN
GREEN

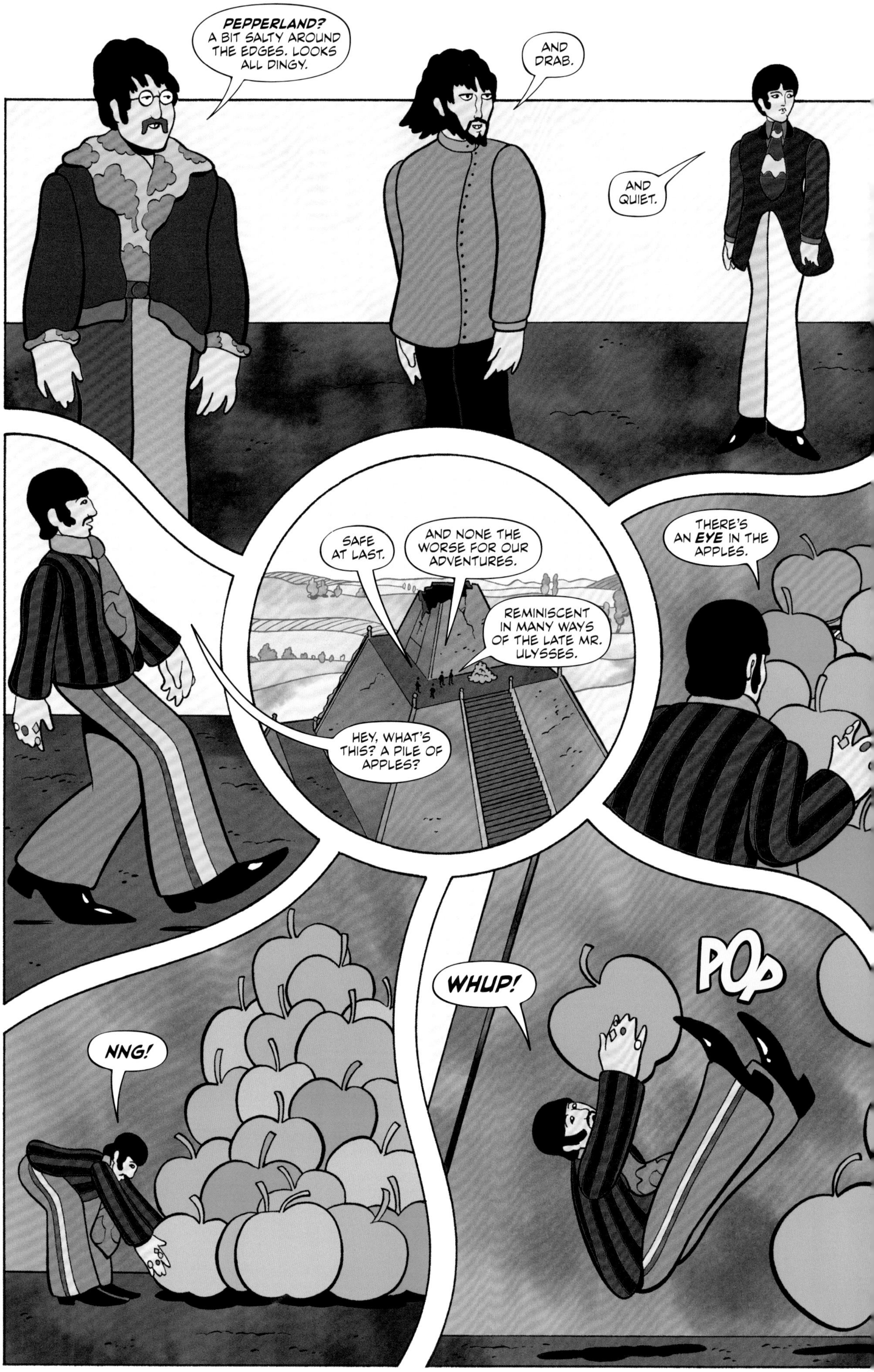

PEPPERLAND? A BIT SALTY AROUND THE EDGES. LOOKS ALL DINGY.
AND DRAB.
AND QUIET.
SAFE AT LAST.
AND NONE THE WORSE FOR OUR ADVENTURES.
REMINISCENT IN MANY WAYS OF THE LATE MR. ULYSSES.
HEY, WHAT'S THIS? A PILE OF APPLES?
THERE'S AN EYE IN THE APPLES.
NNG!
WHUP!
POP

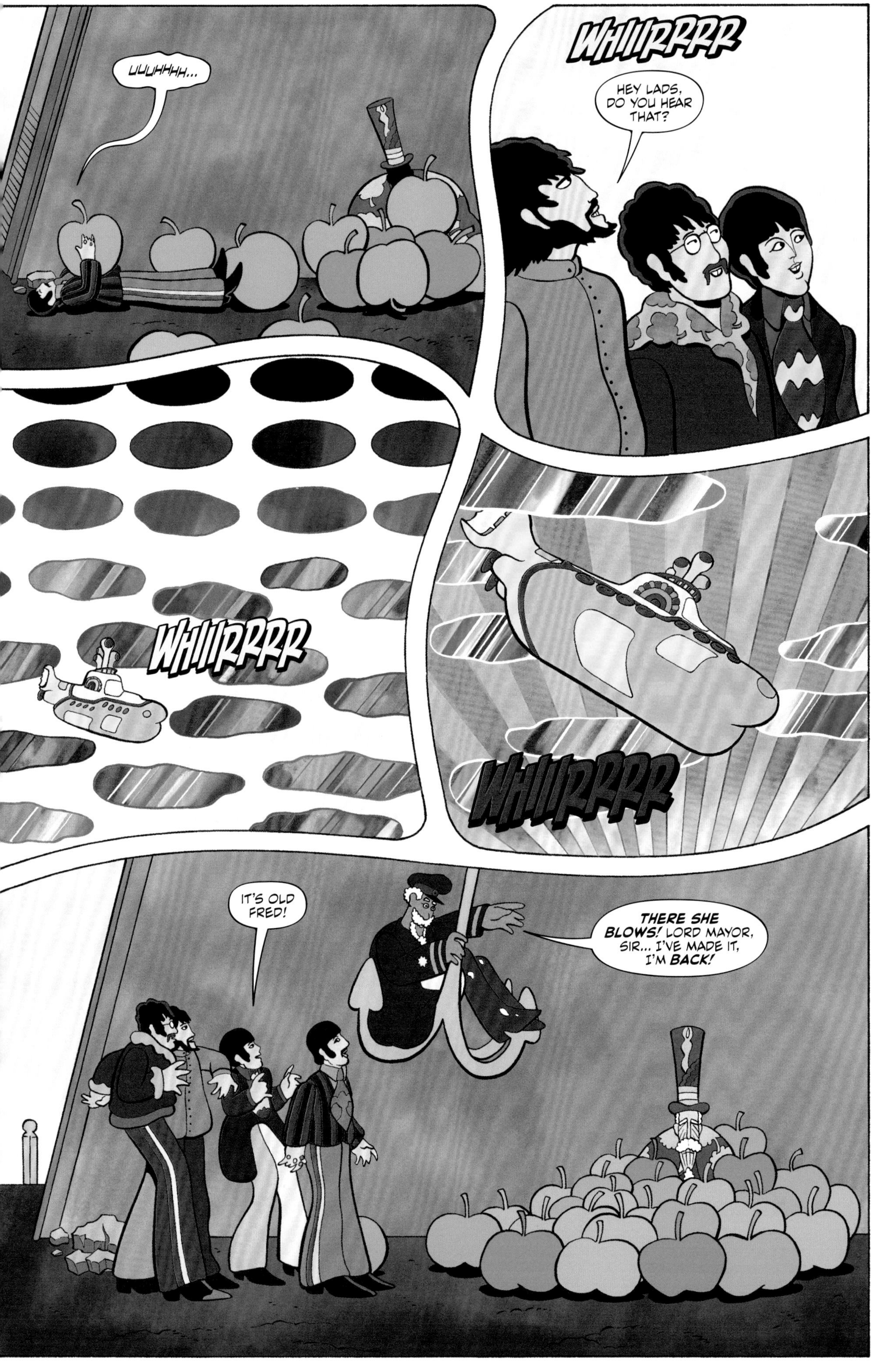

UUUHHHH...
WHIIIRRRR
HEY LADS, DO YOU HEAR THAT?
WHIIIRRRR
WHIIIRRRR
IT'S OLD FRED!
THERE SHE BLOWS! LORD MAYOR, SIR... I'VE MADE IT, I'M **BACK!**

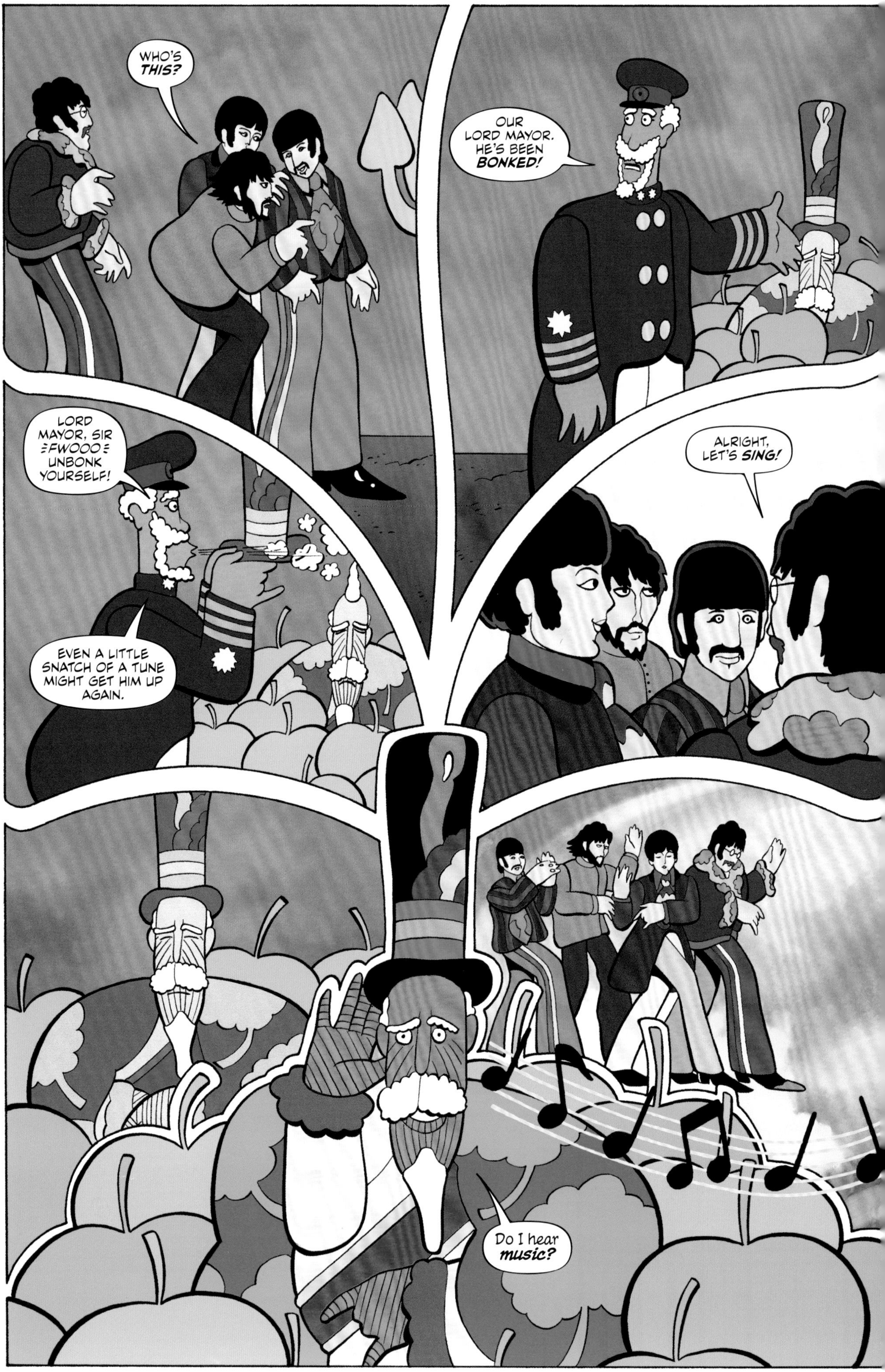
WHO'S THIS?
OUR LORD MAYOR. HE'S BEEN BONKED!
LORD MAYOR, SIR FWOOO UNBONK YOURSELF!
EVEN A LITTLE SNATCH OF A TUNE MIGHT GET HIM UP AGAIN.
ALRIGHT, LET'S SING!
Do I hear music?

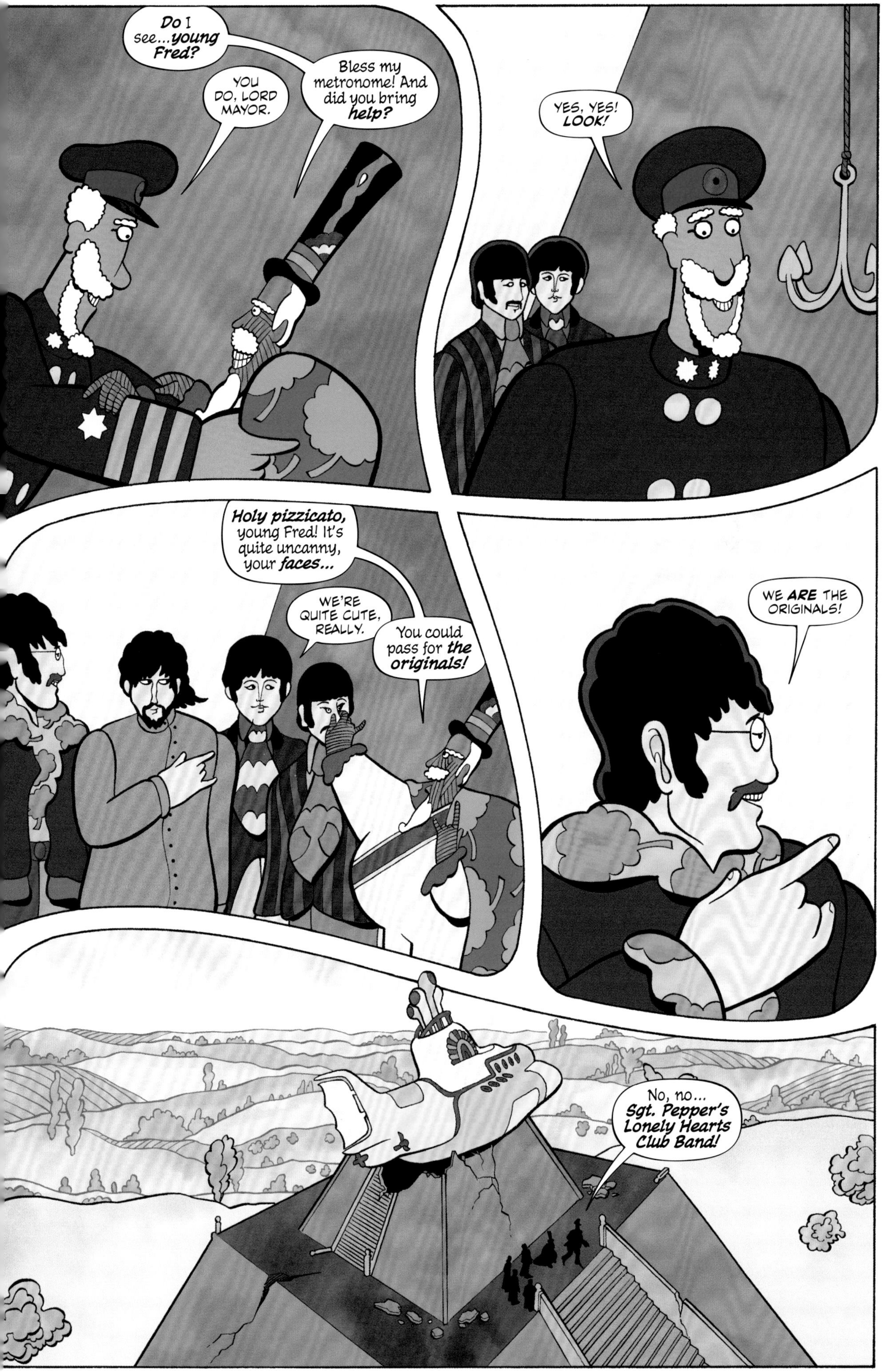

Do I see...young Fred?
YOU DO, LORD MAYOR.
Bless my metronome! And did you bring help?
YES, YES! LOOK!
Holy pizzicato, young Fred! It's quite uncanny, your faces...
WE'RE QUITE CUTE, REALLY.
You could pass for the originals!
WE ARE THE ORIGINALS!
No, no... Sgt. Pepper's Lonely Hearts Club Band!

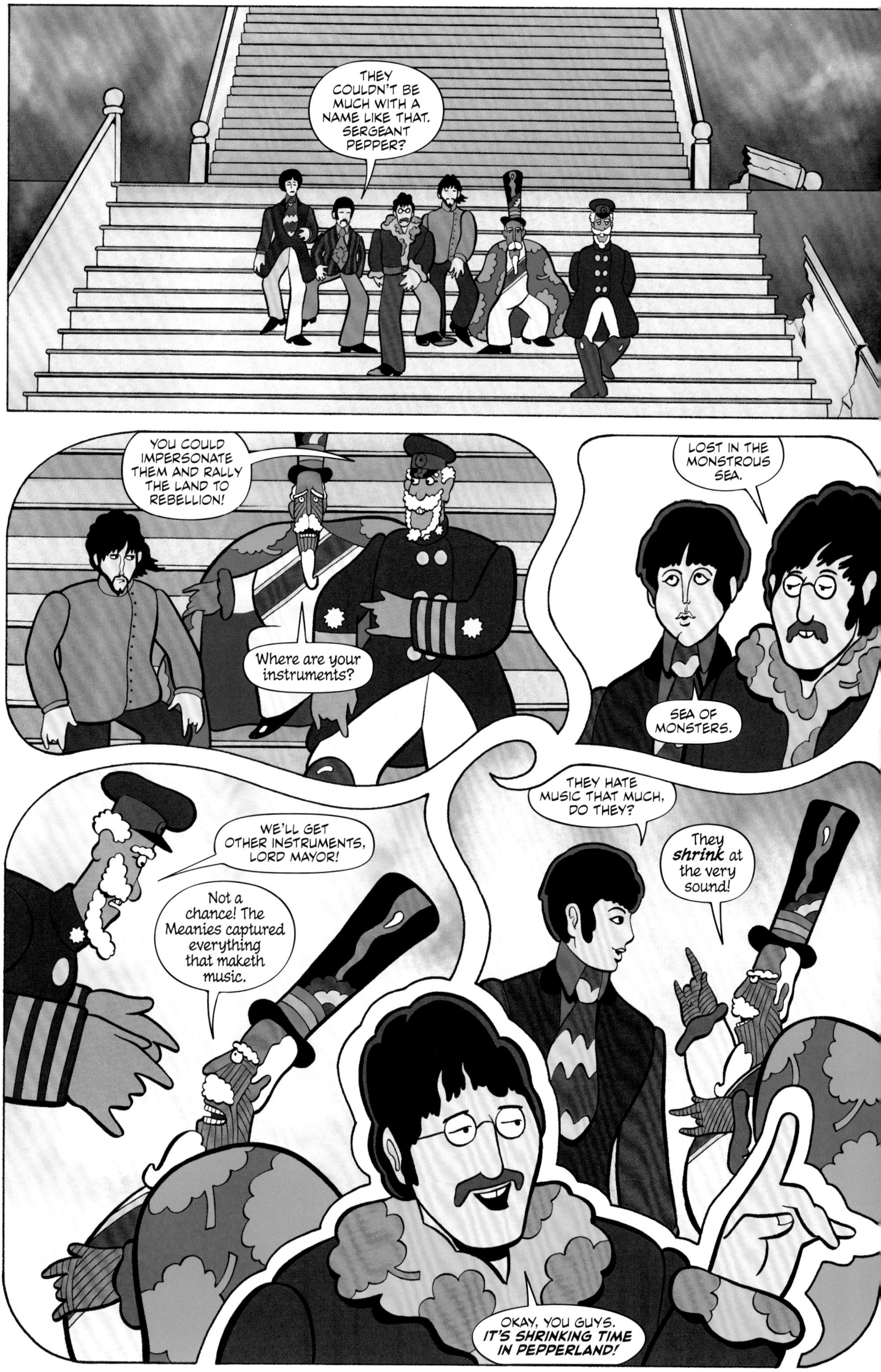
THEY COULDN'T BE MUCH WITH A NAME LIKE THAT. SERGEANT PEPPER?
YOU COULD IMPERSONATE THEM AND RALLY THE LAND TO REBELLION!
Where are your instruments?
LOST IN THE MONSTROUS SEA.
SEA OF MONSTERS.
WE'LL GET OTHER INSTRUMENTS, LORD MAYOR!
Not a chance! The Meanies captured everything that maketh music.
THEY HATE MUSIC THAT MUCH, DO THEY?
They *shrink* at the very sound!
OKAY, YOU GUYS. *IT'S SHRINKING TIME IN PEPPERLAND!*

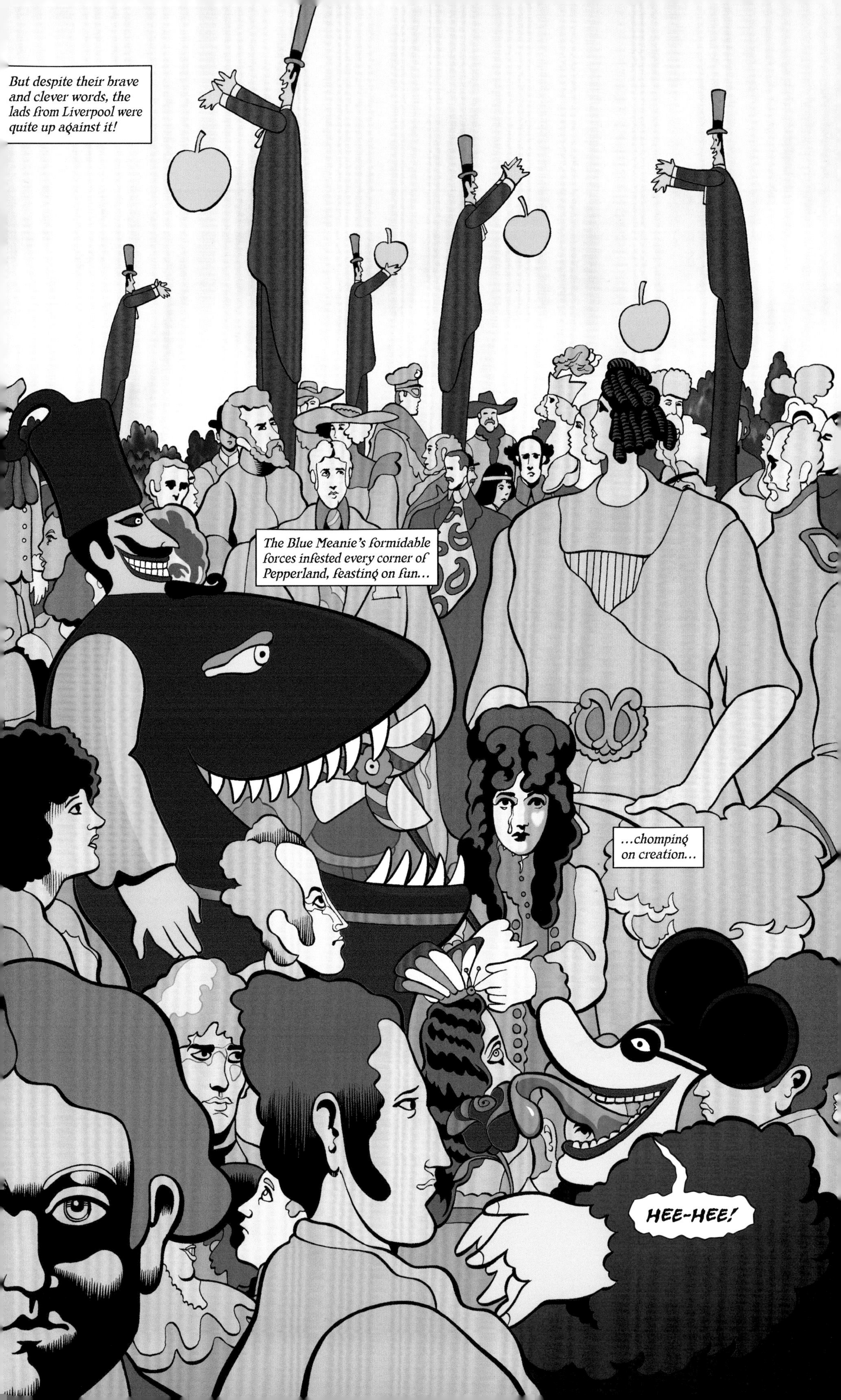

But despite their brave and clever words, the lads from Liverpool were quite up against it!
The Blue Meanie's formidable forces infested every corner of Pepperland, feasting on fun...
...chomping on creation...
HEE-HEE!

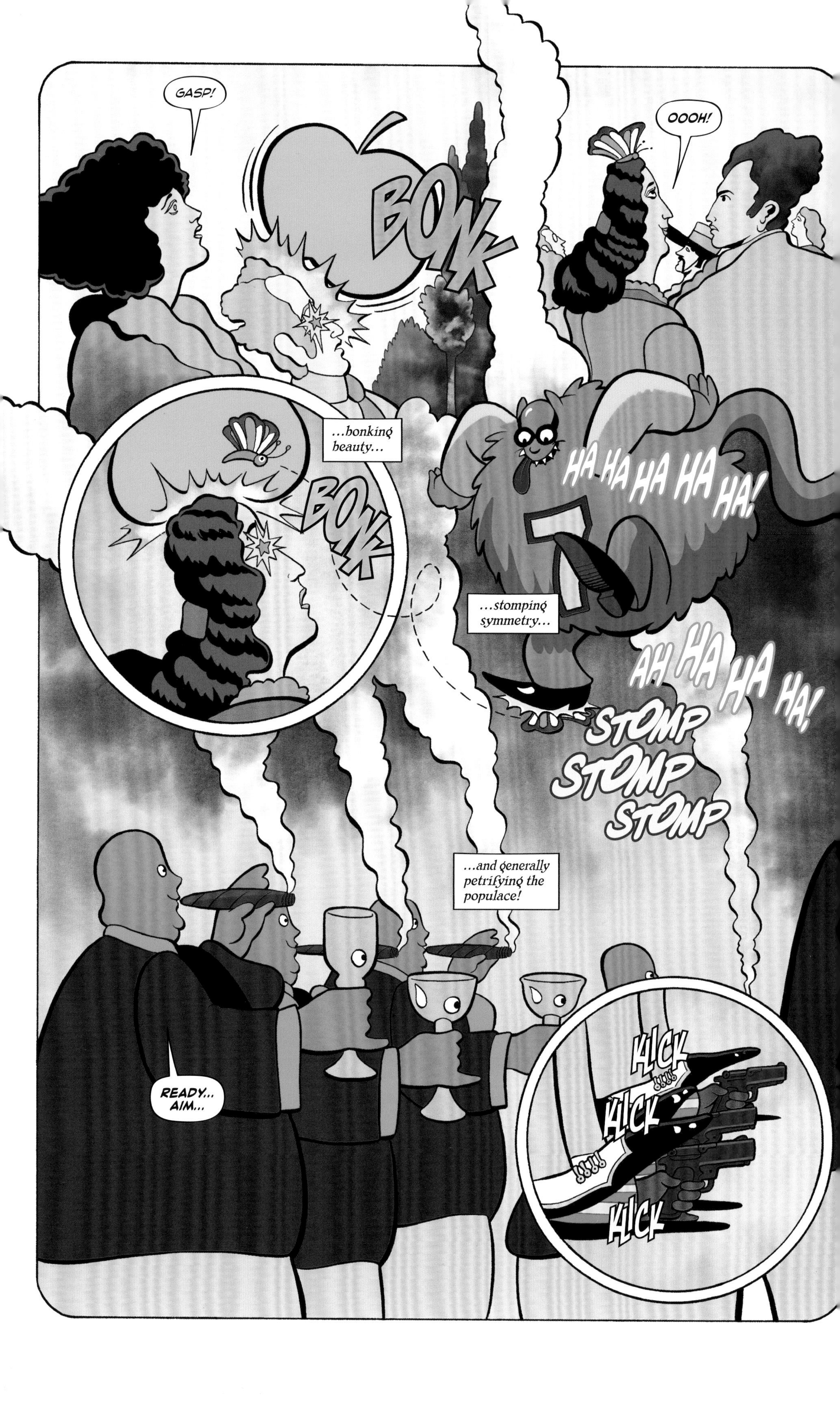
GASP!
BONK
OOOH!
...bonking beauty...
BONK
HA HA HA HA HA HA!
...stomping symmetry...
AH HA HA HA HA!
STOMP
STOMP
STOMP
...and generally petrifying the populace!
READY... AIM...
KLICK
KLICK
KLICK

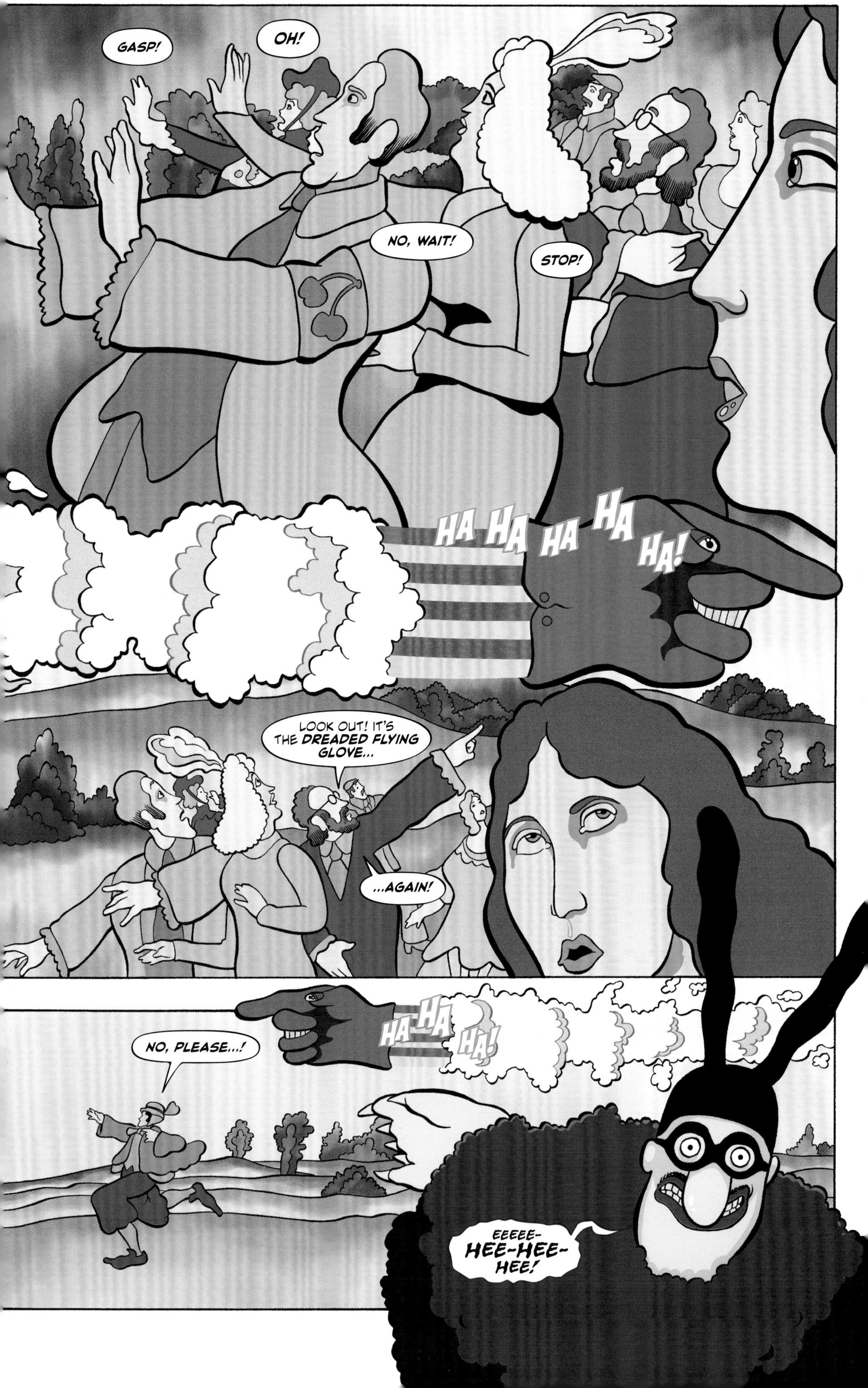
GASP!
OH!
NO, WAIT!
STOP!
HA HA HA HA HA!
LOOK OUT! IT'S THE DREADED FLYING GLOVE...
...AGAIN!
HA-HA HA!
NO, PLEASE...!
EEEEE-HEE-HEE-HEE!

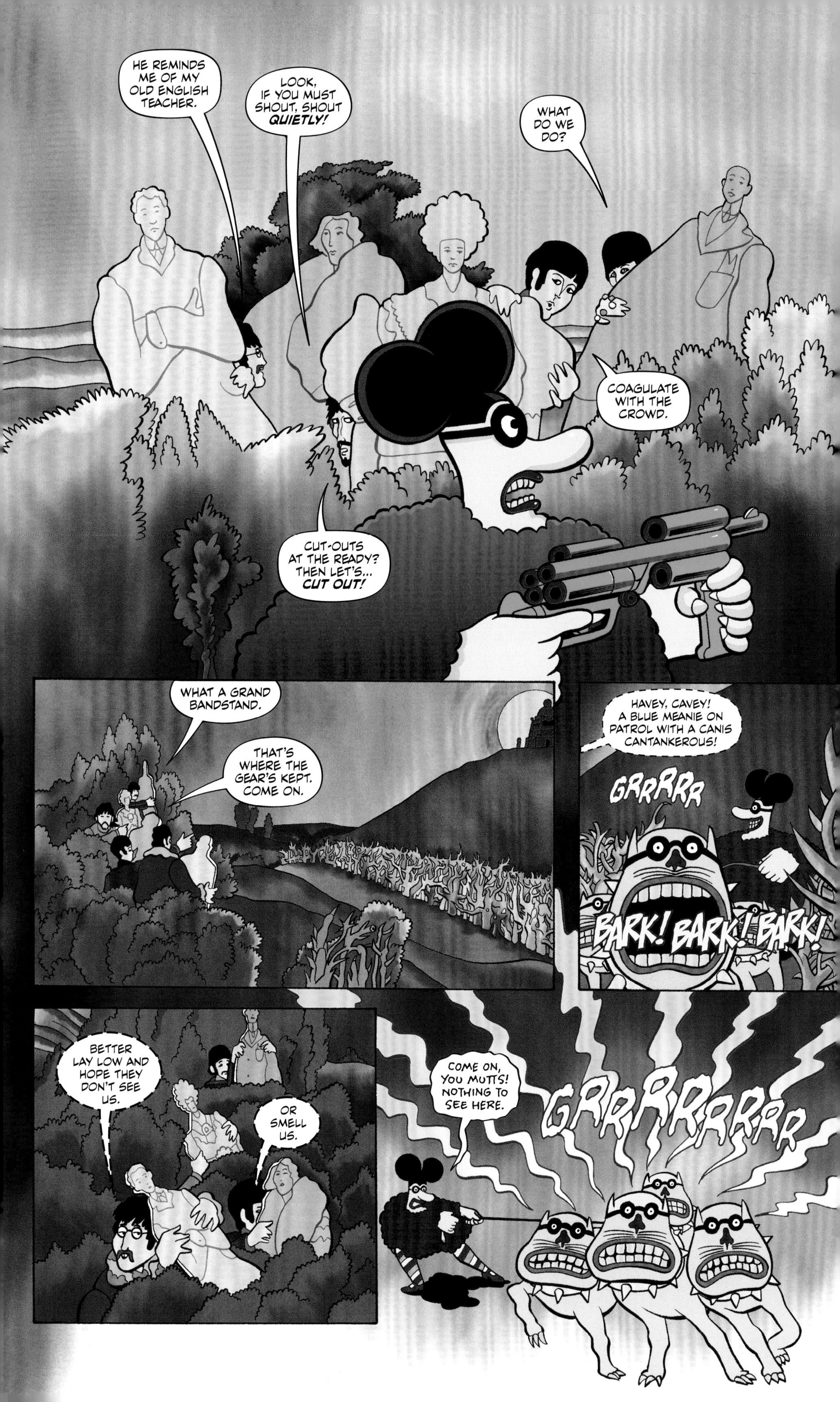

HE REMINDS ME OF MY OLD ENGLISH TEACHER.
LOOK, IF YOU MUST SHOUT, SHOUT QUIETLY!
WHAT DO WE DO?
COAGULATE WITH THE CROWD.
CUT-OUTS AT THE READY? THEN LET'S... CUT OUT!
WHAT A GRAND BANDSTAND.
THAT'S WHERE THE GEAR'S KEPT. COME ON.
HAVEY, CAVEY! A BLUE MEANIE ON PATROL WITH A CANIS CANTANKEROUS!
GRRRRR
BARK! BARK! BARK!
BETTER LAY LOW AND HOPE THEY DON'T SEE US.
OR SMELL US.
COME ON, YOU MUTTS! NOTHING TO SEE HERE.
GRRRRRRRRR

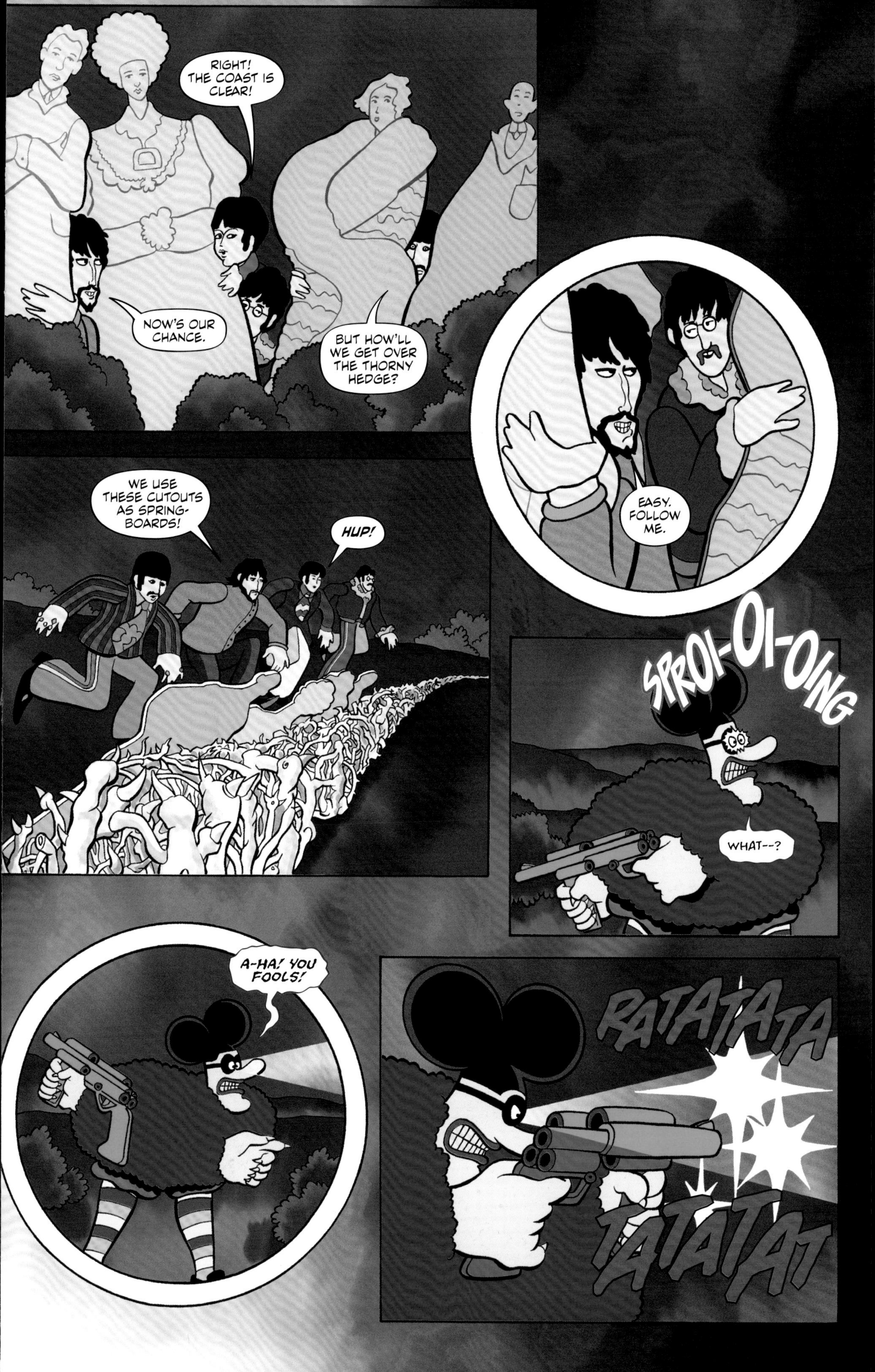
RIGHT! THE COAST IS CLEAR!
NOW'S OUR CHANCE.
BUT HOW'LL WE GET OVER THE THORNY HEDGE?
EASY. FOLLOW ME.
WE USE THESE CUTOUTS AS SPRING-BOARDS!
HUP!
SPROI-OI-OING
WHAT--?
A-HA! YOU FOOLS!
RATATATATA
TATATAT

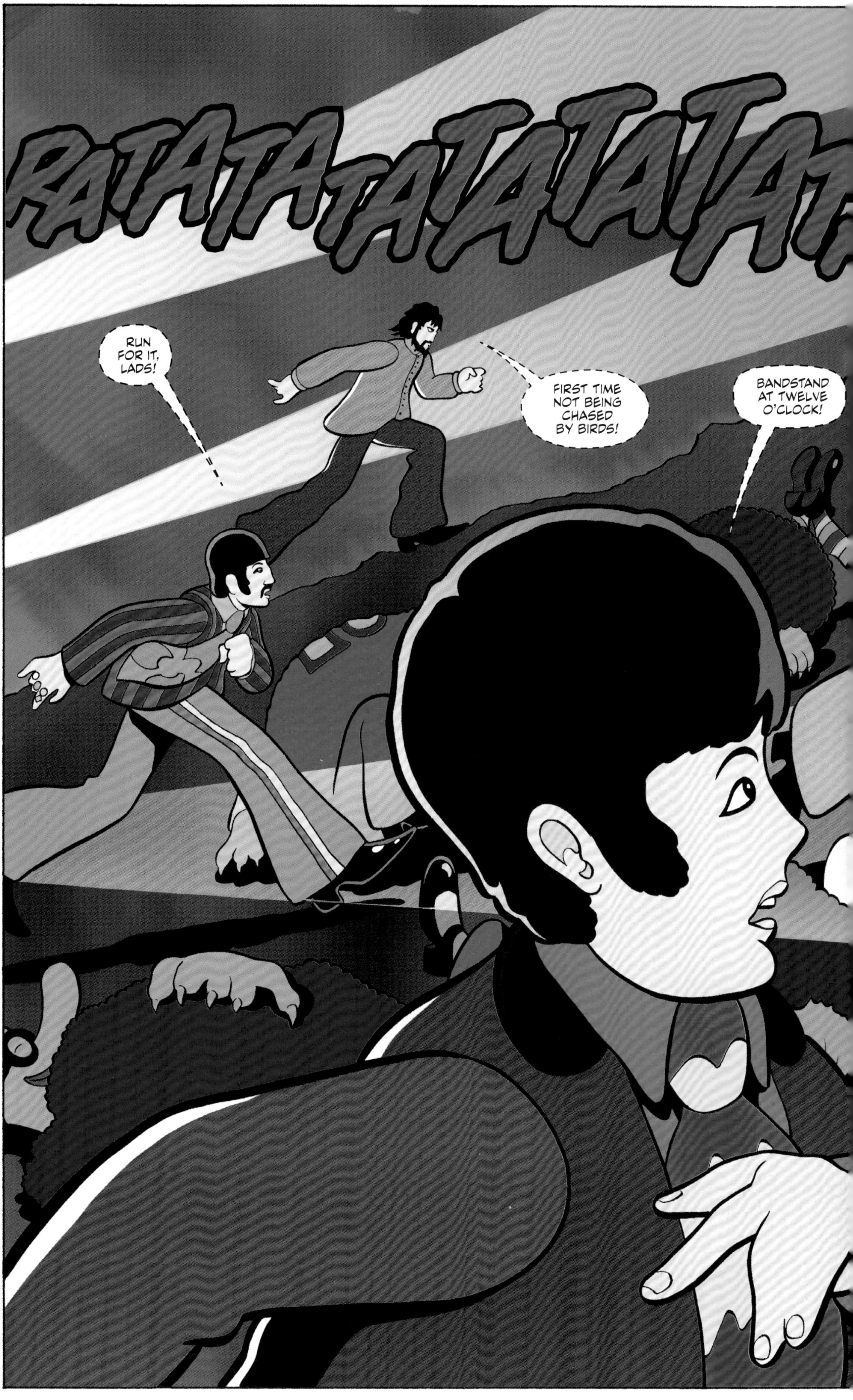
RATATATATATATATA
RUN FOR IT, LADS!
FIRST TIME NOT BEING CHASED BY BIRDS!
BANDSTAND AT TWELVE O'CLOCK!

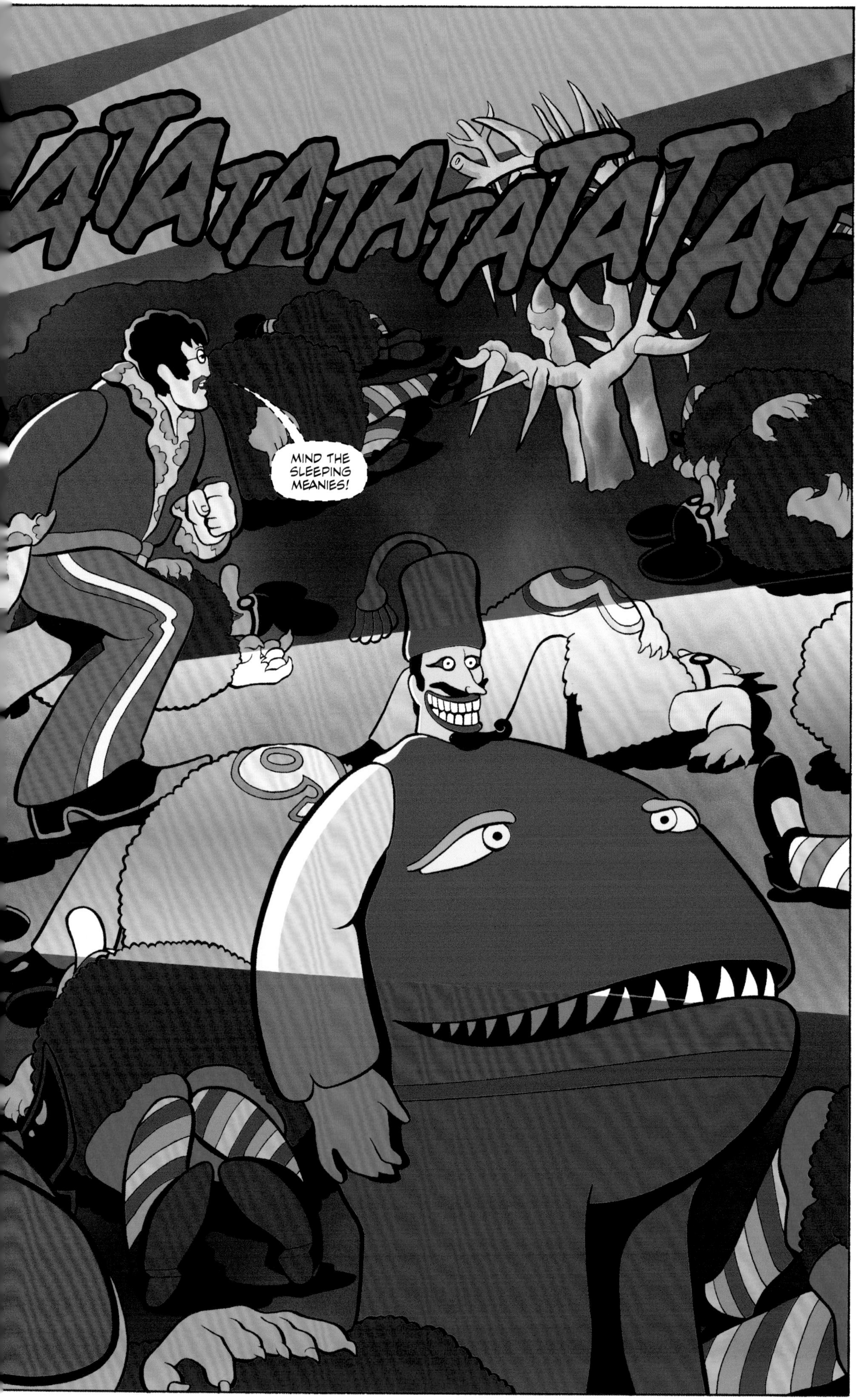
TATATATATATATATAT
MIND THE SLEEPING MEANIES!

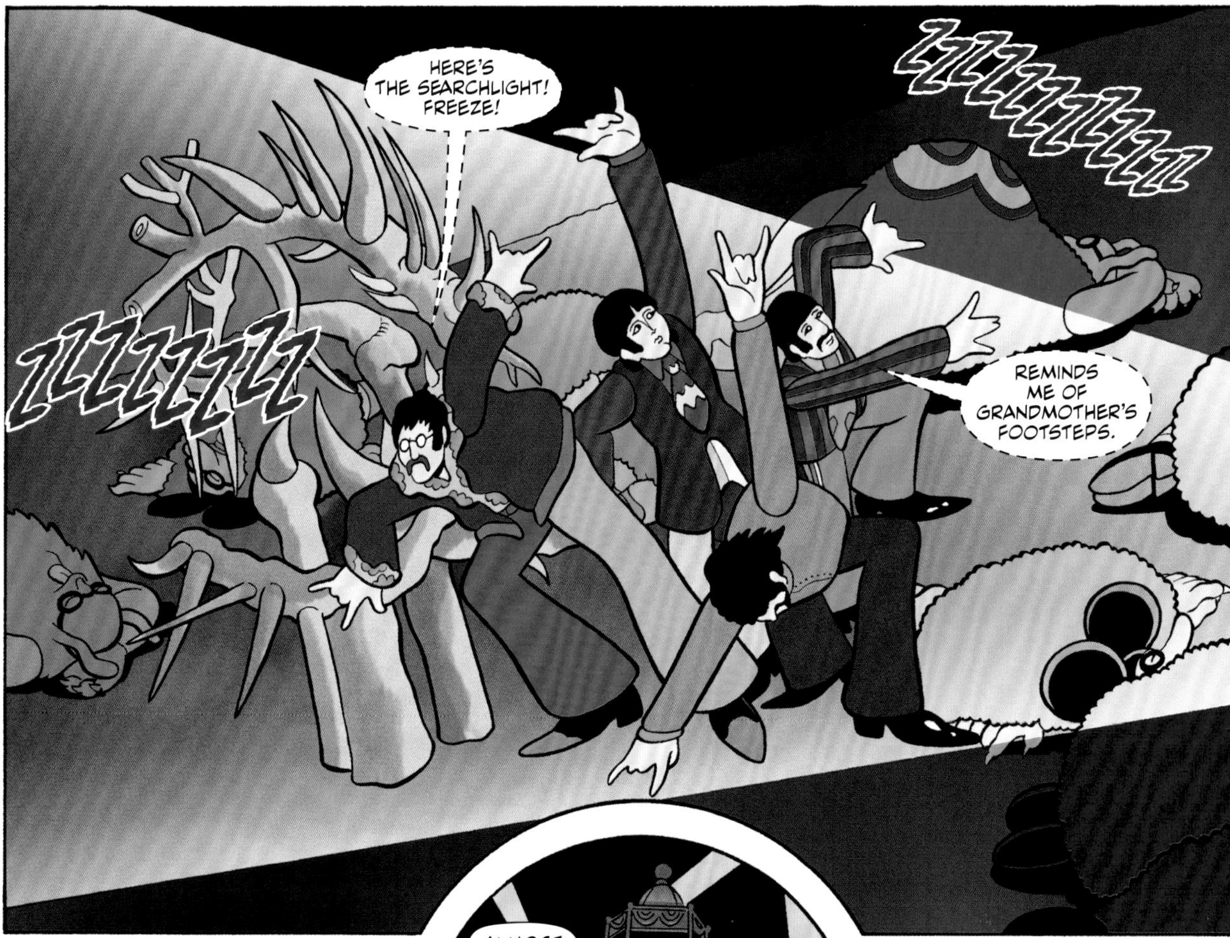
HERE'S THE SEARCHLIGHT! FREEZE!
ZZZZZZZZZZ
ZZZZZZZZZ
REMINDS ME OF GRANDMOTHER'S FOOTSTEPS.

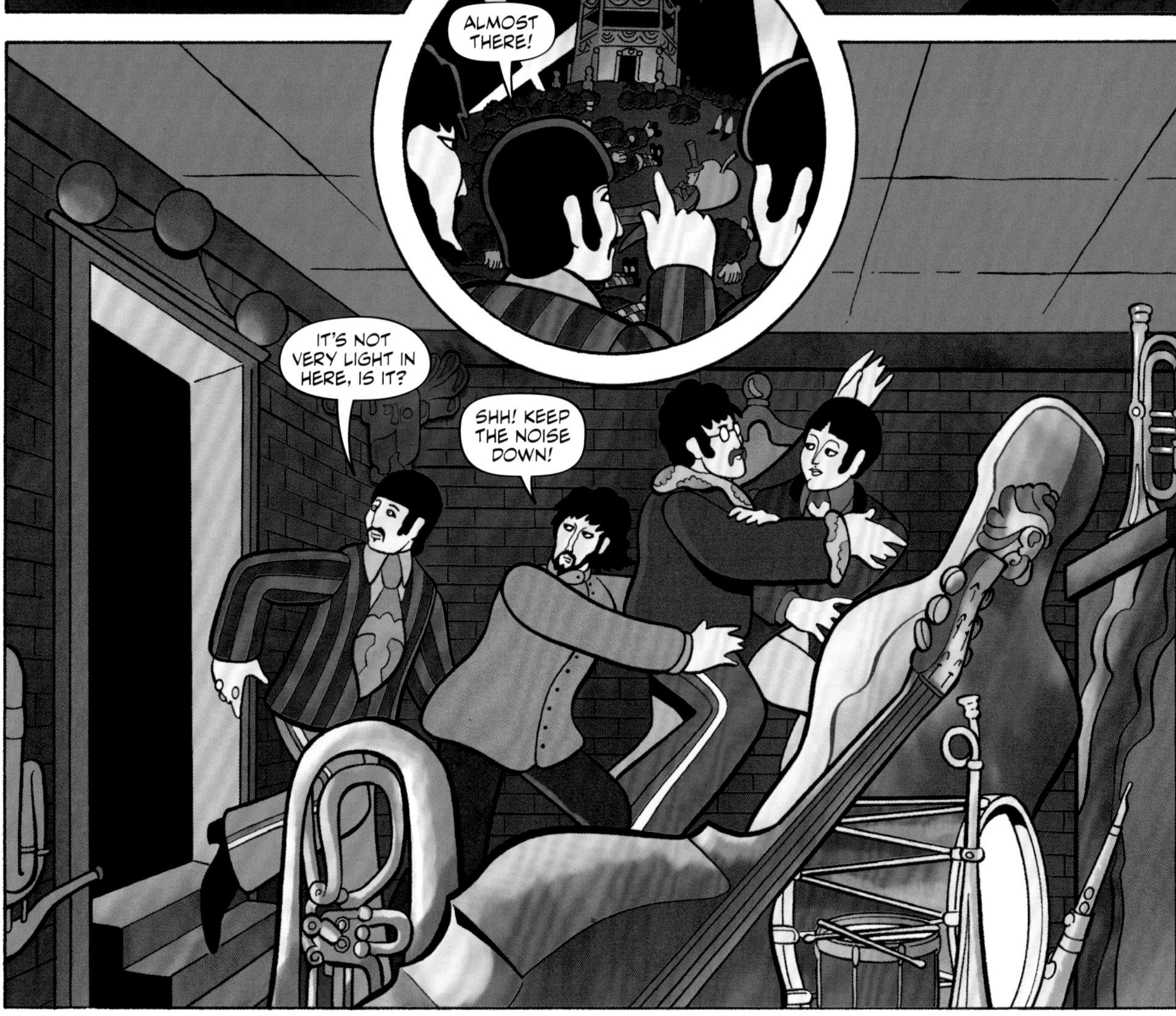
ALMOST THERE!
IT'S NOT VERY LIGHT IN HERE, IS IT?
SHH! KEEP THE NOISE DOWN!

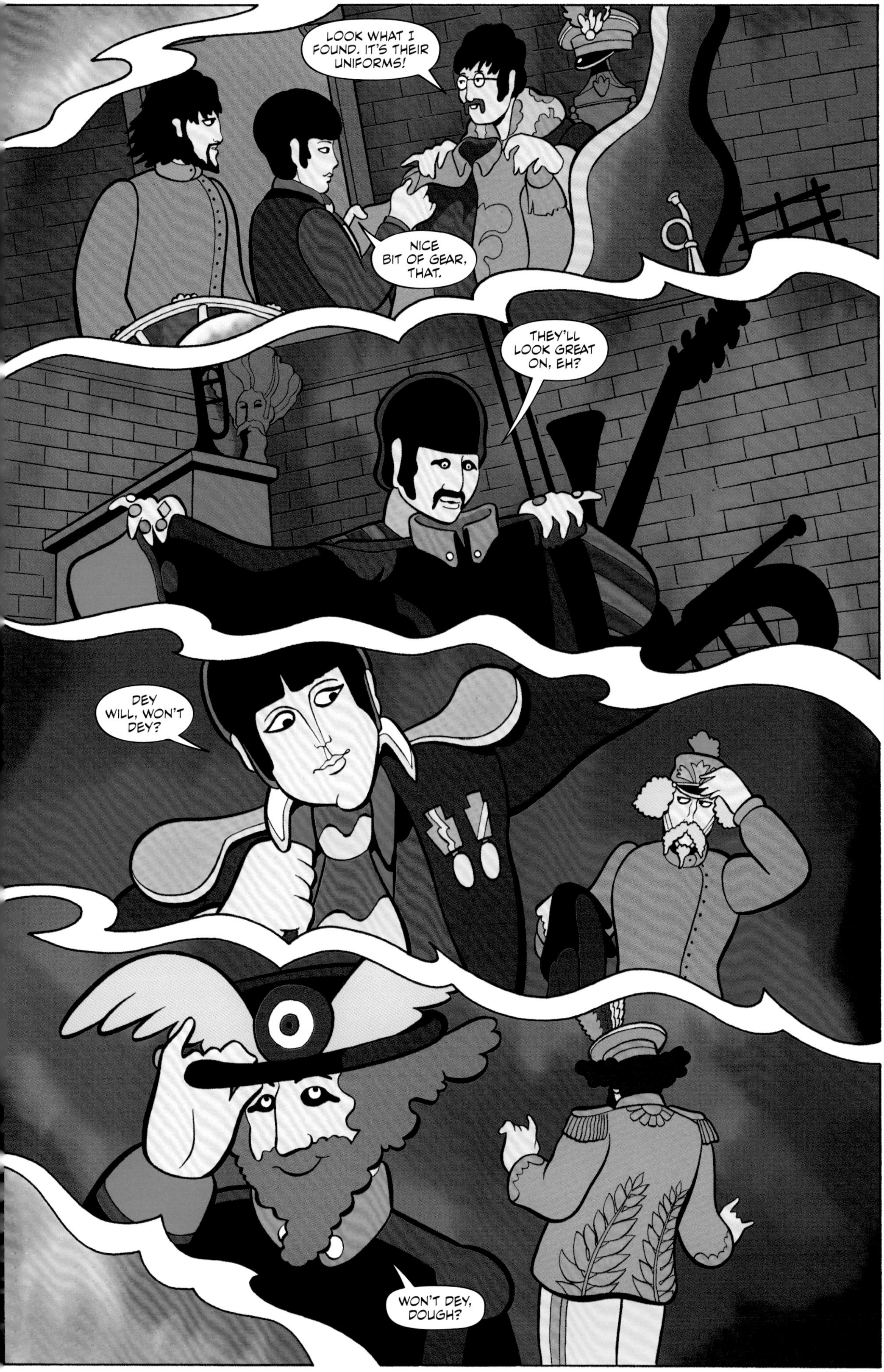
LOOK WHAT I FOUND. IT'S THEIR UNIFORMS!
NICE BIT OF GEAR, THAT.
THEY'LL LOOK GREAT ON, EH?
DEY WILL, WON'T DEY?
WON'T DEY, DOUGH?

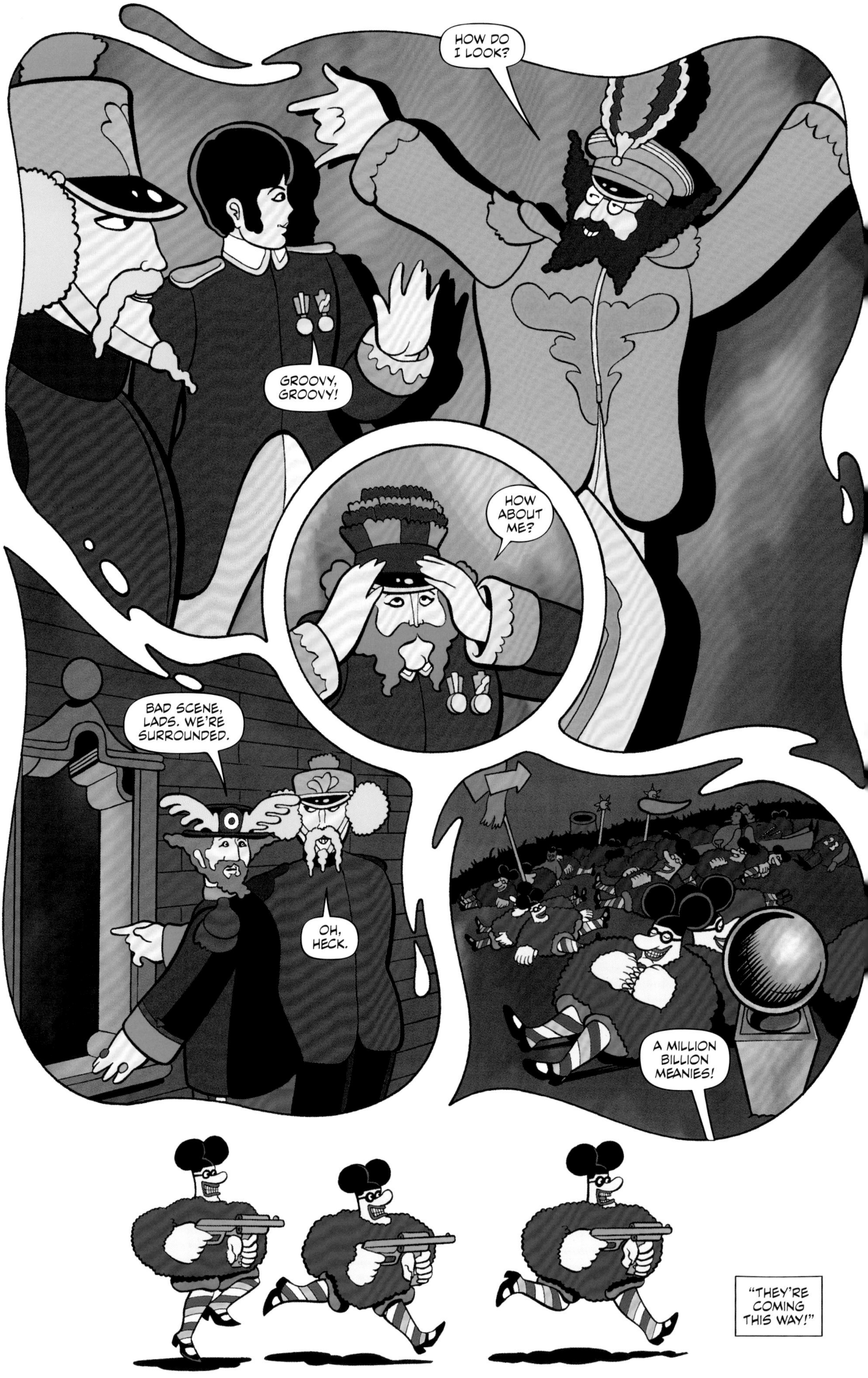
HOW DO I LOOK?
GROOVY, GROOVY!
HOW ABOUT ME?
BAD SCENE, LADS. WE'RE SURROUNDED.
OH, HECK.
A MILLION BILLION MEANIES!
"THEY'RE COMING THIS WAY!"

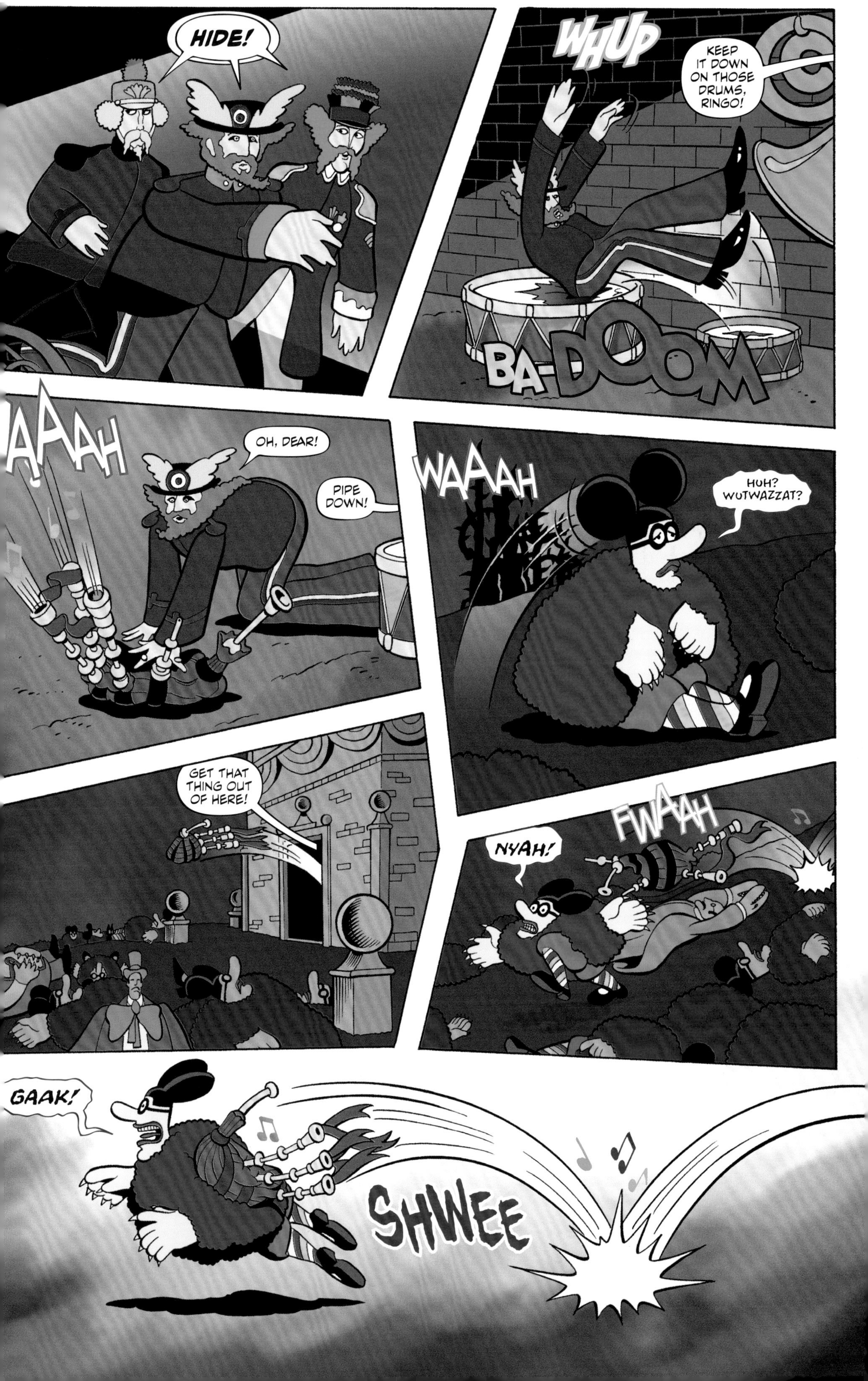

HIDE!
WHUP
KEEP IT DOWN ON THOSE DRUMS, RINGO!
BA-DOOM
AAAAH
OH, DEAR!
PIPE DOWN!
WAAAAH
HUH? WUTWAZZAT?
GET THAT THING OUT OF HERE!
NYAH!
FWAAAH
GAAK!
SHWEE

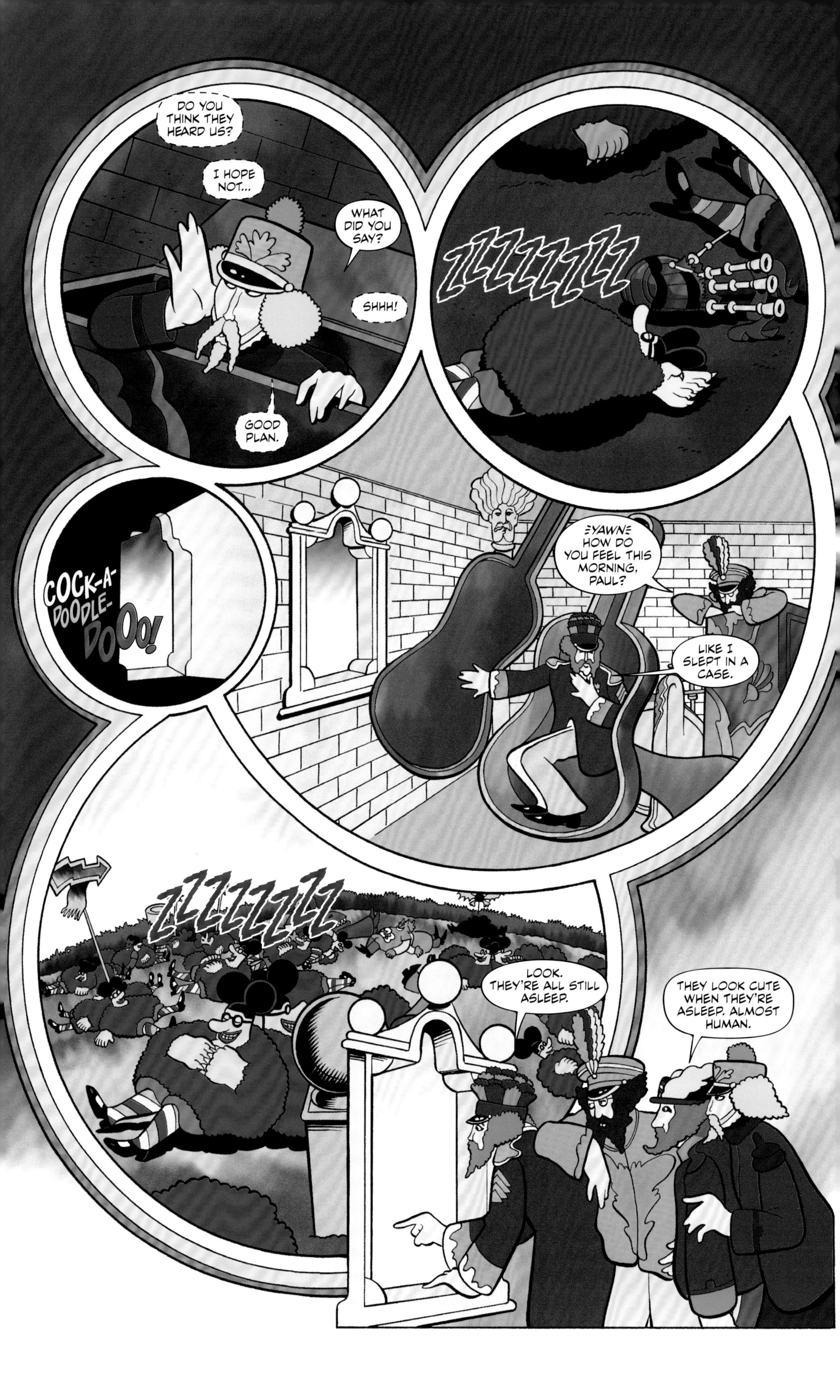
DO YOU THINK THEY HEARD US?
I HOPE NOT...
WHAT DID YOU SAY?
SHHH!
GOOD PLAN.
ZZZZZZZZ
COCK-A-DOODLE-DOOO!
=YAWN= HOW DO YOU FEEL THIS MORNING, PAUL?
LIKE I SLEPT IN A CASE.
ZZZZZZZZ
LOOK. THEY'RE ALL STILL ASLEEP.
THEY LOOK CUTE WHEN THEY'RE ASLEEP. ALMOST HUMAN.

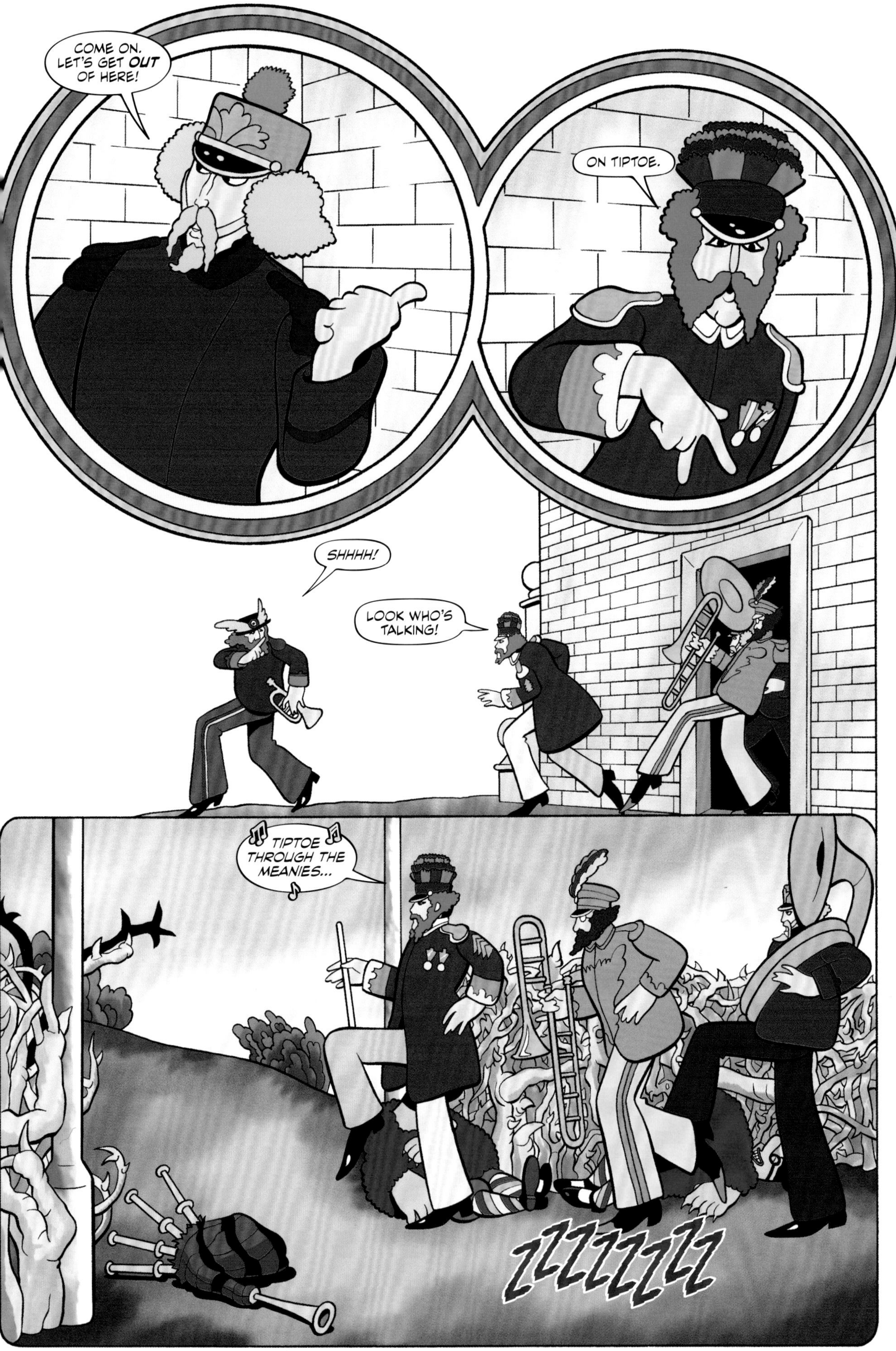
COME ON. LET'S GET OUT OF HERE!
ON TIPTOE.
SHHHH!
LOOK WHO'S TALKING!
TIPTOE THROUGH THE MEANIES...
ZZZZZZZZ

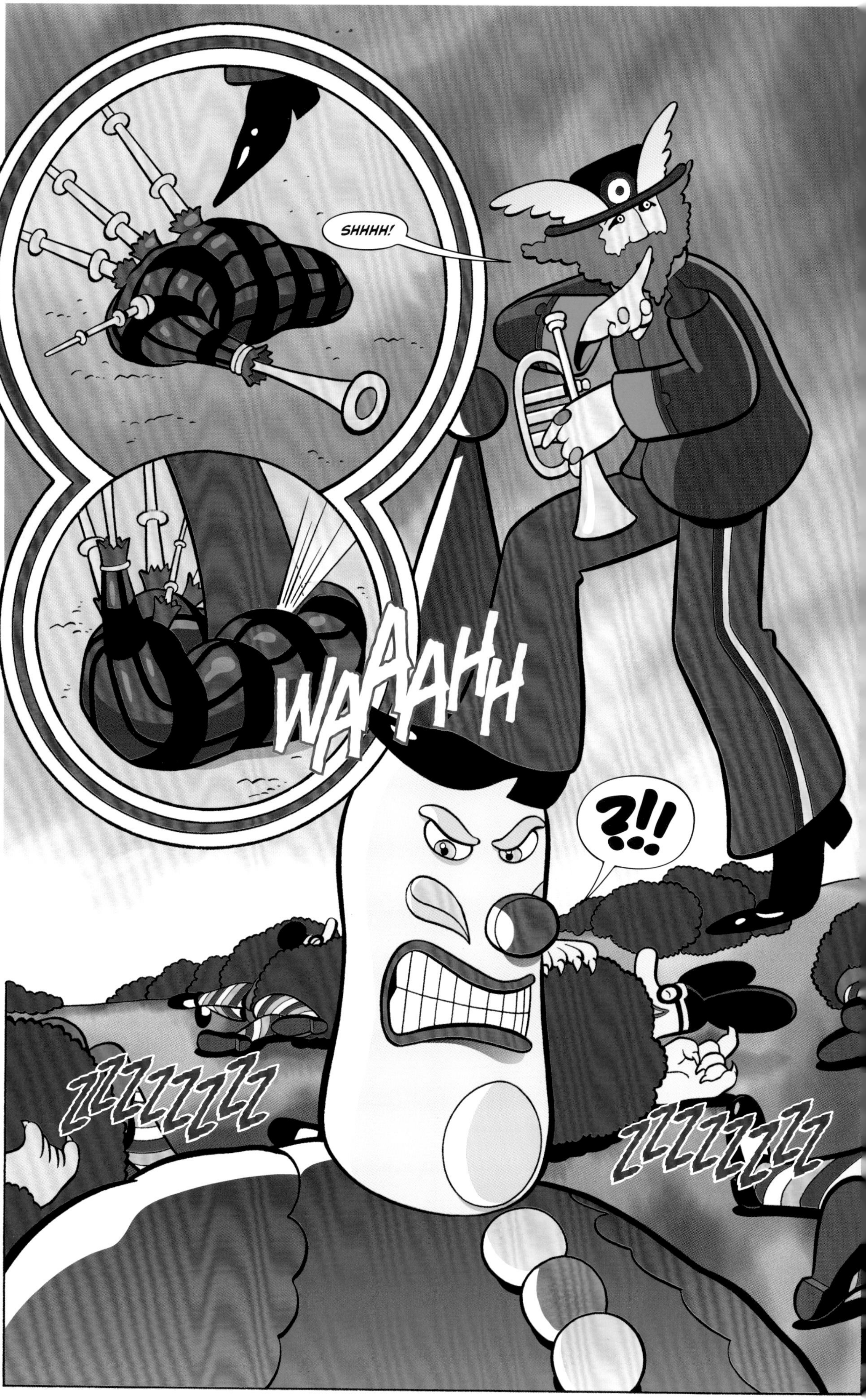
SHHHH!
WAAAHH
?!!
ZZZZZZZ
ZZZZZZZ

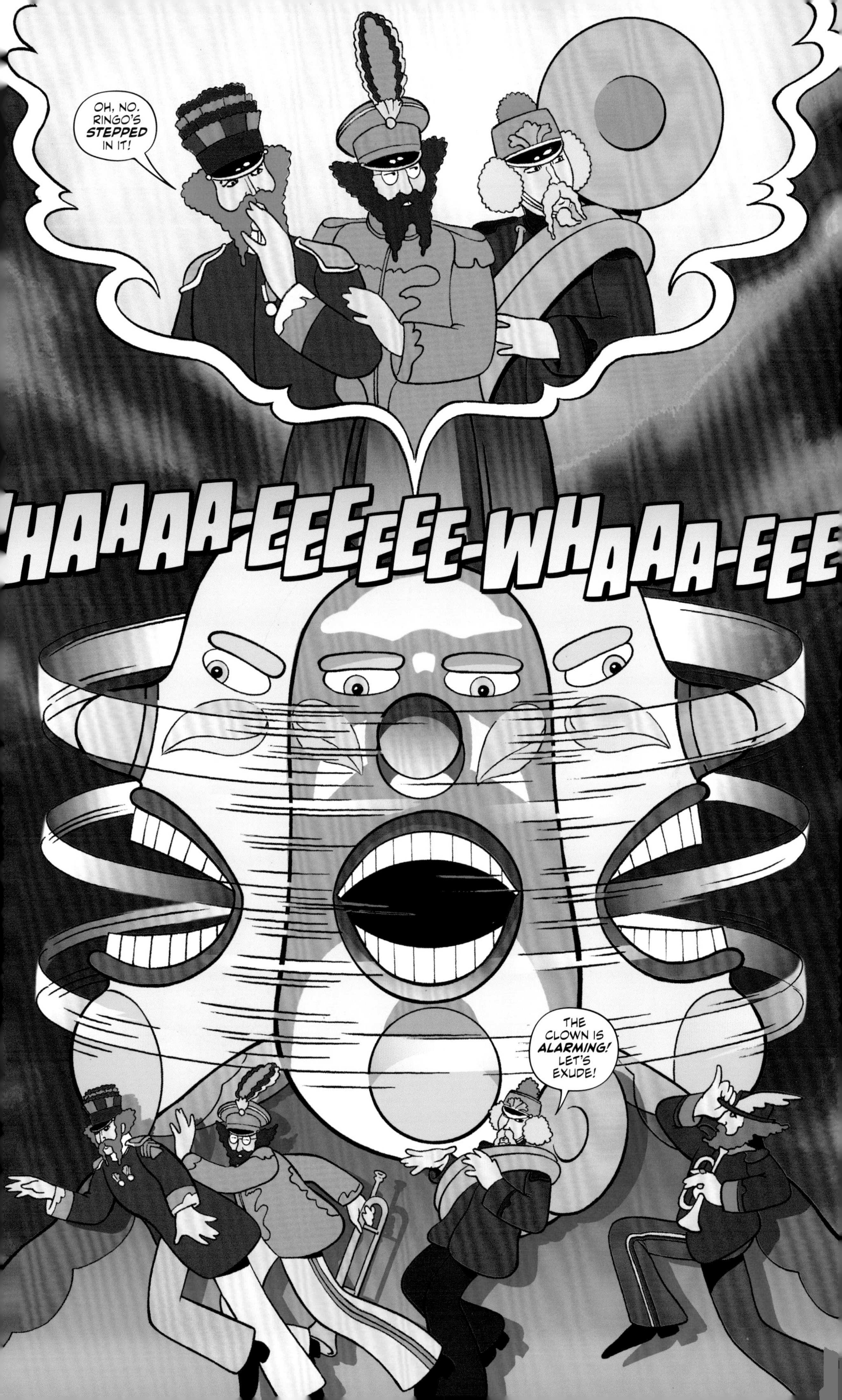
OH, NO. RINGO'S STEPPED IN IT!
HAAAA-EEEEEE-WHAAAA-EEE
THE CLOWN IS ALARMING! LET'S EXUDE!

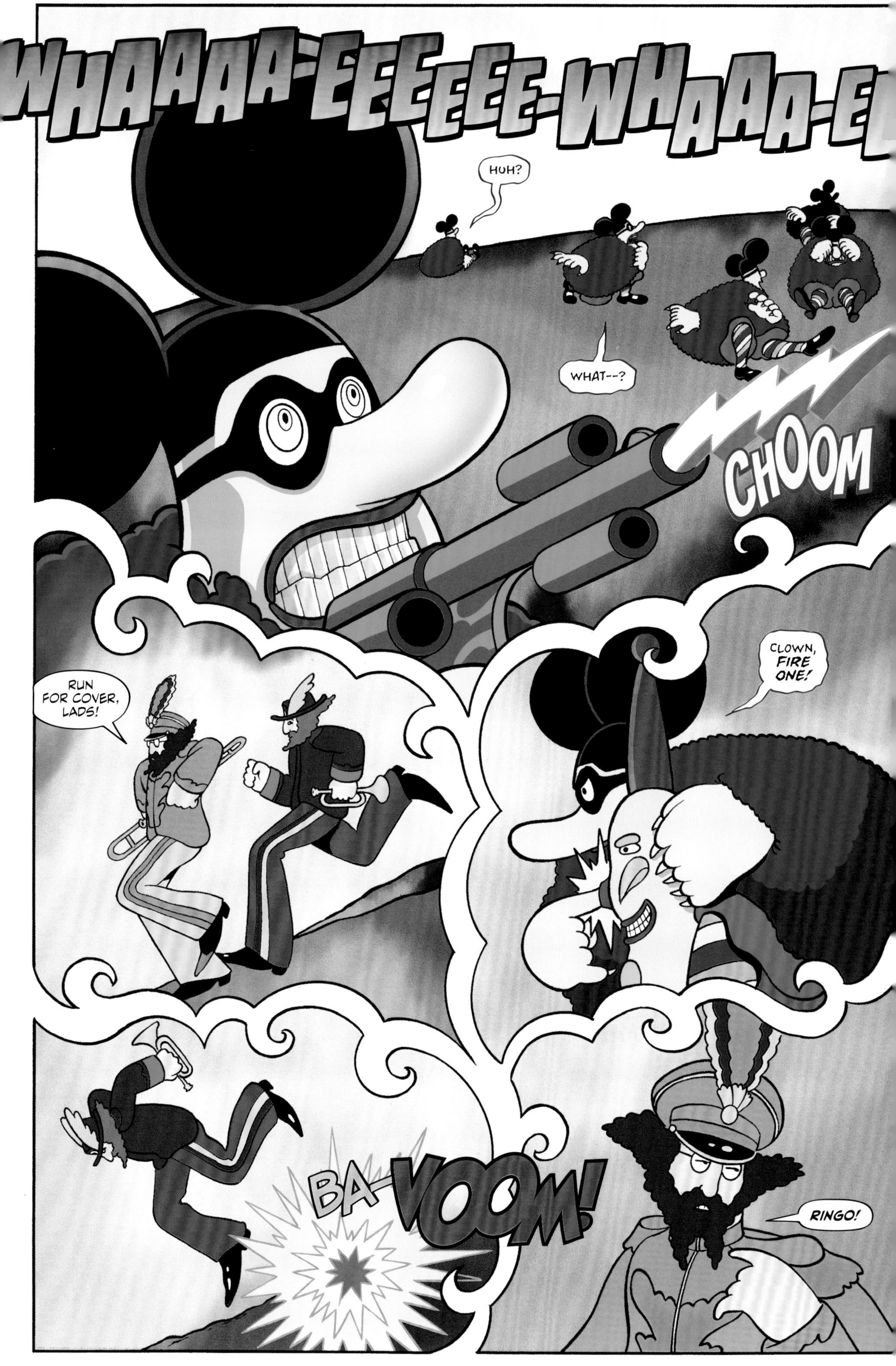
WHAAAA-EEEEEEE-WHAAAA-EE
HUH?
WHAT--?
CHOOM
RUN FOR COVER, LADS!
CLOWN, FIRE ONE!
BA-VOOM!
RINGO!

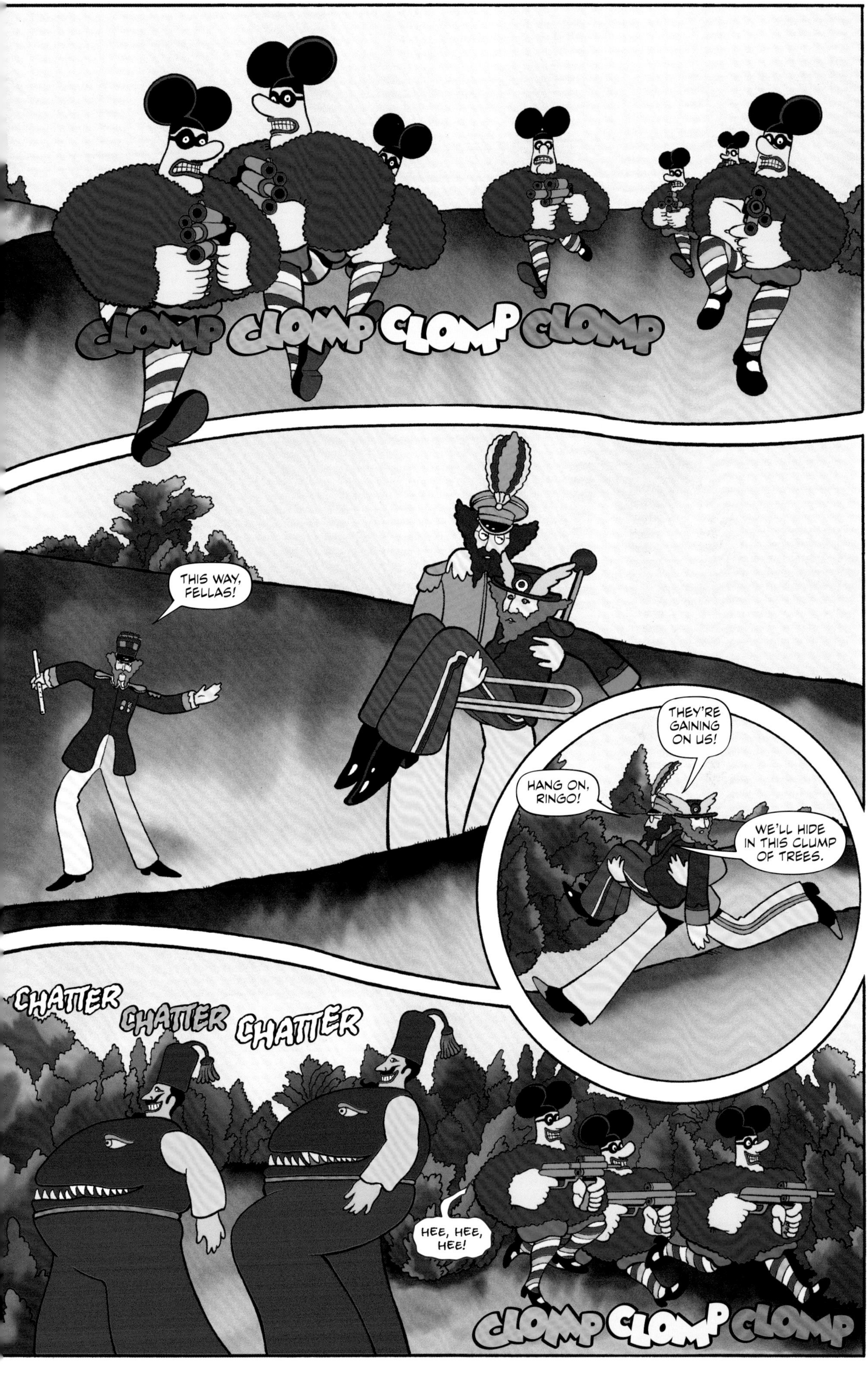
CLOMP CLOMP CLOMP CLOMP
THIS WAY, FELLAS!
THEY'RE GAINING ON US!
HANG ON, RINGO!
WE'LL HIDE IN THIS CLUMP OF TREES.
CHATTER CHATTER CHATTER
HEE, HEE, HEE!
CLOMP CLOMP CLOMP

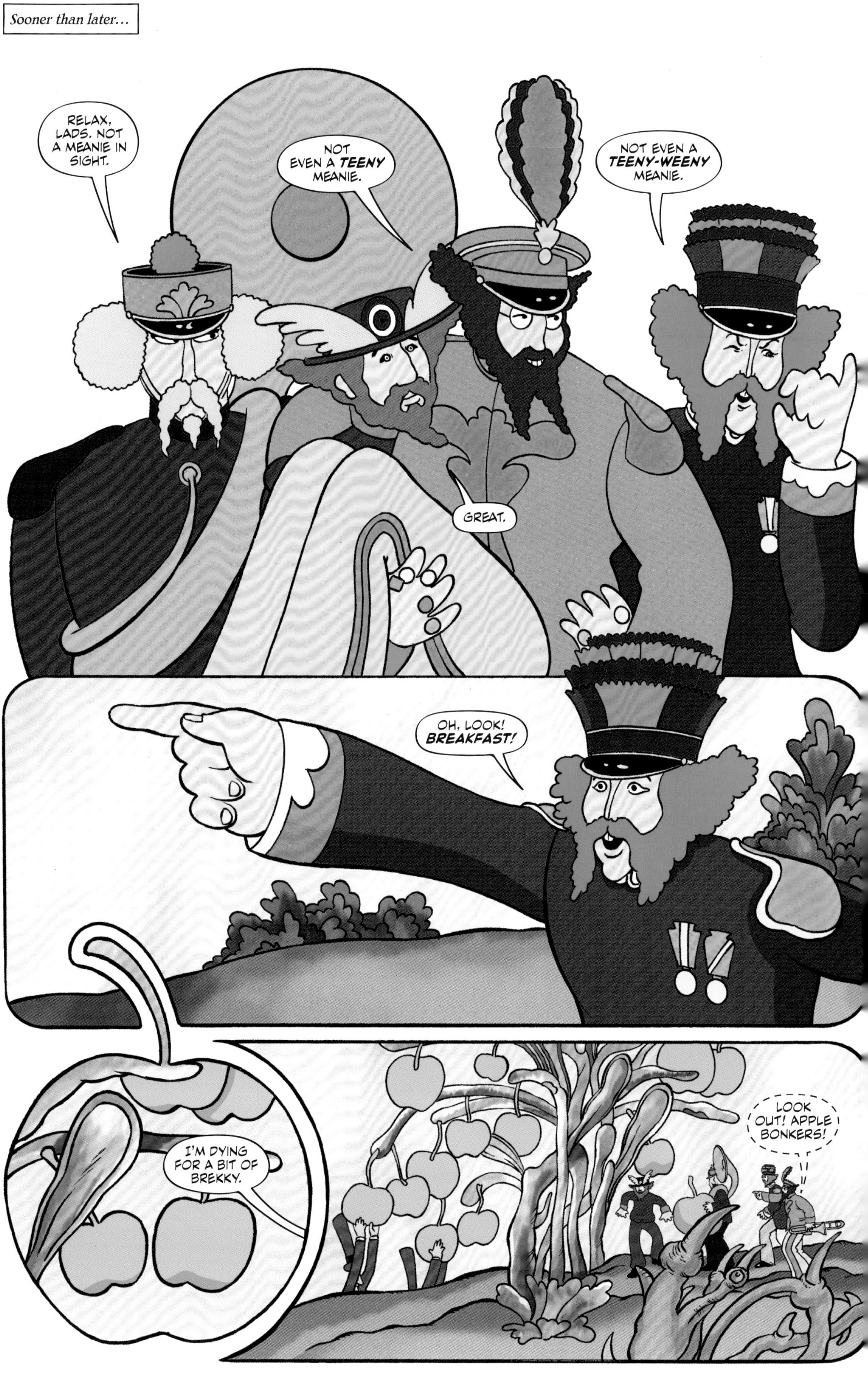
Sooner than later…
RELAX, LADS. NOT A MEANIE IN SIGHT.
NOT EVEN A TEENY MEANIE.
NOT EVEN A TEENY-WEENY MEANIE.
GREAT.
OH, LOOK! BREAKFAST!
I'M DYING FOR A BIT OF BREKKY.
LOOK OUT! APPLE BONKERS!

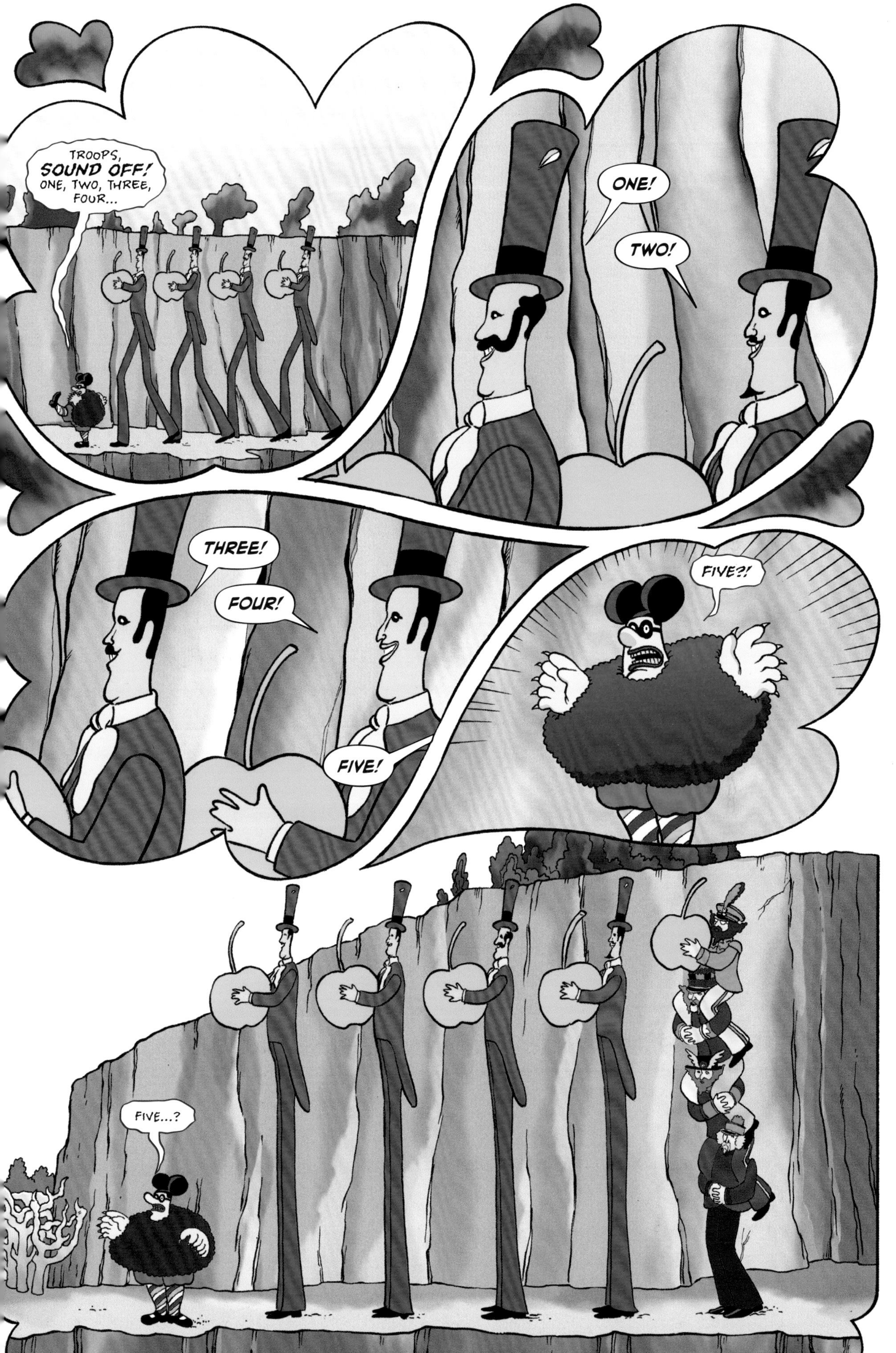

TROOPS, **SOUND OFF!** ONE, TWO, THREE, FOUR...
ONE!
TWO!
THREE!
FOUR!
FIVE!
FIVE?!
FIVE...?

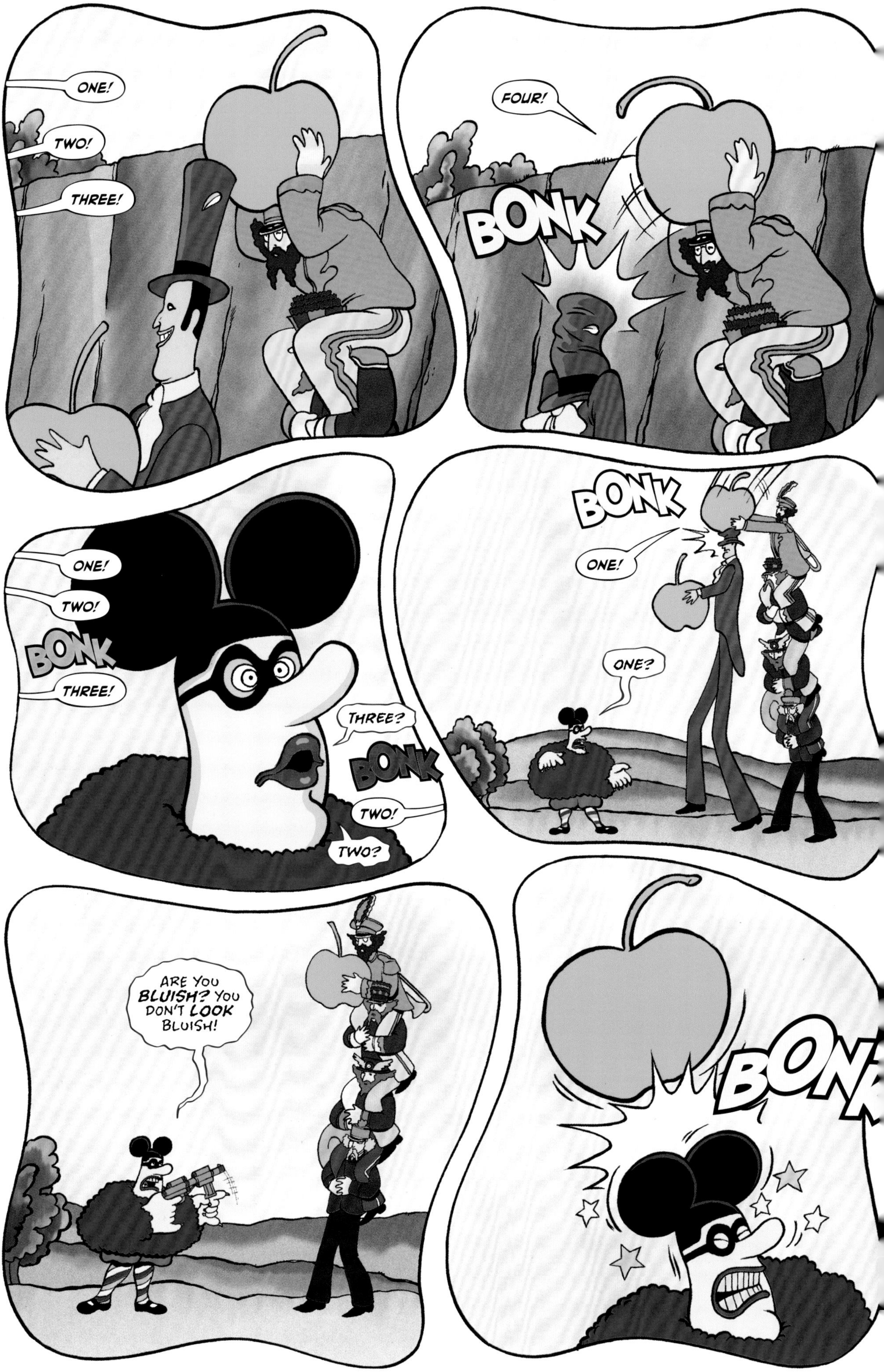
ONE!
TWO!
THREE!
FOUR!
BONK
ONE!
TWO!
BONK
THREE!
THREE?
BONK
TWO!
TWO?
BONK
ONE!
ONE?
ARE YOU BLUISH? YOU DON'T LOOK BLUISH!
BONK

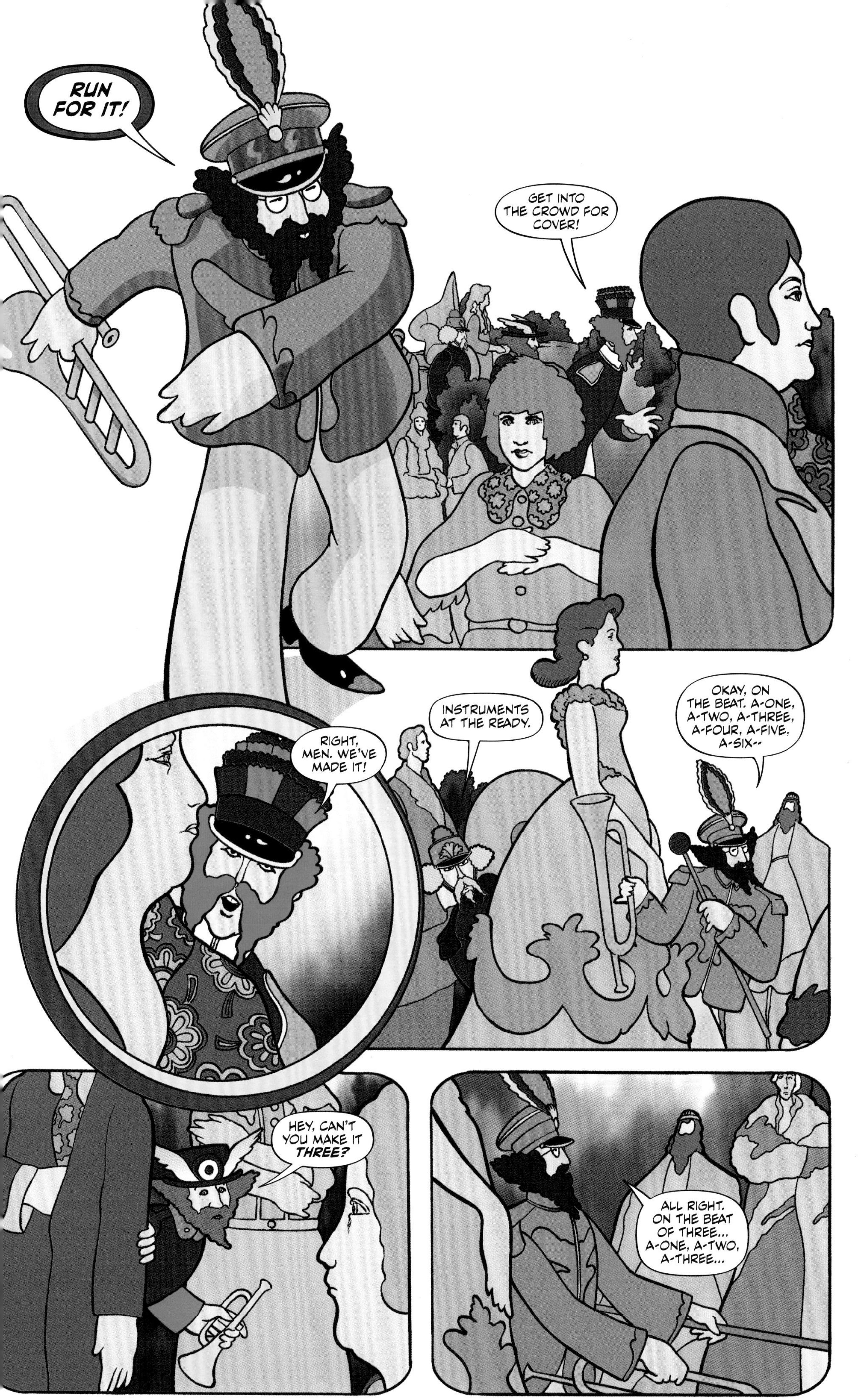
RUN FOR IT!
GET INTO THE CROWD FOR COVER!
RIGHT, MEN. WE'VE MADE IT!
INSTRUMENTS AT THE READY.
OKAY, ON THE BEAT. A-ONE, A-TWO, A-THREE, A-FOUR, A-FIVE, A-SIX--
HEY, CAN'T YOU MAKE IT *THREE?*
ALL RIGHT. ON THE BEAT OF THREE... A-ONE, A-TWO, A-THREE...

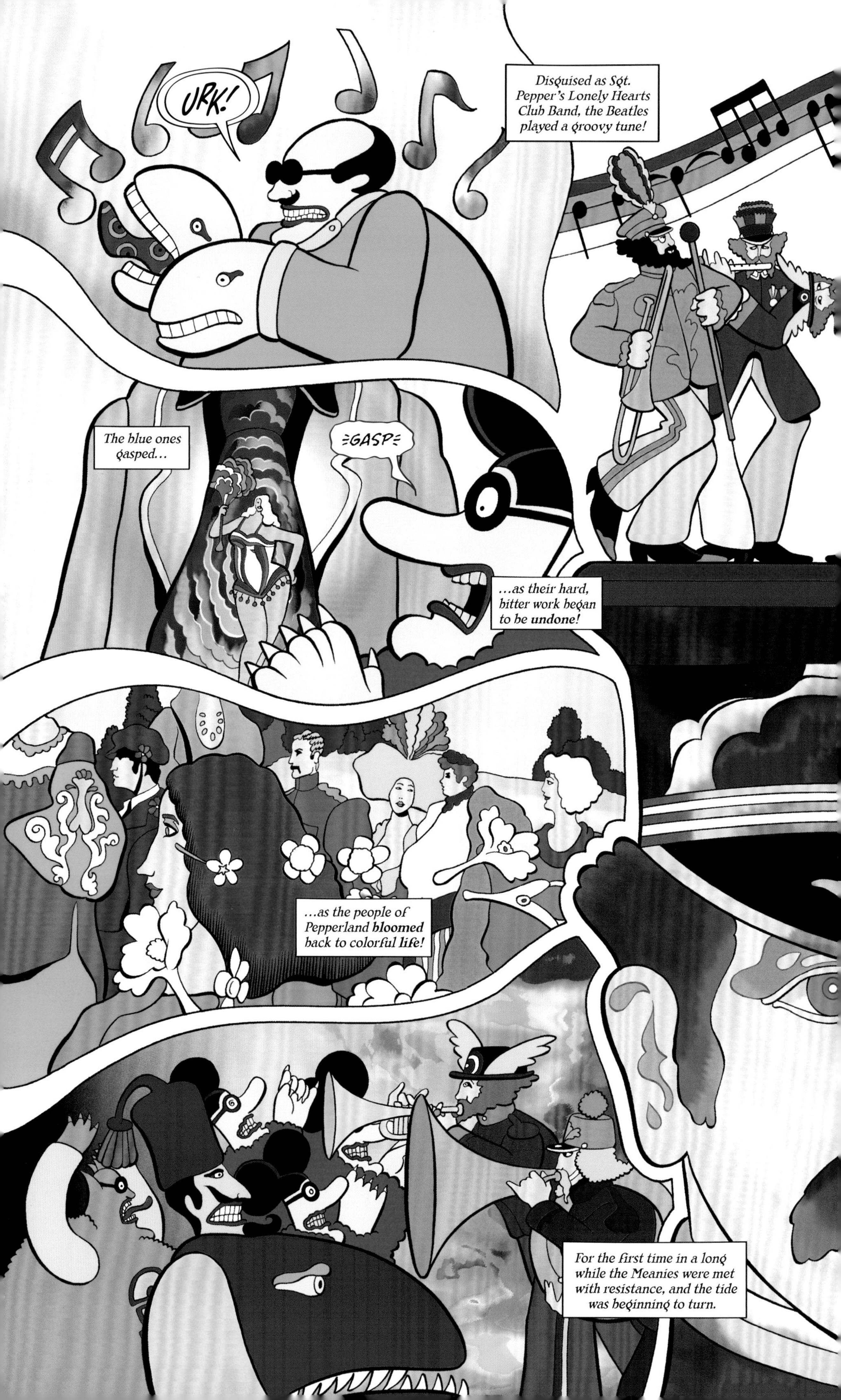
URK!
Disguised as Sgt. Pepper's Lonely Hearts Club Band, the Beatles played a groovy tune!
The blue ones gasped...
GASP
...as their hard, bitter work began to be undone!
...as the people of Pepperland bloomed back to colorful life!
For the first time in a long while the Meanies were met with resistance, and the tide was beginning to turn.

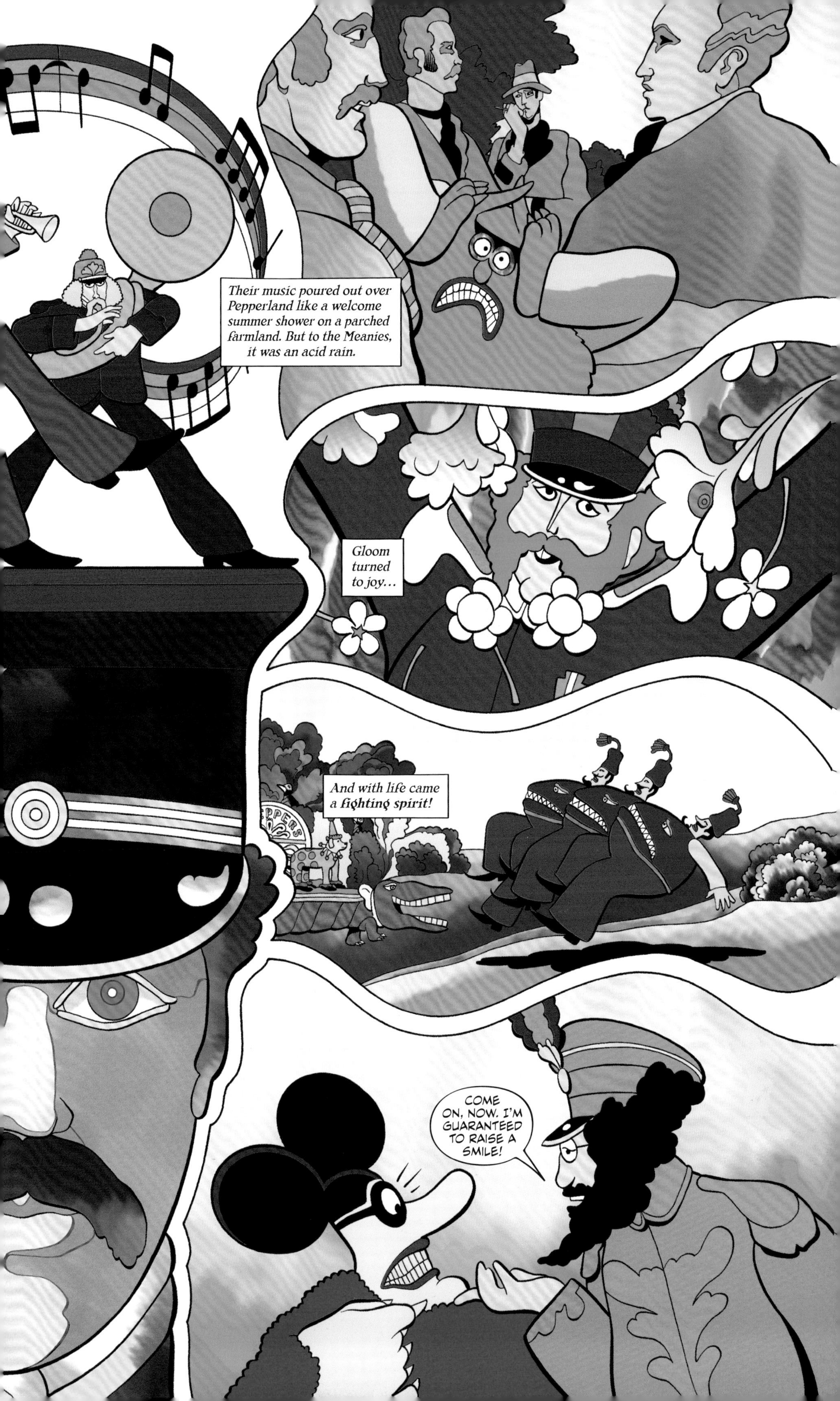
Their music poured out over Pepperland like a welcome summer shower on a parched farmland. But to the Meanies, it was an acid rain.
Gloom turned to joy...
And with life came a fighting spirit!
COME ON, NOW. I'M GUARANTEED TO RAISE A SMILE!

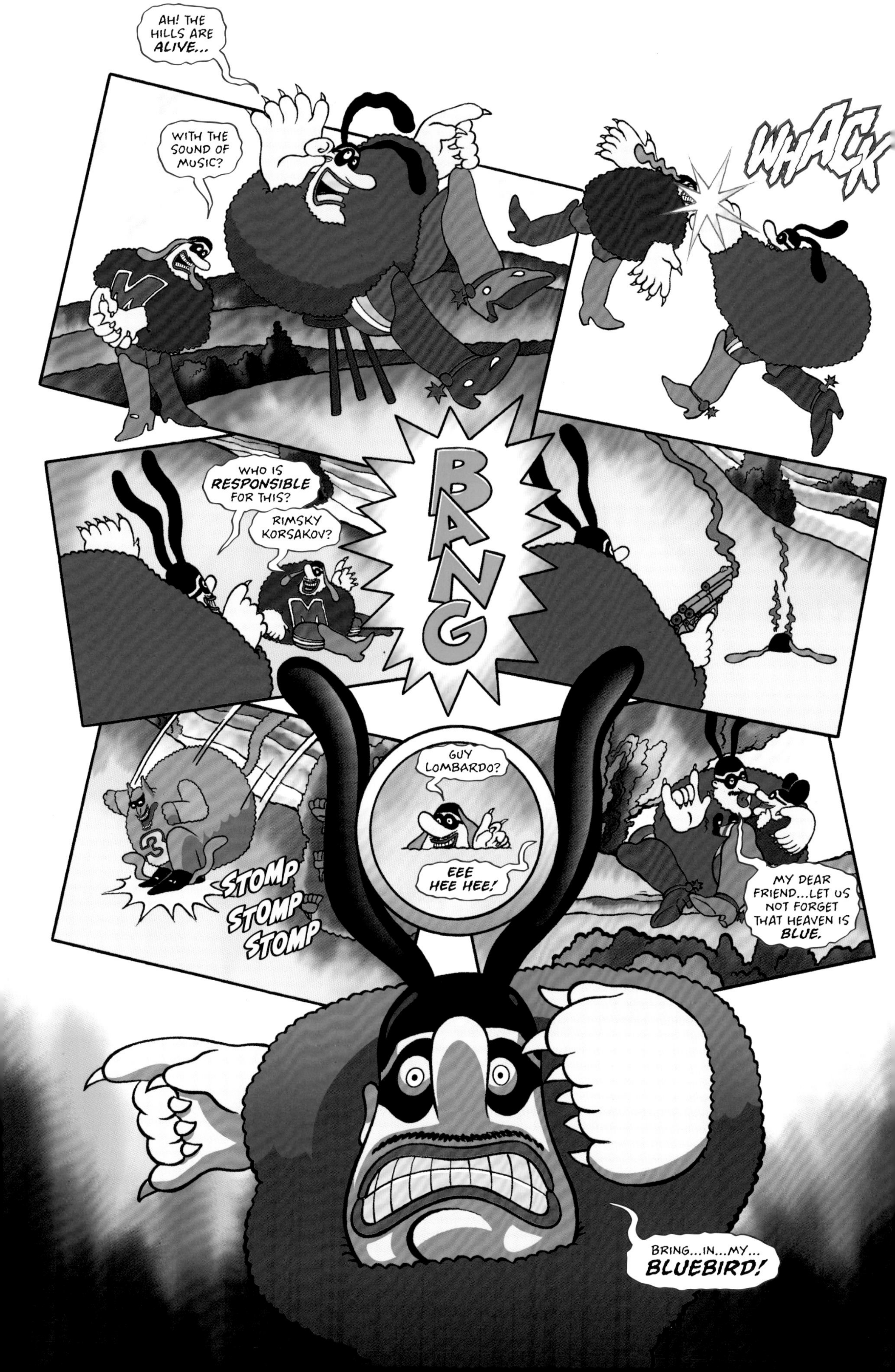

AH! THE HILLS ARE ALIVE...
WITH THE SOUND OF MUSIC?
WHACK
WHO IS RESPONSIBLE FOR THIS?
RIMSKY KORSAKOV?
BANG
STOMP STOMP STOMP
GUY LOMBARDO?
EEE HEE HEE!
MY DEAR FRIEND...LET US NOT FORGET THAT HEAVEN IS BLUE.
BRING...IN...MY... BLUEBIRD!

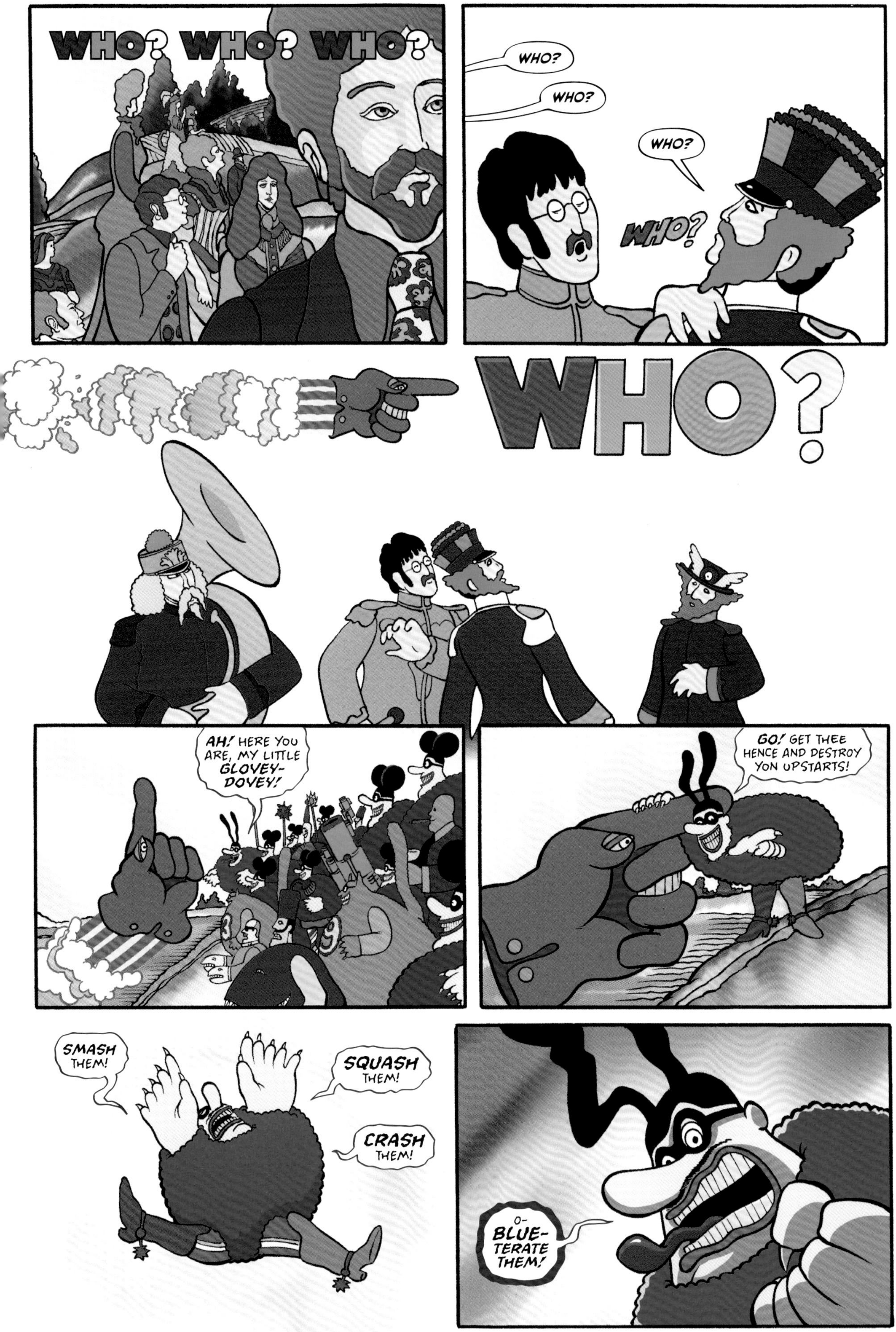
WHO? WHO? WHO?
WHO?
WHO?
WHO?
WHO?
WHO?
AH! HERE YOU ARE, MY LITTLE GLOVEY-DOVEY!
GO! GET THEE HENCE AND DESTROY YON UPSTARTS!
SMASH THEM!
SQUASH THEM!
CRASH THEM!
O-BLUE-TERATE THEM!

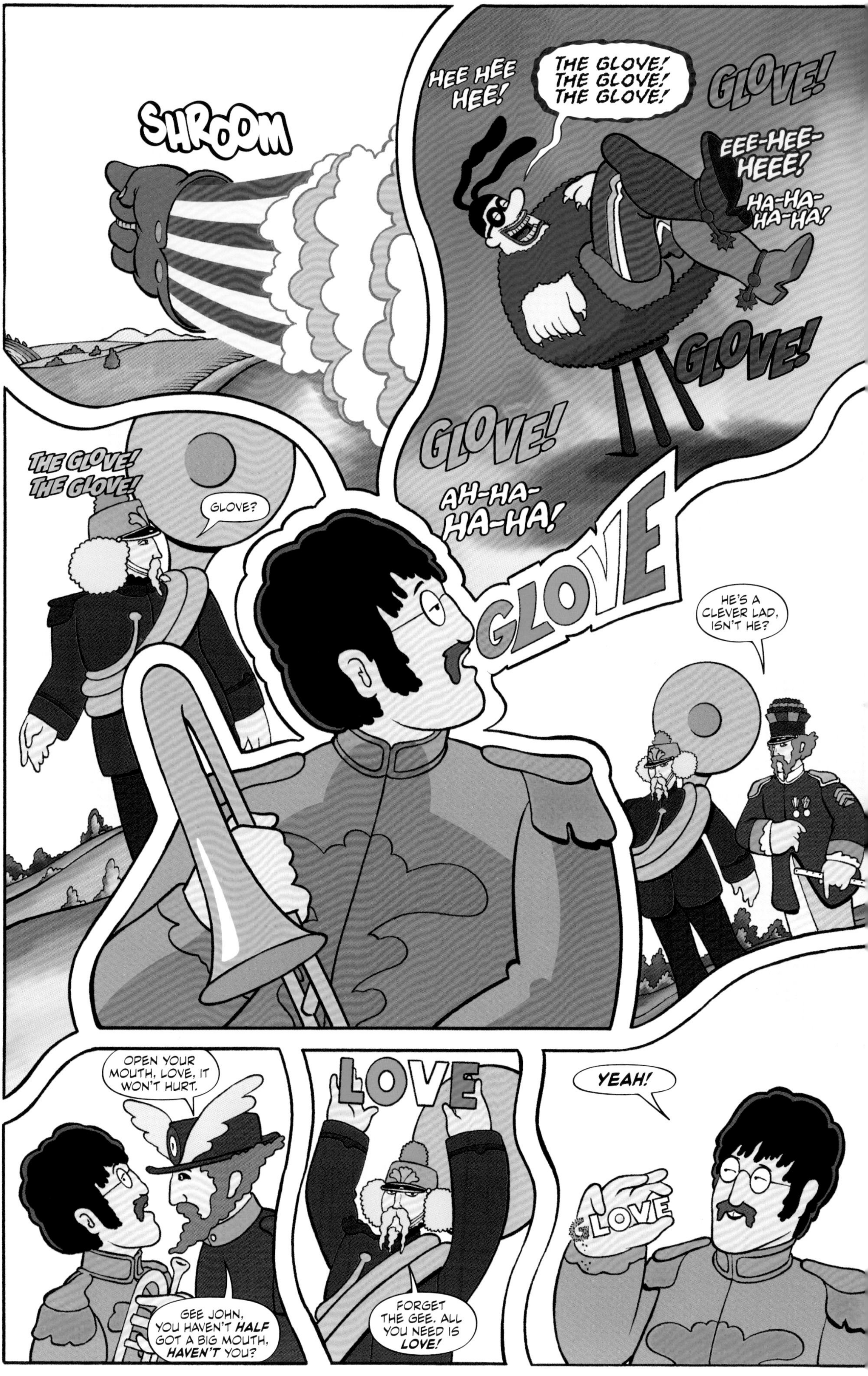
SHROOM
HEE HEE HEE!
THE GLOVE! THE GLOVE! THE GLOVE!
GLOVE!
EEE-HEE-HEEE!
HA-HA-HA-HA!
GLOVE!
GLOVE!
AH-HA-HA-HA!
THE GLOVE! THE GLOVE!
GLOVE?
GLOVE
HE'S A CLEVER LAD, ISN'T HE?
OPEN YOUR MOUTH, LOVE, IT WON'T HURT.
GEE JOHN, YOU HAVEN'T **HALF** GOT A BIG MOUTH, **HAVEN'T** YOU?
LOVE
FORGET THE GEE. ALL YOU NEED IS **LOVE!**
YEAH!
GLOVE

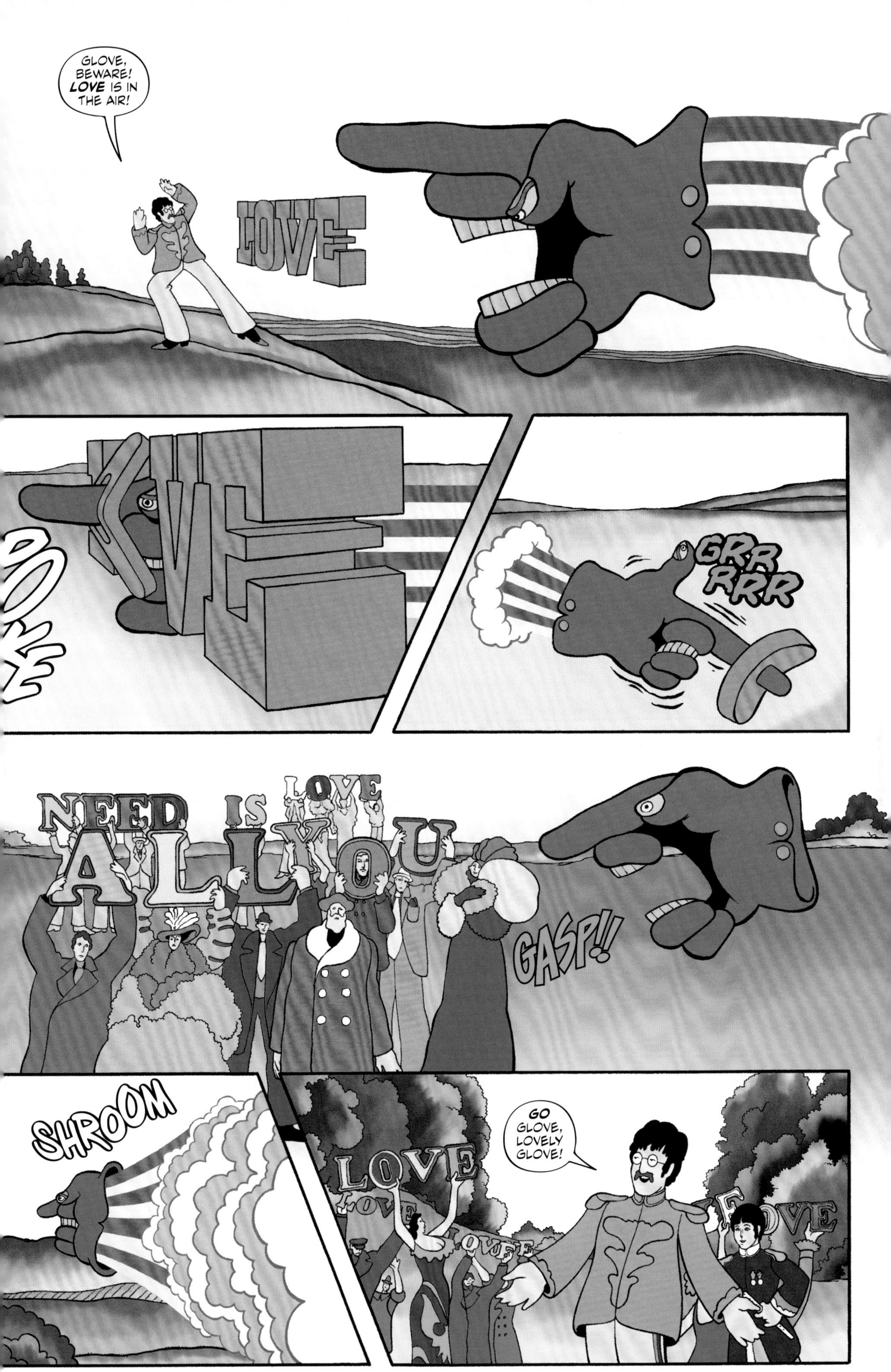
GLOVE, BEWARE! **LOVE** IS IN THE AIR!
LOVE
GRR RRR
ALL YOU NEED IS LOVE
GASP!!
SHROOM
LOVE
GO GLOVE, LOVELY GLOVE!

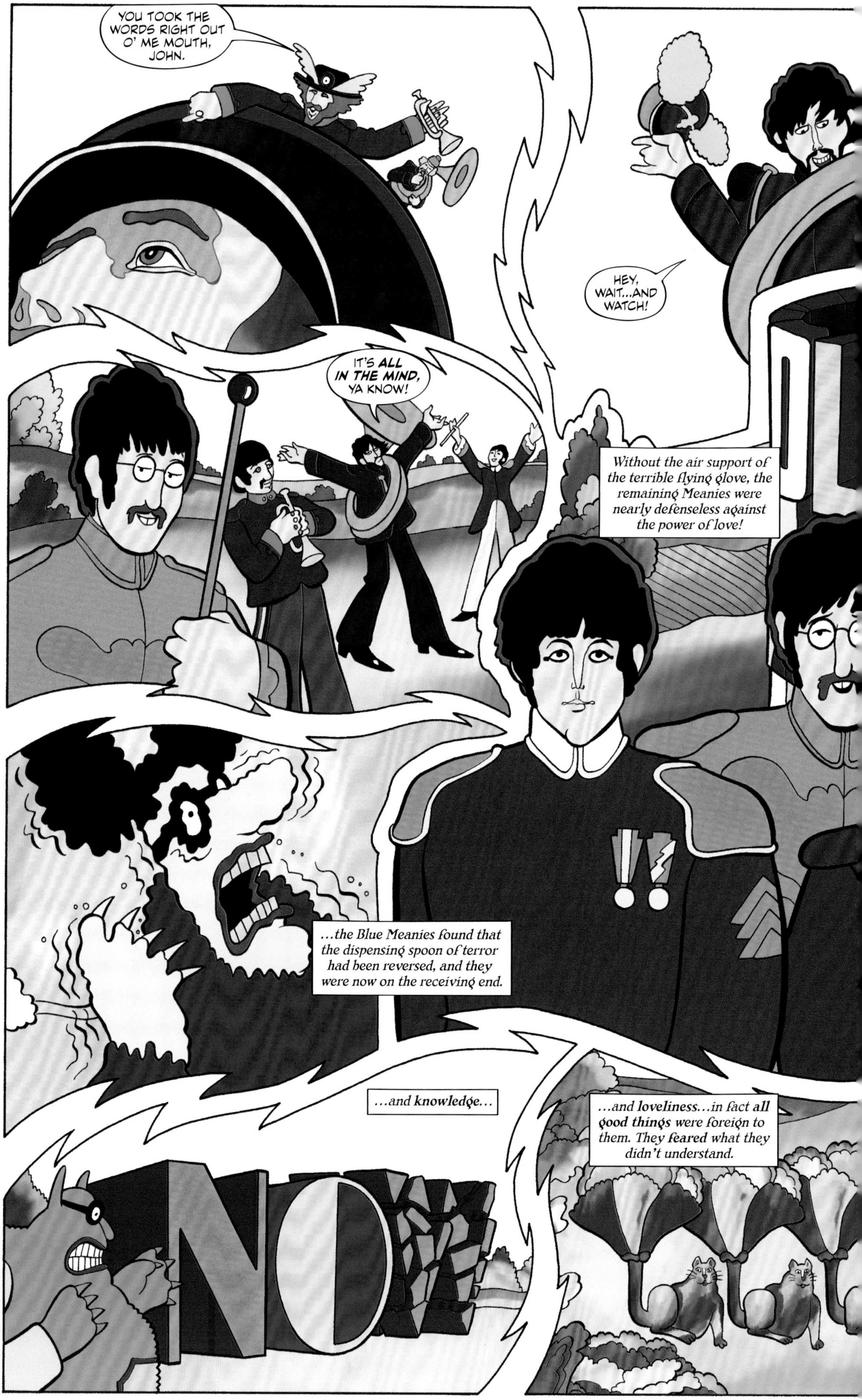

YOU TOOK THE WORDS RIGHT OUT O' ME MOUTH, JOHN.
HEY, WAIT...AND WATCH!
IT'S **ALL IN THE MIND,** YA KNOW!
Without the air support of the terrible flying glove, the remaining Meanies were nearly defenseless against the power of love!
...the Blue Meanies found that the dispensing spoon of terror had been reversed, and they were now on the receiving end.
*...and **knowledge**...*
*...and **loveliness**...in fact **all good things** were foreign to them. They **feared** what they didn't understand.*
NO

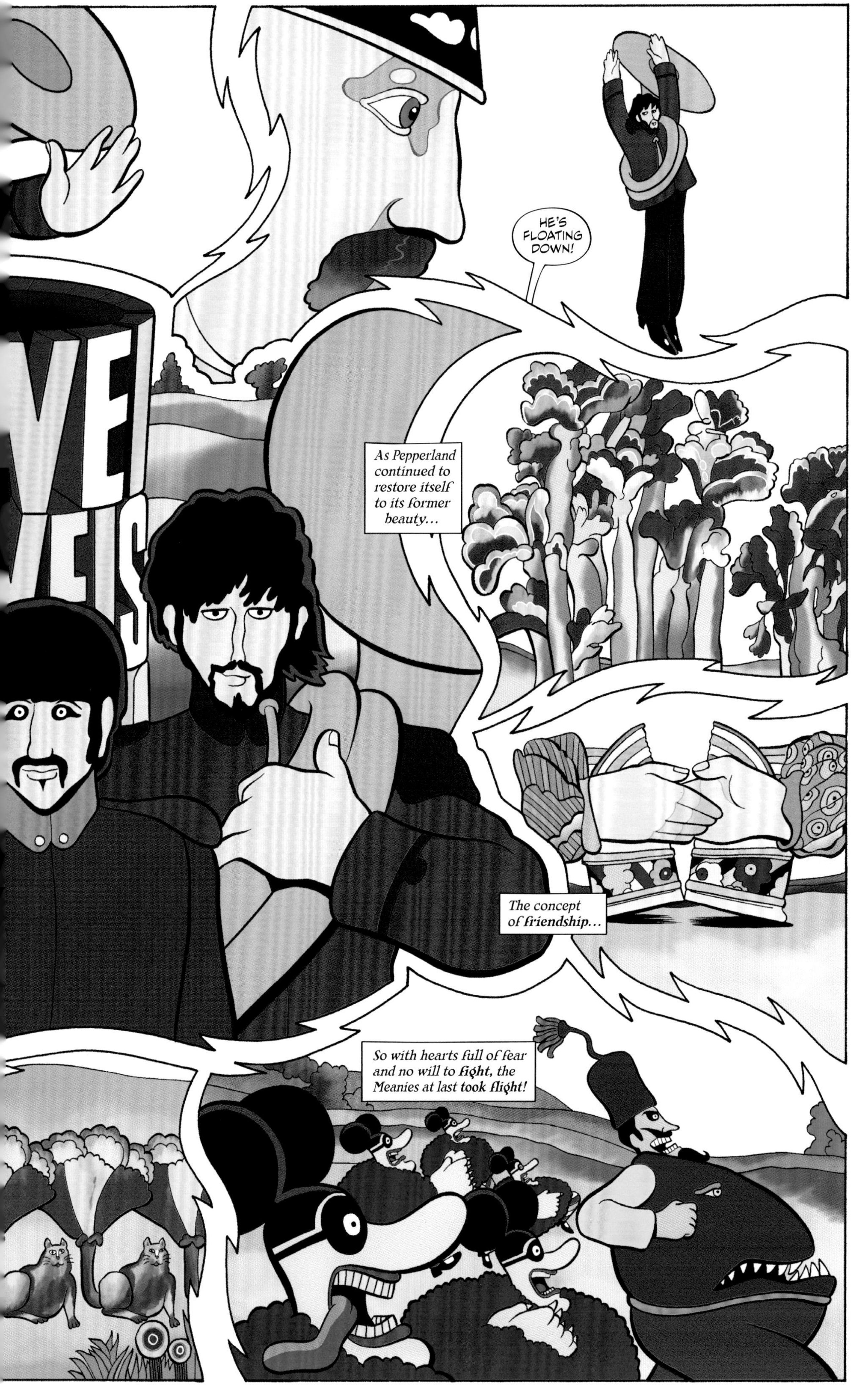
HE'S FLOATING DOWN!
As Pepperland continued to restore itself to its former beauty...
The concept of friendship...
So with hearts full of fear and no will to fight, the Meanies at last took flight!

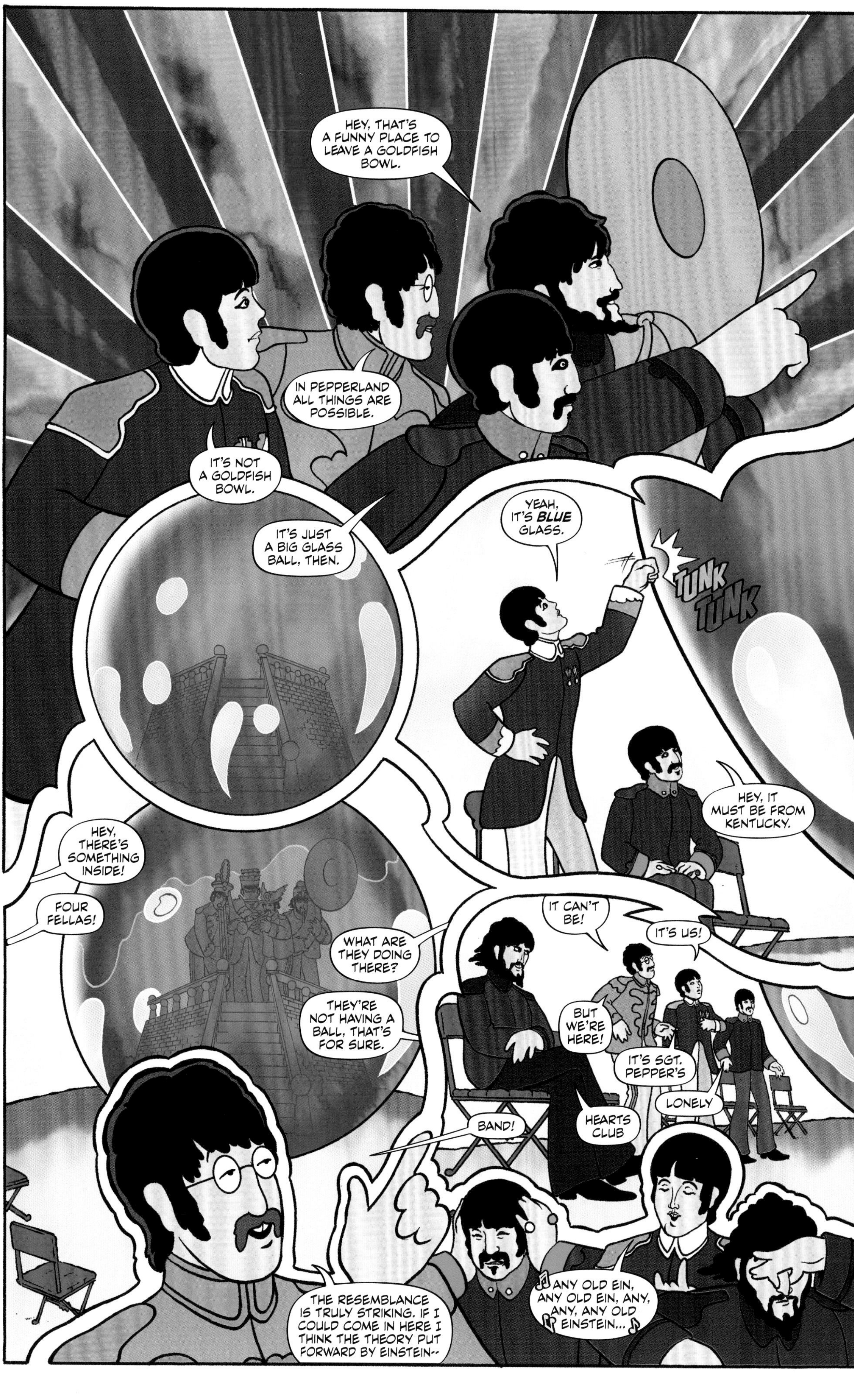
HEY, THAT'S A FUNNY PLACE TO LEAVE A GOLDFISH BOWL.
IN PEPPERLAND ALL THINGS ARE POSSIBLE.
IT'S NOT A GOLDFISH BOWL.
IT'S JUST A BIG GLASS BALL, THEN.
YEAH, IT'S BLUE GLASS.
TUNK TUNK
HEY, IT MUST BE FROM KENTUCKY.
HEY, THERE'S SOMETHING INSIDE!
FOUR FELLAS!
WHAT ARE THEY DOING THERE?
THEY'RE NOT HAVING A BALL, THAT'S FOR SURE.
IT CAN'T BE!
IT'S US!
BUT WE'RE HERE!
IT'S SGT. PEPPER'S
LONELY
HEARTS CLUB
BAND!
THE RESEMBLANCE IS TRULY STRIKING. IF I COULD COME IN HERE I THINK THE THEORY PUT FORWARD BY EINSTEIN--
ANY OLD EIN, ANY OLD EIN, ANY, ANY, ANY OLD EINSTEIN...

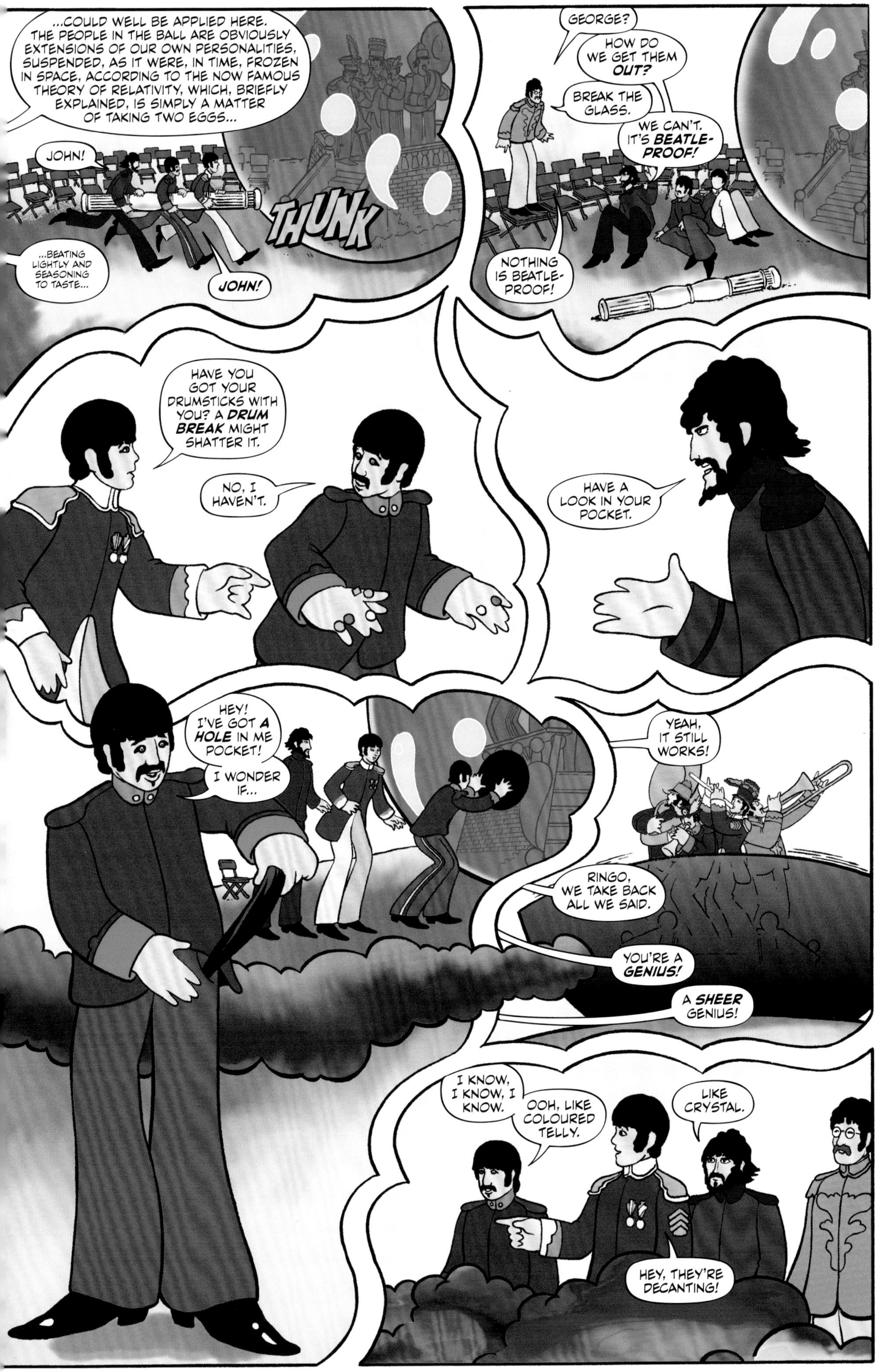
...COULD WELL BE APPLIED HERE. THE PEOPLE IN THE BALL ARE OBVIOUSLY EXTENSIONS OF OUR OWN PERSONALITIES, SUSPENDED, AS IT WERE, IN TIME, FROZEN IN SPACE, ACCORDING TO THE NOW FAMOUS THEORY OF RELATIVITY, WHICH, BRIEFLY EXPLAINED, IS SIMPLY A MATTER OF TAKING TWO EGGS...
JOHN!
THUNK
...BEATING LIGHTLY AND SEASONING TO TASTE...
JOHN!
GEORGE?
HOW DO WE GET THEM OUT?
BREAK THE GLASS.
WE CAN'T. IT'S BEATLE-PROOF!
NOTHING IS BEATLE-PROOF!
HAVE YOU GOT YOUR DRUMSTICKS WITH YOU? A DRUM BREAK MIGHT SHATTER IT.
NO, I HAVEN'T.
HAVE A LOOK IN YOUR POCKET.
HEY! I'VE GOT A HOLE IN ME POCKET!
I WONDER IF...
YEAH, IT STILL WORKS!
RINGO, WE TAKE BACK ALL WE SAID.
YOU'RE A GENIUS!
A SHEER GENIUS!
I KNOW, I KNOW, I KNOW.
OOH, LIKE COLOURED TELLY.
LIKE CRYSTAL.
HEY, THEY'RE DECANTING!

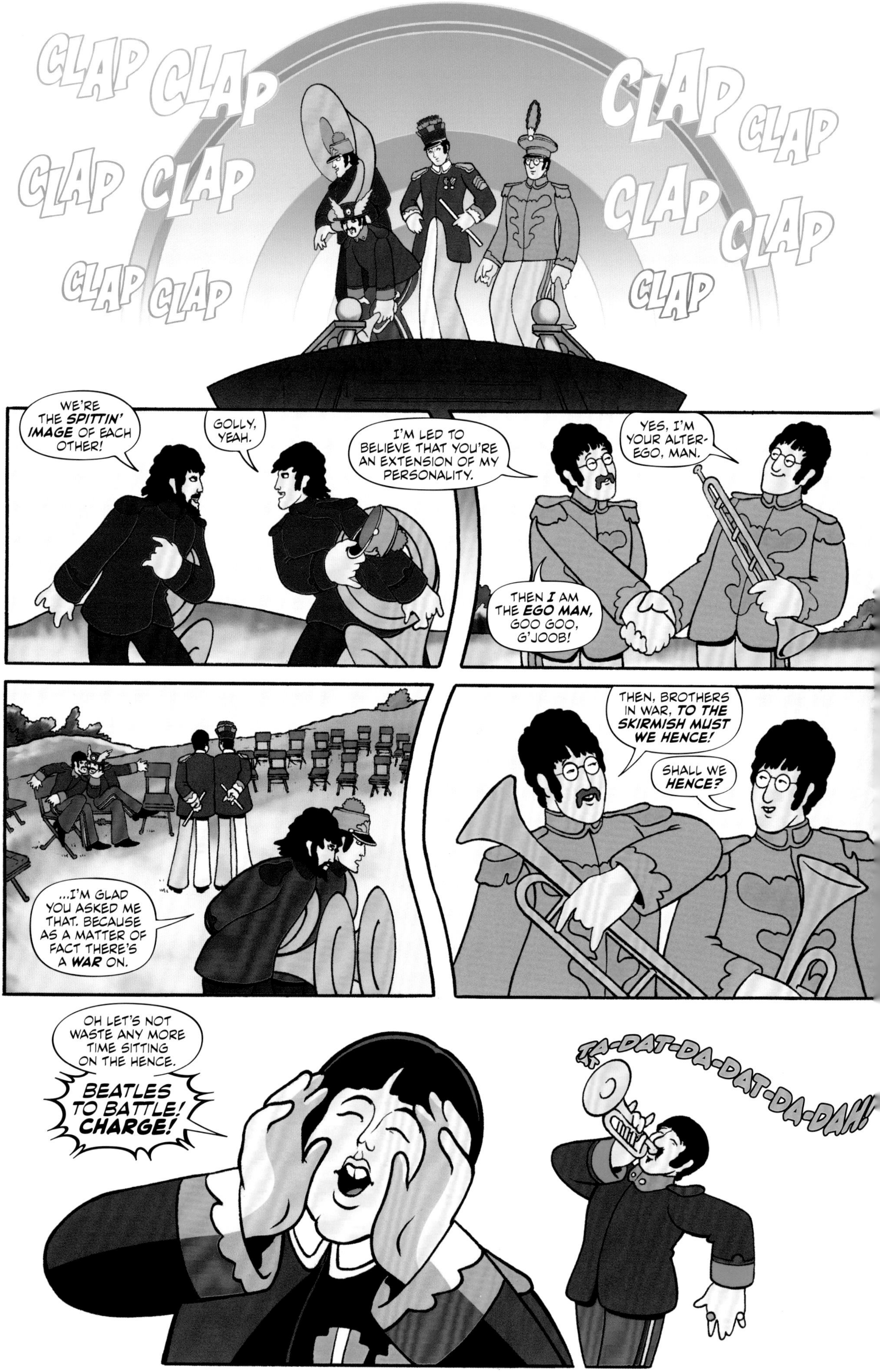
CLAP CLAP
CLAP CLAP
CLAP CLAP
CLAP CLAP
CLAP CLAP
CLAP
WE'RE THE SPITTIN' IMAGE OF EACH OTHER!
GOLLY, YEAH.
I'M LED TO BELIEVE THAT YOU'RE AN EXTENSION OF MY PERSONALITY.
YES, I'M YOUR ALTER-EGO, MAN.
THEN I AM THE EGO MAN, GOO GOO, G'JOOB!
...I'M GLAD YOU ASKED ME THAT. BECAUSE AS A MATTER OF FACT THERE'S A WAR ON.
THEN, BROTHERS IN WAR, TO THE SKIRMISH MUST WE HENCE!
SHALL WE HENCE?
OH LET'S NOT WASTE ANY MORE TIME SITTING ON THE HENCE.
BEATLES TO BATTLE! CHARGE!
TA-DAT-DA-DAT-DA-DAH!

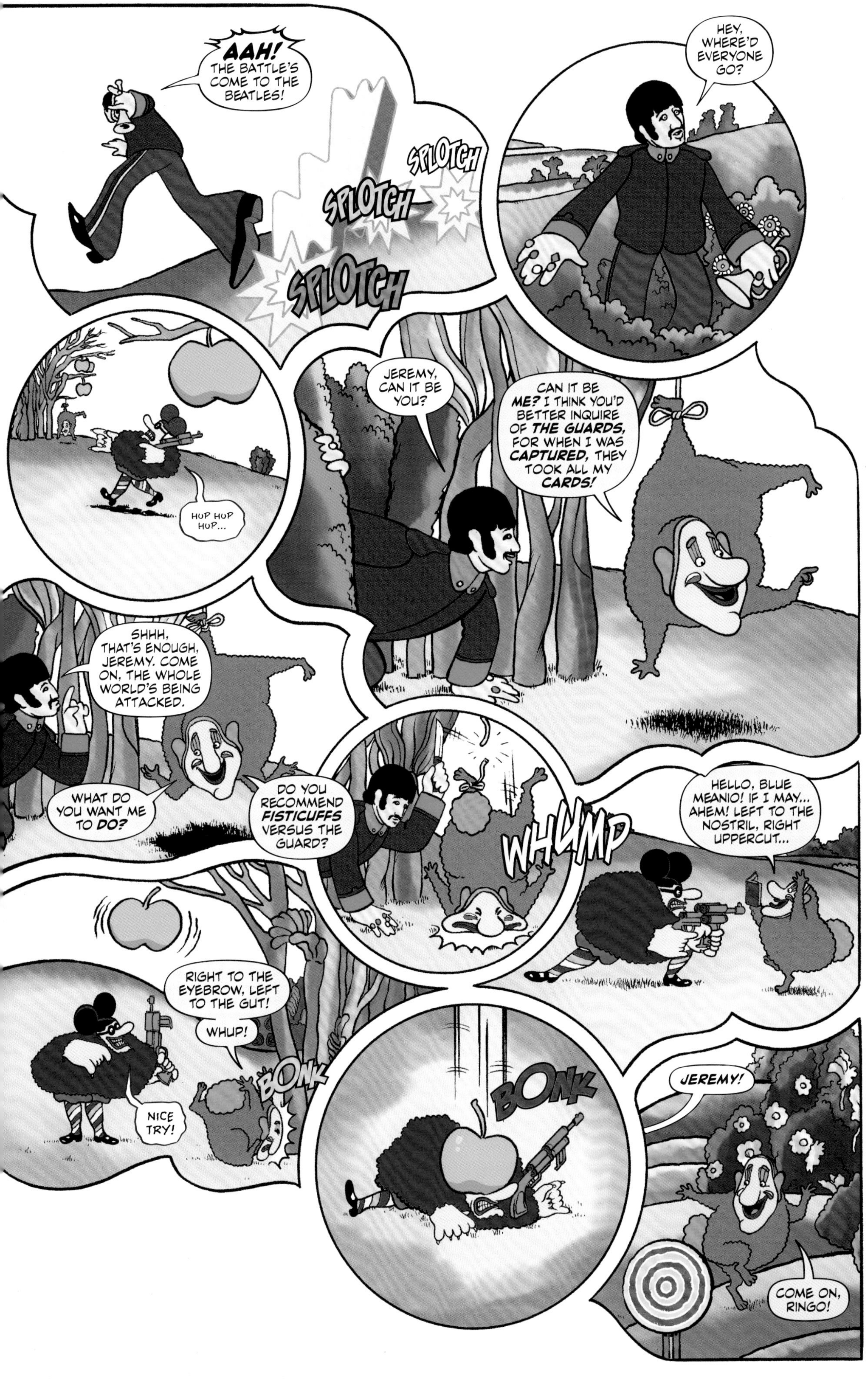
AAH! THE BATTLE'S COME TO THE BEATLES!
SPLOTCH
SPLOTCH
SPLOTCH
HEY, WHERE'D EVERYONE GO?
HUP HUP HUP...
JEREMY, CAN IT BE YOU?
CAN IT BE ME? I THINK YOU'D BETTER INQUIRE OF THE GUARDS, FOR WHEN I WAS CAPTURED, THEY TOOK ALL MY CARDS!
SHHH, THAT'S ENOUGH, JEREMY. COME ON, THE WHOLE WORLD'S BEING ATTACKED.
WHAT DO YOU WANT ME TO DO?
DO YOU RECOMMEND FISTICUFFS VERSUS THE GUARD?
WHUMP
HELLO, BLUE MEANIO! IF I MAY... AHEM! LEFT TO THE NOSTRIL, RIGHT UPPERCUT...
RIGHT TO THE EYEBROW, LEFT TO THE GUT!
WHUP!
NICE TRY!
BONK
BONK
JEREMY!
COME ON, RINGO!

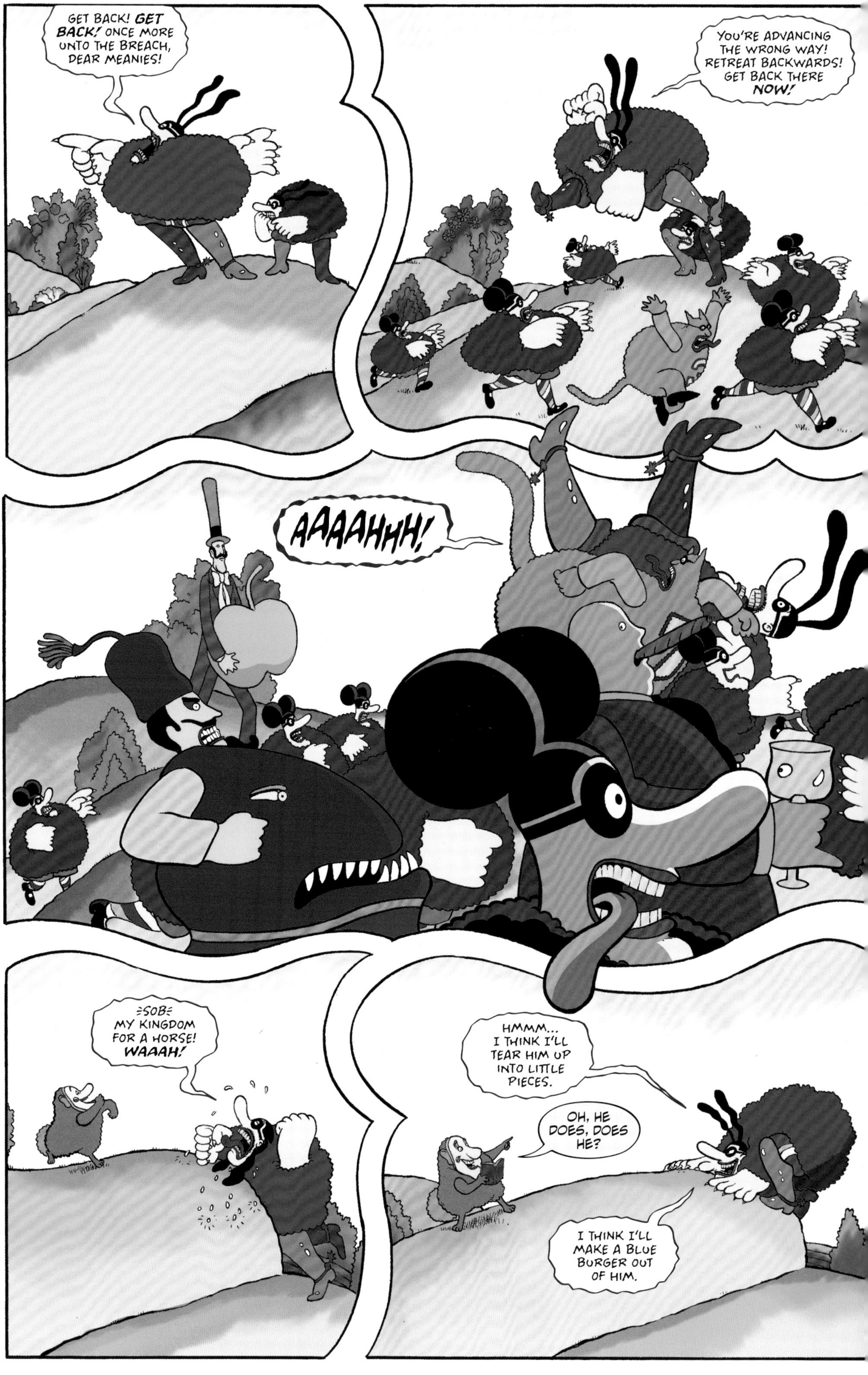
GET BACK! GET BACK! ONCE MORE UNTO THE BREACH, DEAR MEANIES!
YOU'RE ADVANCING THE WRONG WAY! RETREAT BACKWARDS! GET BACK THERE NOW!
AAAAHHH!
SOB MY KINGDOM FOR A HORSE! WAAAH!
HMMM... I THINK I'LL TEAR HIM UP INTO LITTLE PIECES.
OH, HE DOES, DOES HE?
I THINK I'LL MAKE A BLUE BURGER OUT OF HIM.

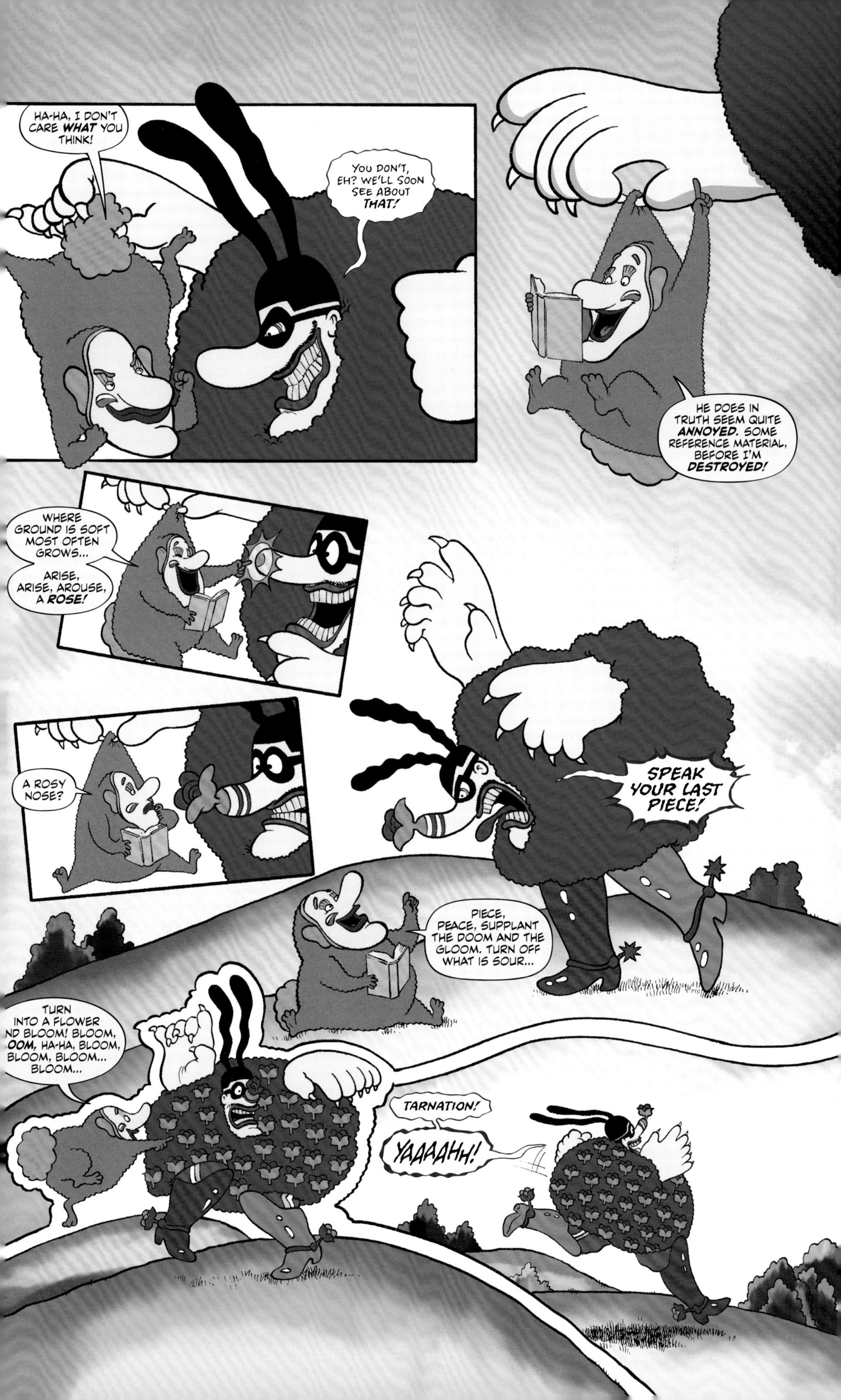
HA-HA, I DON'T CARE **WHAT** YOU THINK!
YOU DON'T, EH? WE'LL SOON SEE ABOUT **THAT!**
HE DOES IN TRUTH SEEM QUITE **ANNOYED.** SOME REFERENCE MATERIAL, BEFORE I'M **DESTROYED!**
WHERE GROUND IS SOFT MOST OFTEN GROWS...
ARISE, ARISE, AROUSE, A **ROSE!**
A ROSY NOSE?
SPEAK YOUR LAST PIECE!
PIECE, PEACE, SUPPLANT THE DOOM AND THE GLOOM. TURN OFF WHAT IS SOUR...
TURN INTO A FLOWER ND BLOOM! BLOOM, **OOM,** HA-HA, BLOOM, BLOOM, BLOOM... BLOOM...
TARNATION!
YAAAAHH!

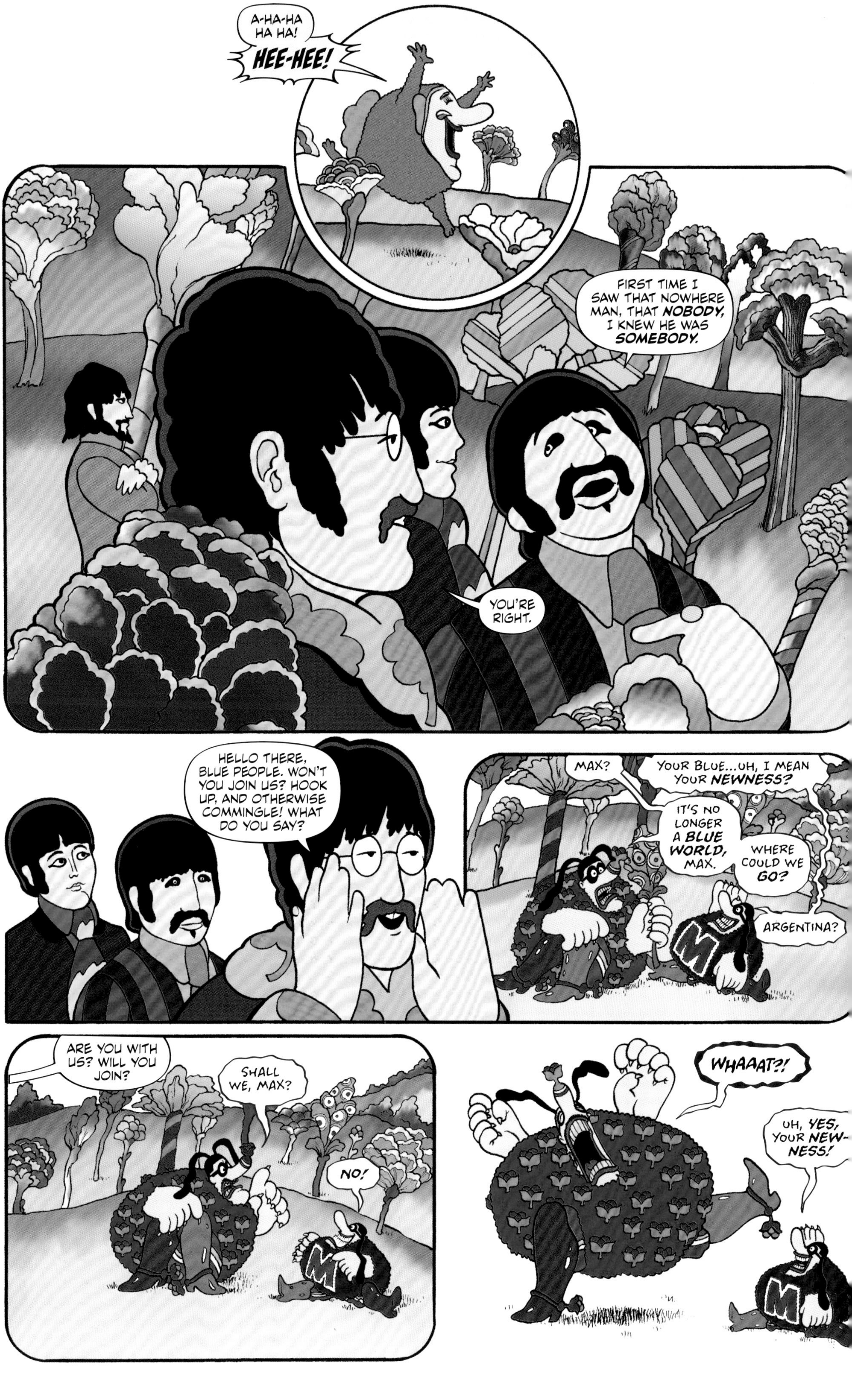
A-HA-HA HA HA!
HEE-HEE!
FIRST TIME I SAW THAT NOWHERE MAN, THAT NOBODY, I KNEW HE WAS SOMEBODY.
YOU'RE RIGHT.
HELLO THERE, BLUE PEOPLE. WON'T YOU JOIN US? HOOK UP, AND OTHERWISE COMMINGLE! WHAT DO YOU SAY?
MAX?
YOUR BLUE...UH, I MEAN YOUR NEWNESS?
IT'S NO LONGER A BLUE WORLD, MAX.
WHERE COULD WE GO?
ARGENTINA?
ARE YOU WITH US? WILL YOU JOIN?
SHALL WE, MAX?
NO!
WHAAAT?!
UH, YES, YOUR NEW-NESS!

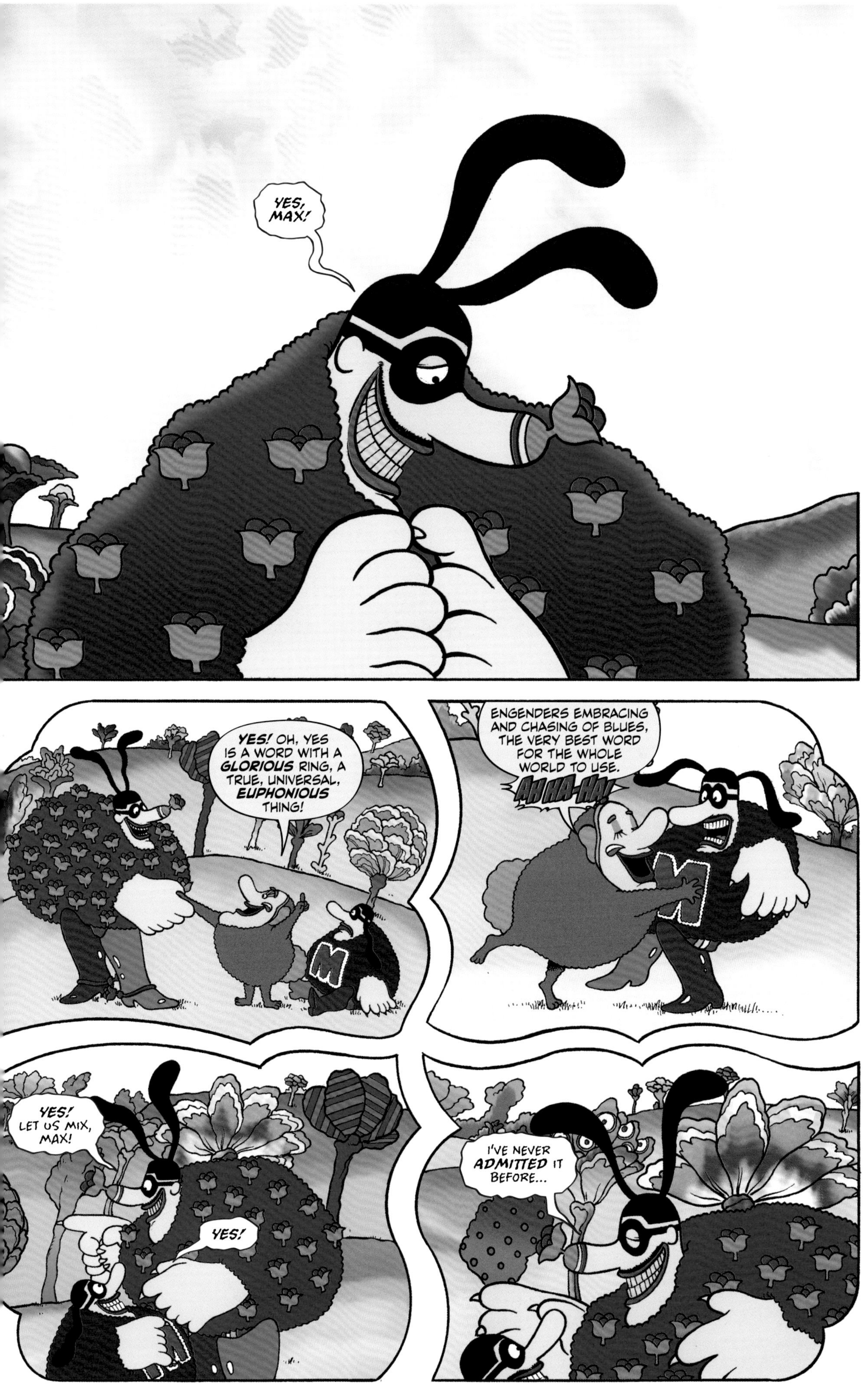
YES, MAX!
YES! OH, YES IS A WORD WITH A GLORIOUS RING, A TRUE, UNIVERSAL, EUPHONIOUS THING!
ENGENDERS EMBRACING AND CHASING OF BLUES, THE VERY BEST WORD FOR THE WHOLE WORLD TO USE.
AH HA-HA!
YES! LET US MIX, MAX!
YES!
I'VE NEVER ADMITTED IT BEFORE...

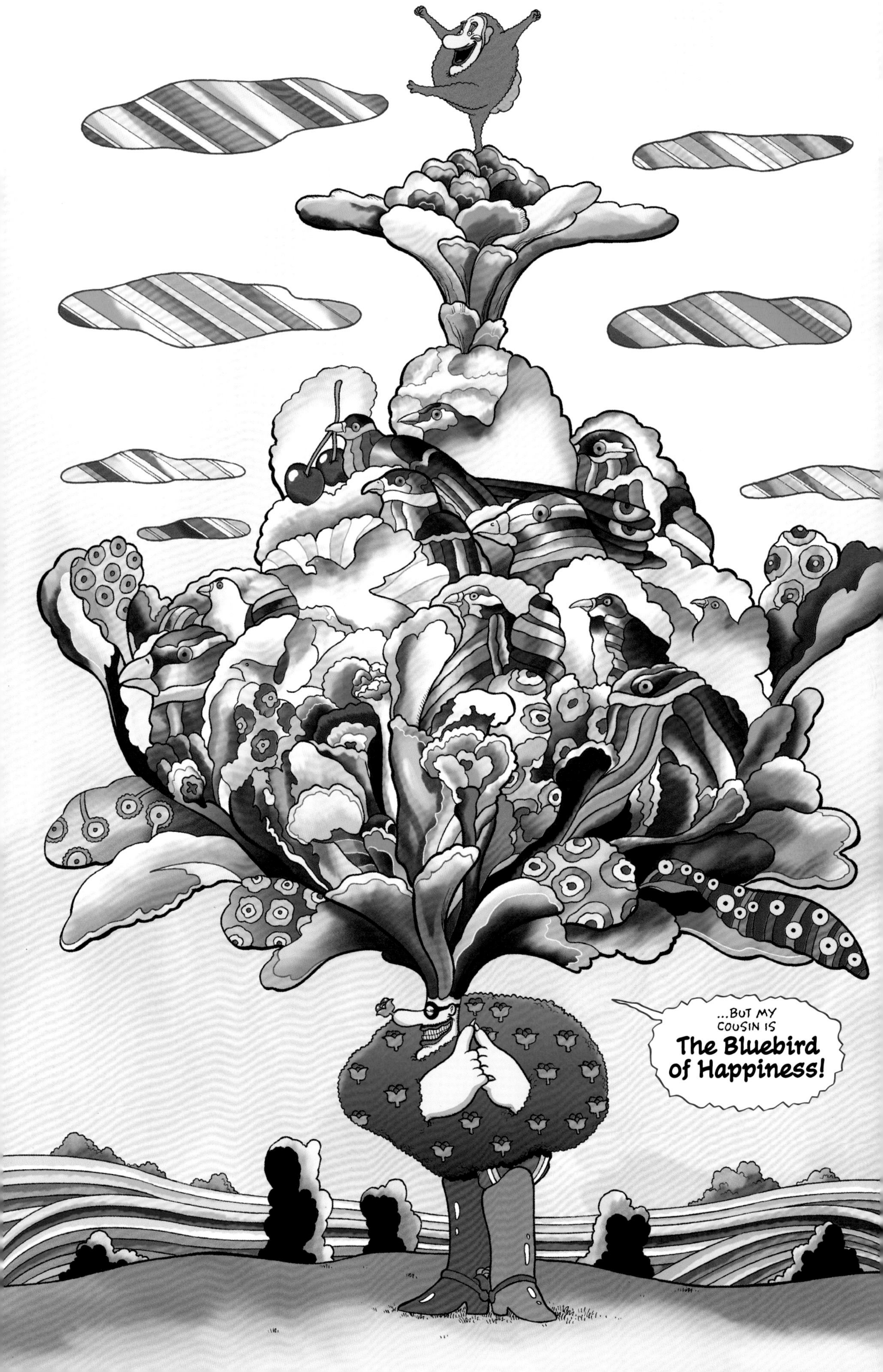
...BUT MY COUSIN IS The Bluebird of Happiness!

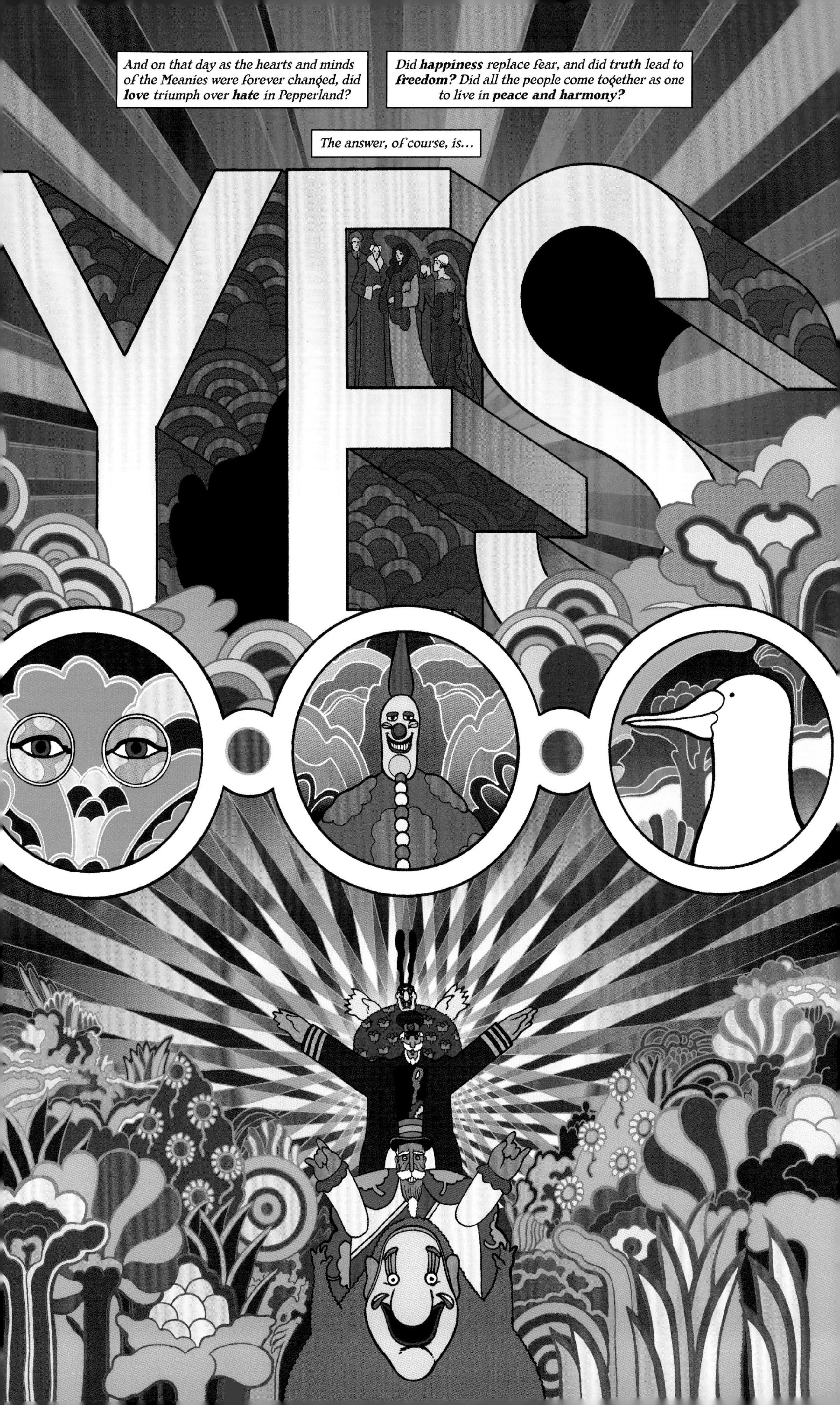

And on that day as the hearts and minds of the Meanies were forever changed, did **love** triumph over **hate** in Pepperland?
Did **happiness** replace fear, and did **truth** lead to **freedom?** Did all the people come together as one to live in **peace and harmony?**
The answer, of course, is...
YES

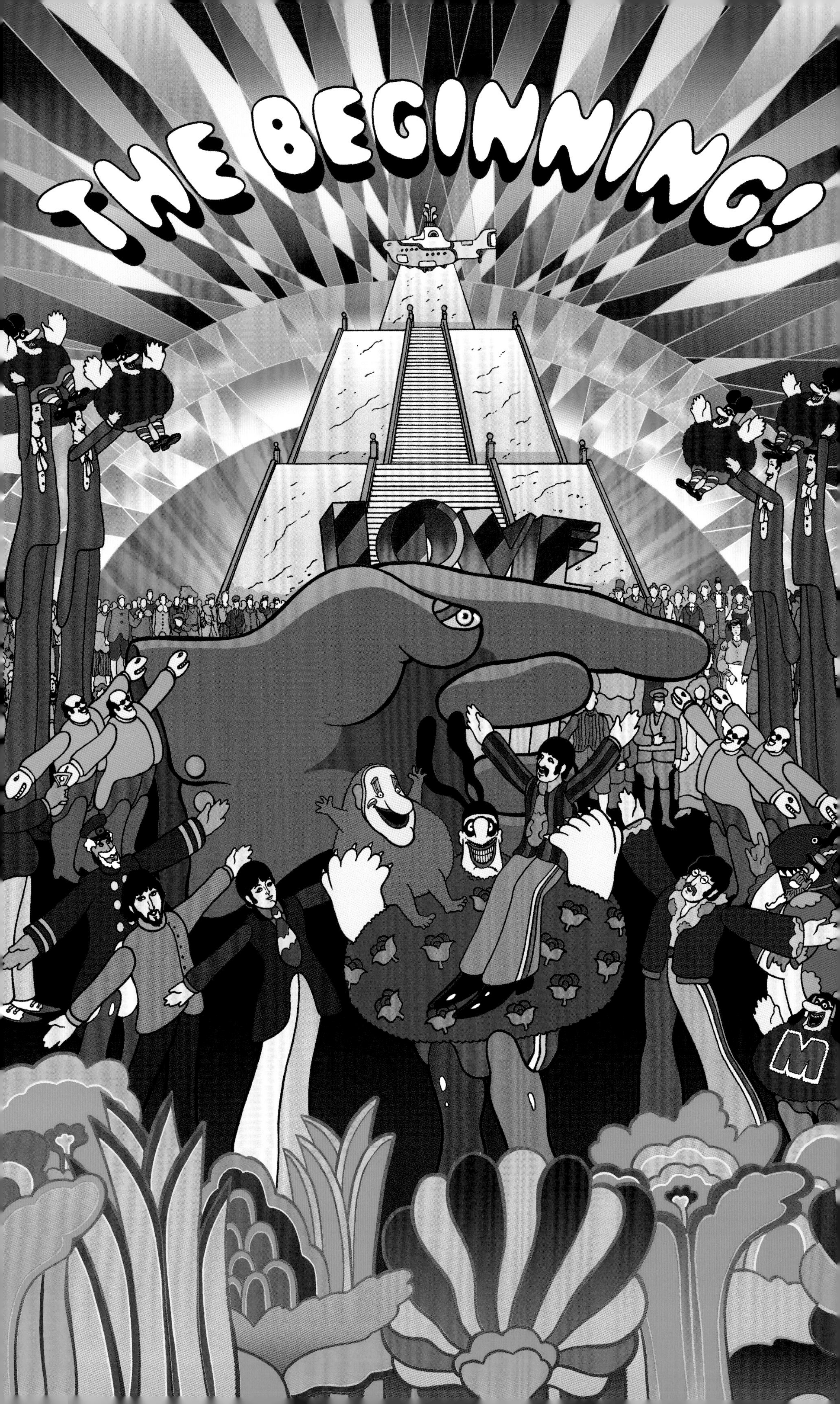
THE BEGINNING!
LOVE
M

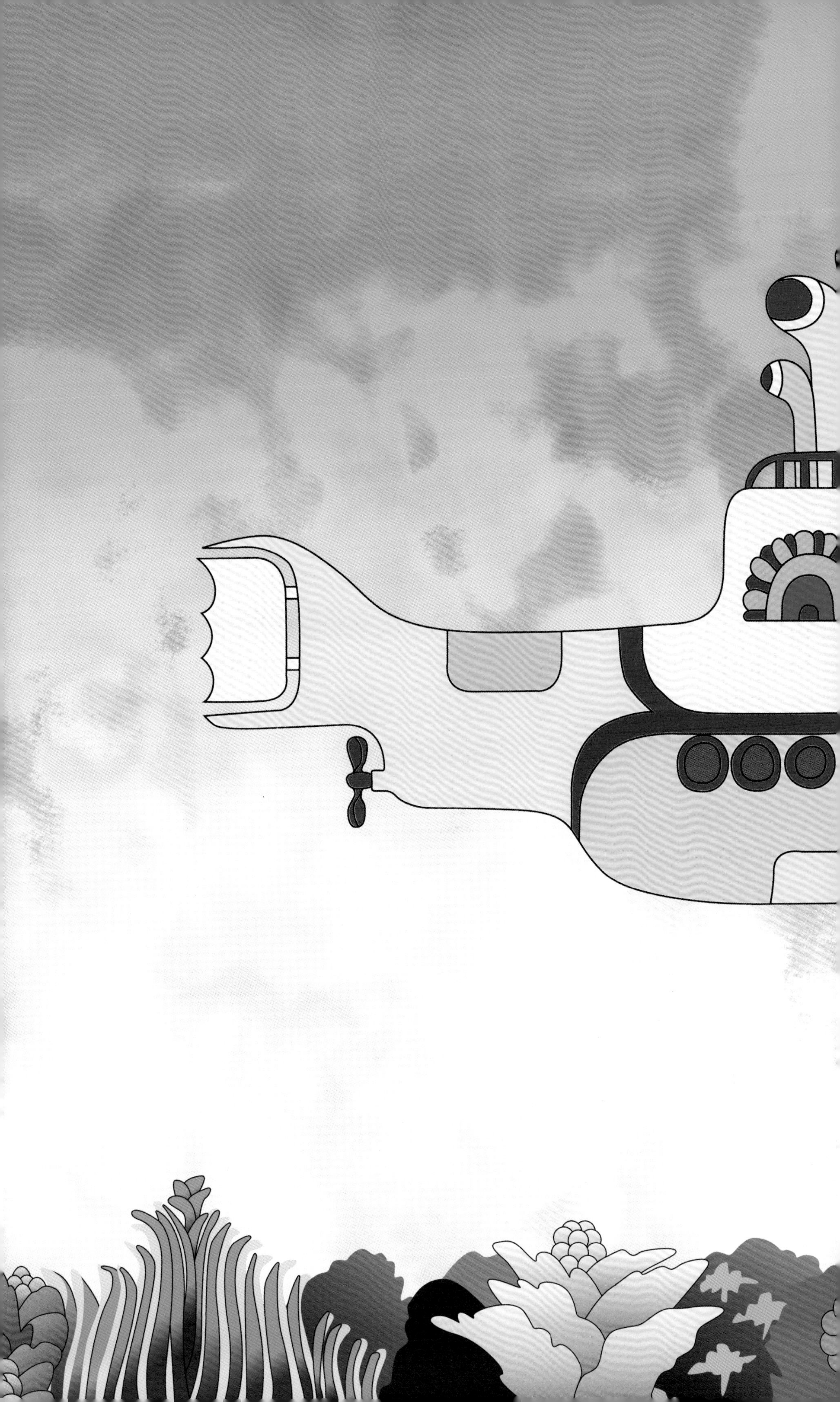

Concept Art and Sketches

Here's a peek at some of the *Yellow Submarine* graphic novel pages in their early stages, plus pencil art for the cover and for an alternative cover for the project, and, finally, pictures from Bill Morrison's sketchbook

PG. 2-3

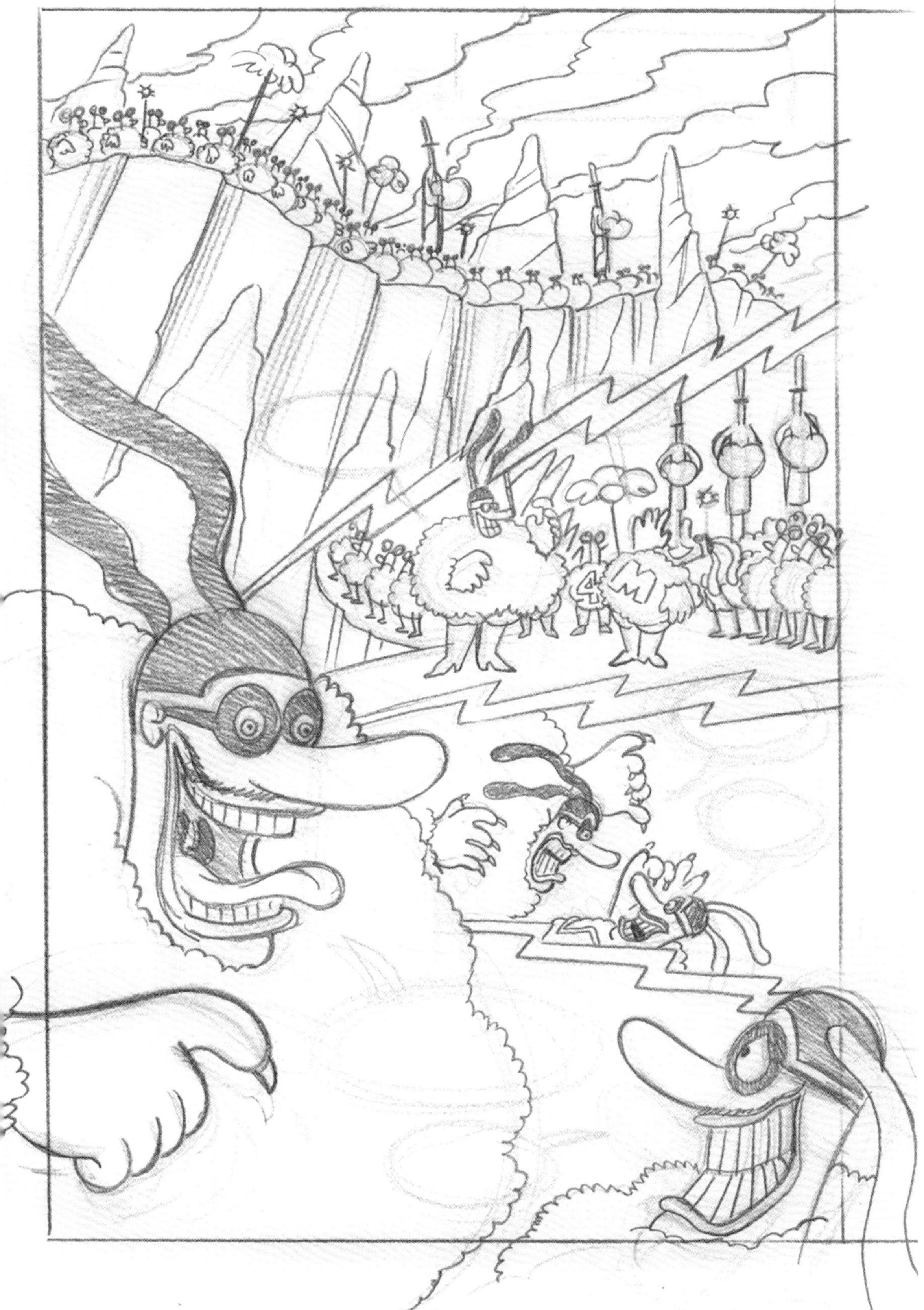

PG 4

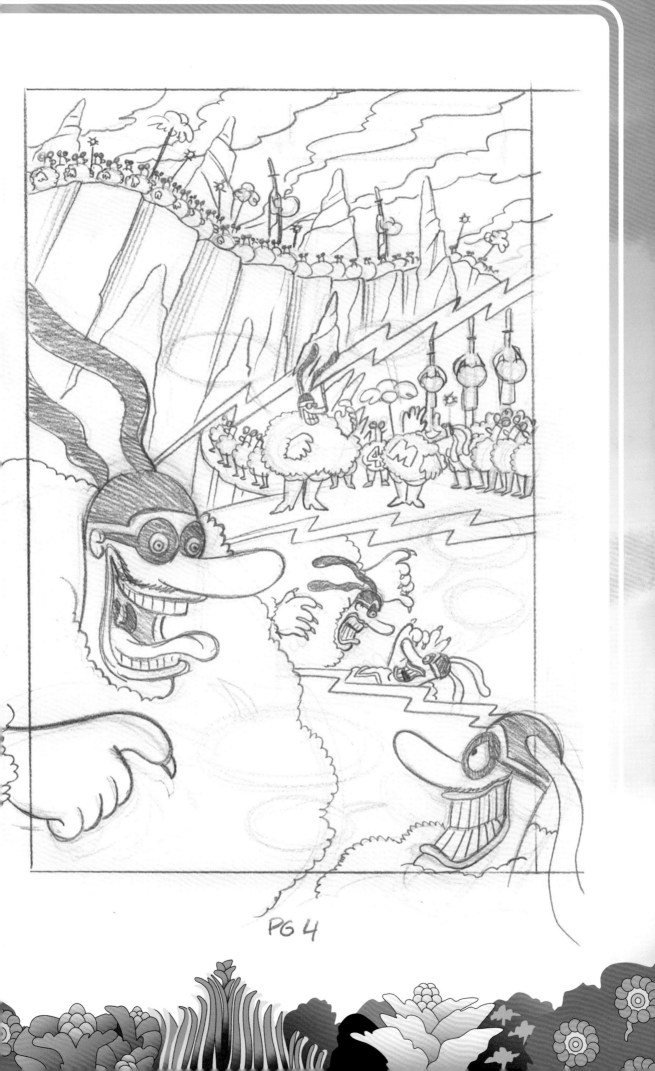

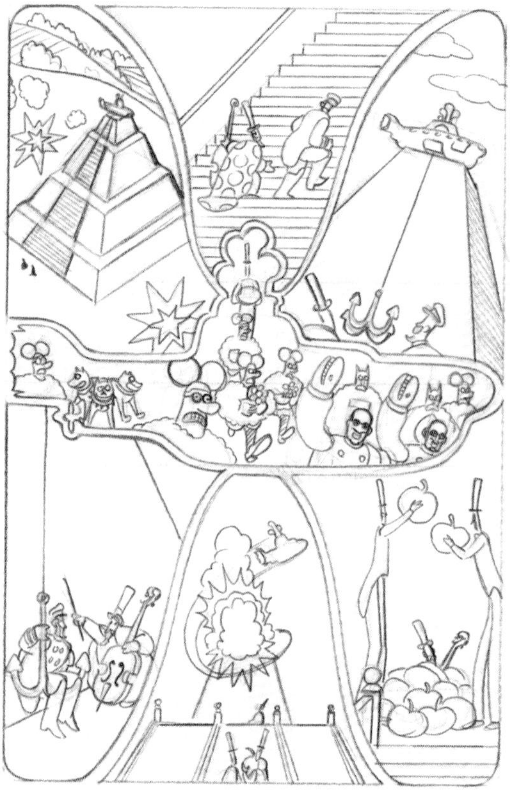

PG. 12

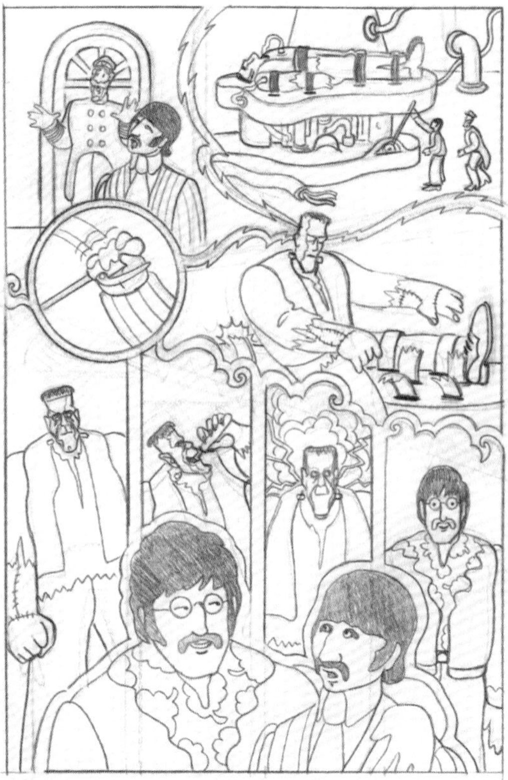

PG.15

PG 24

PG 25

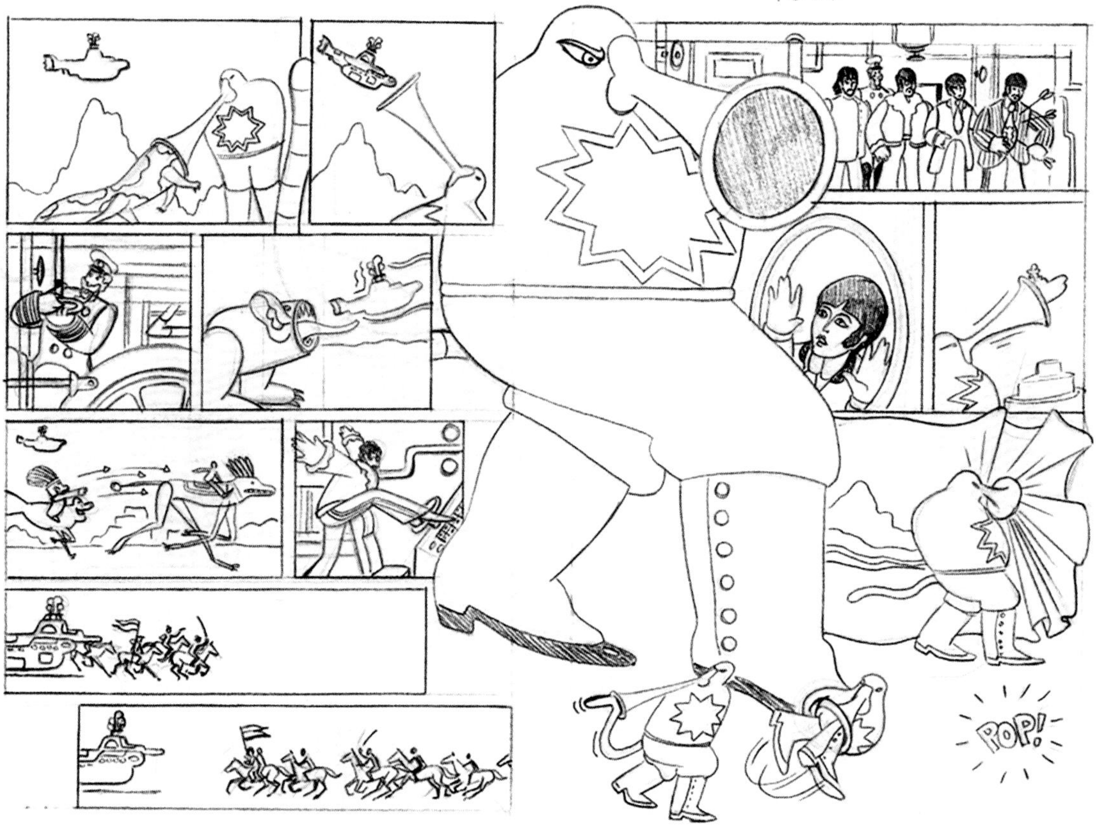
POP!

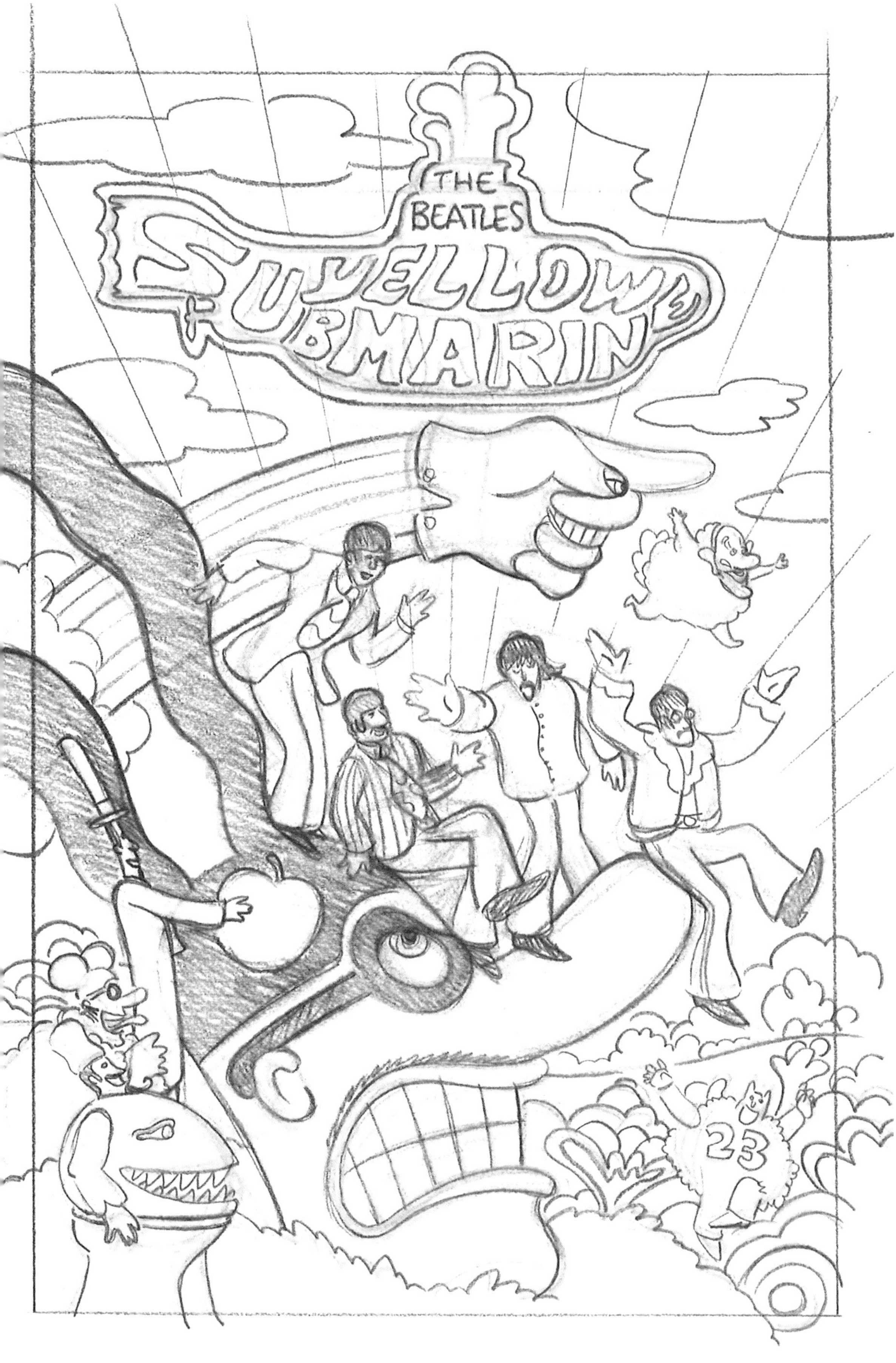
THE
BEATLES
YELLOW SUBMARINE
23

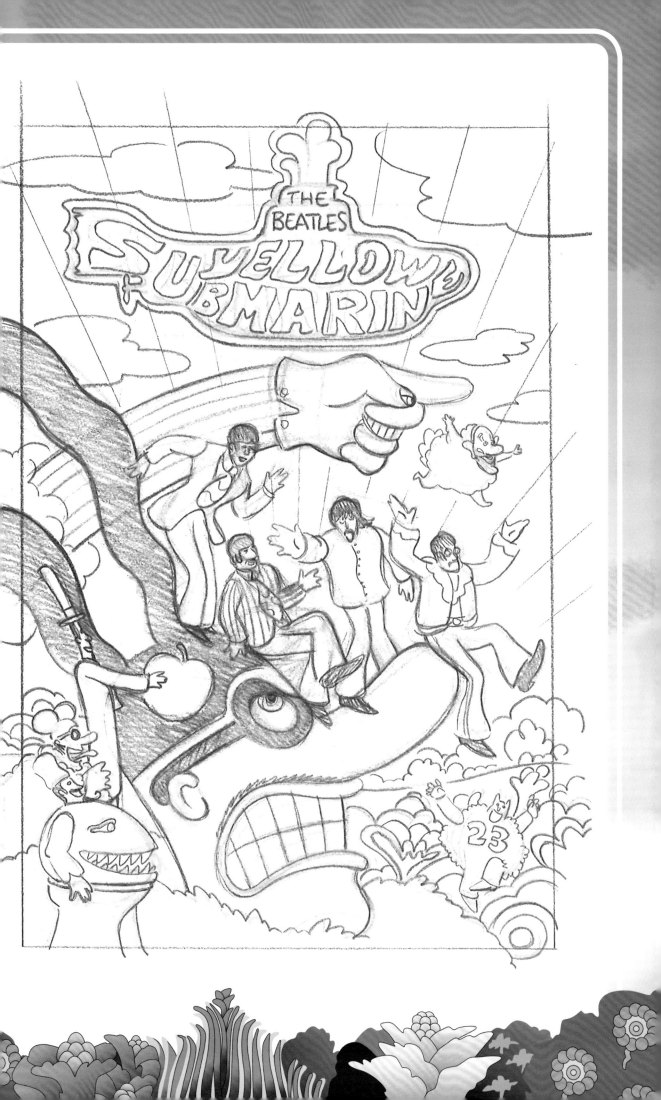

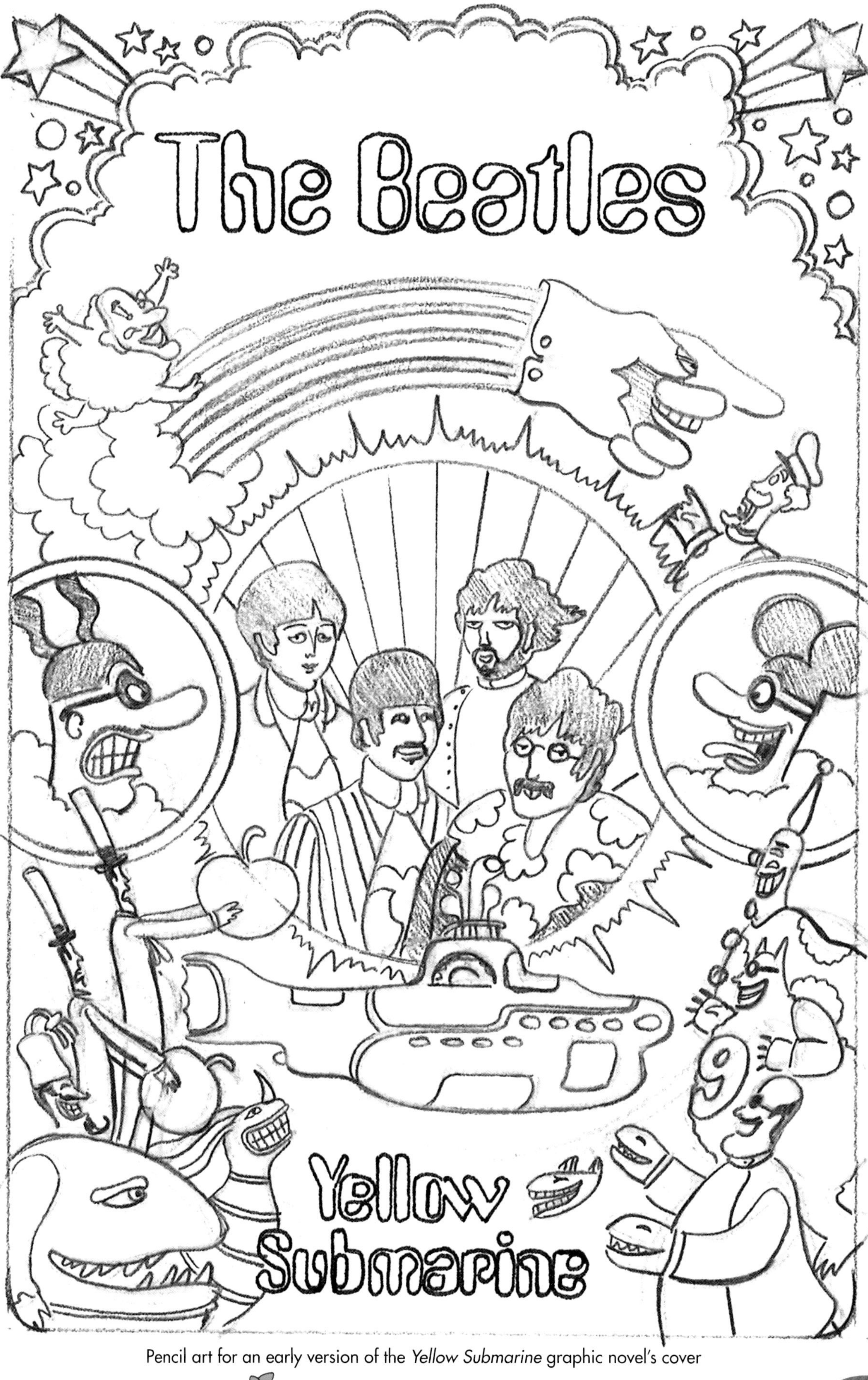
The Beatles
Yellow Submarine

Pencil art for an early version of the *Yellow Submarine* graphic novel's cover

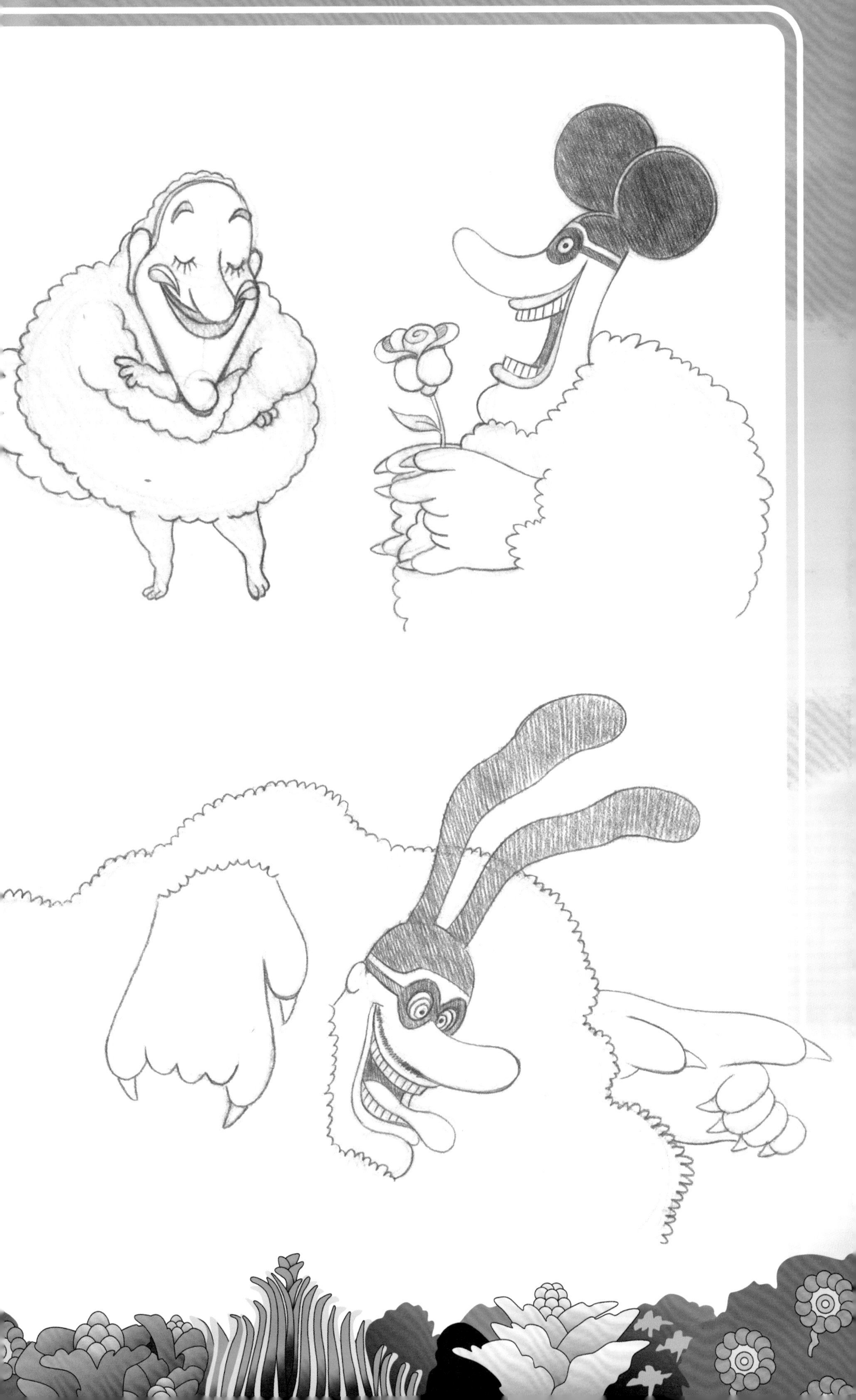

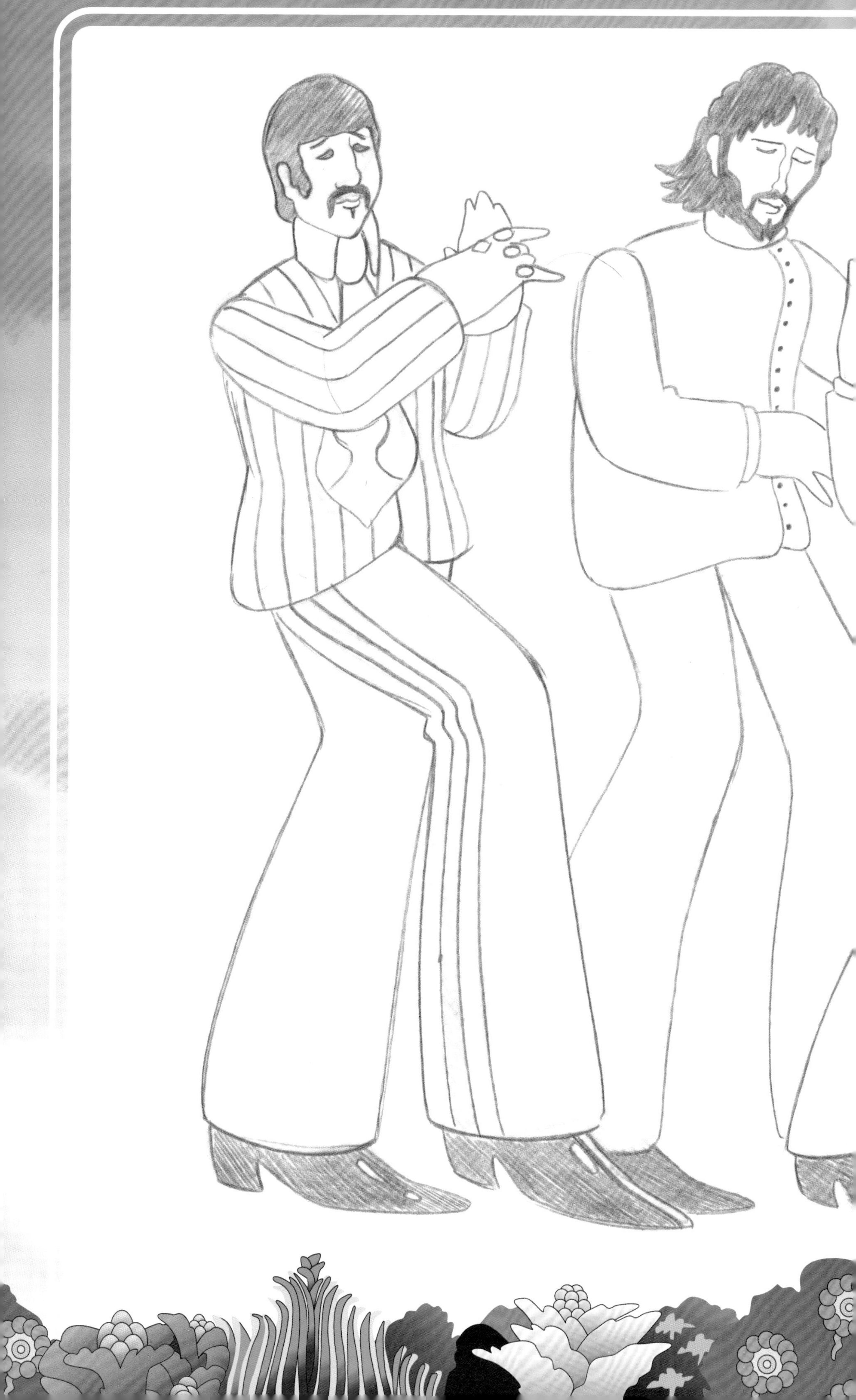

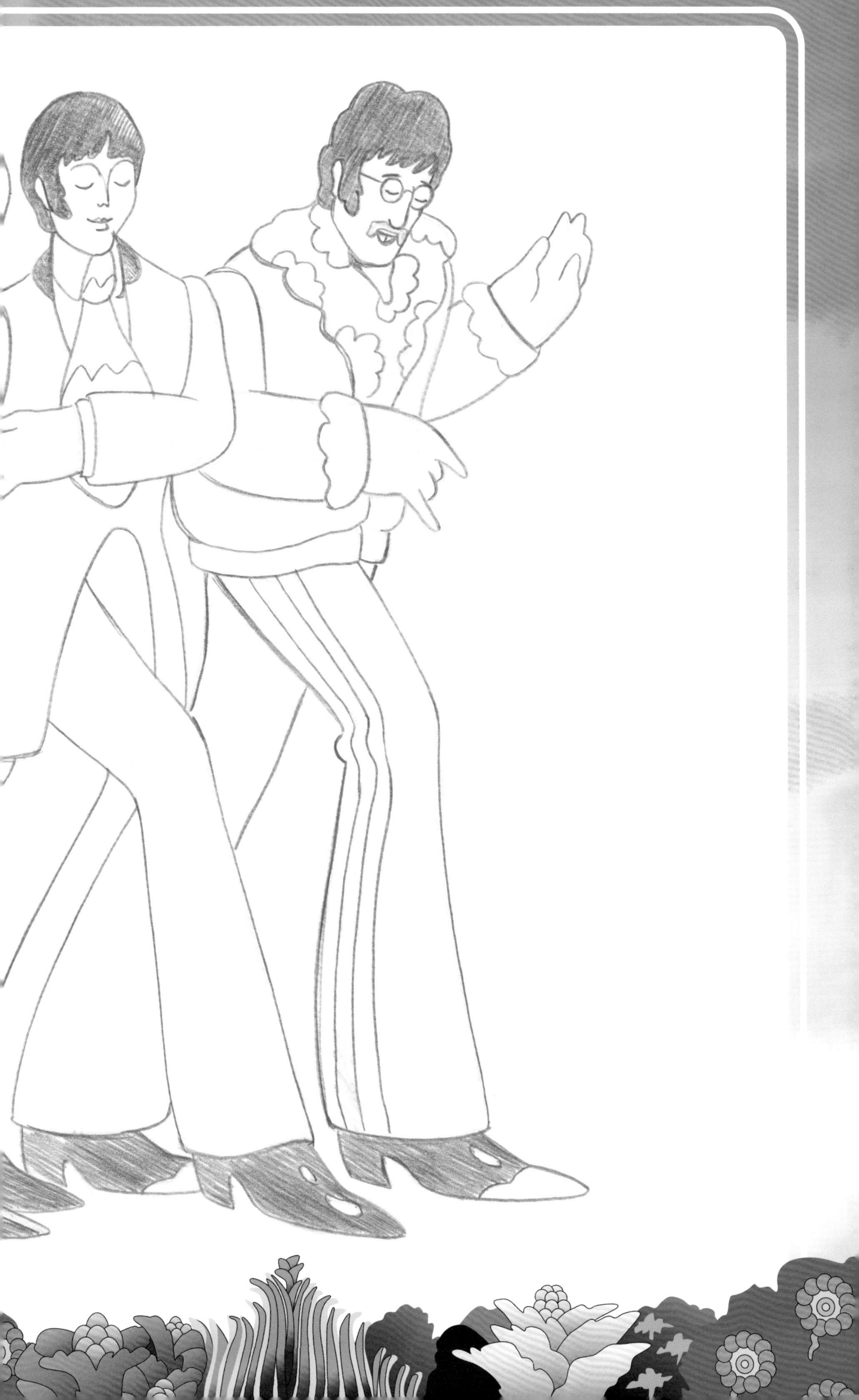

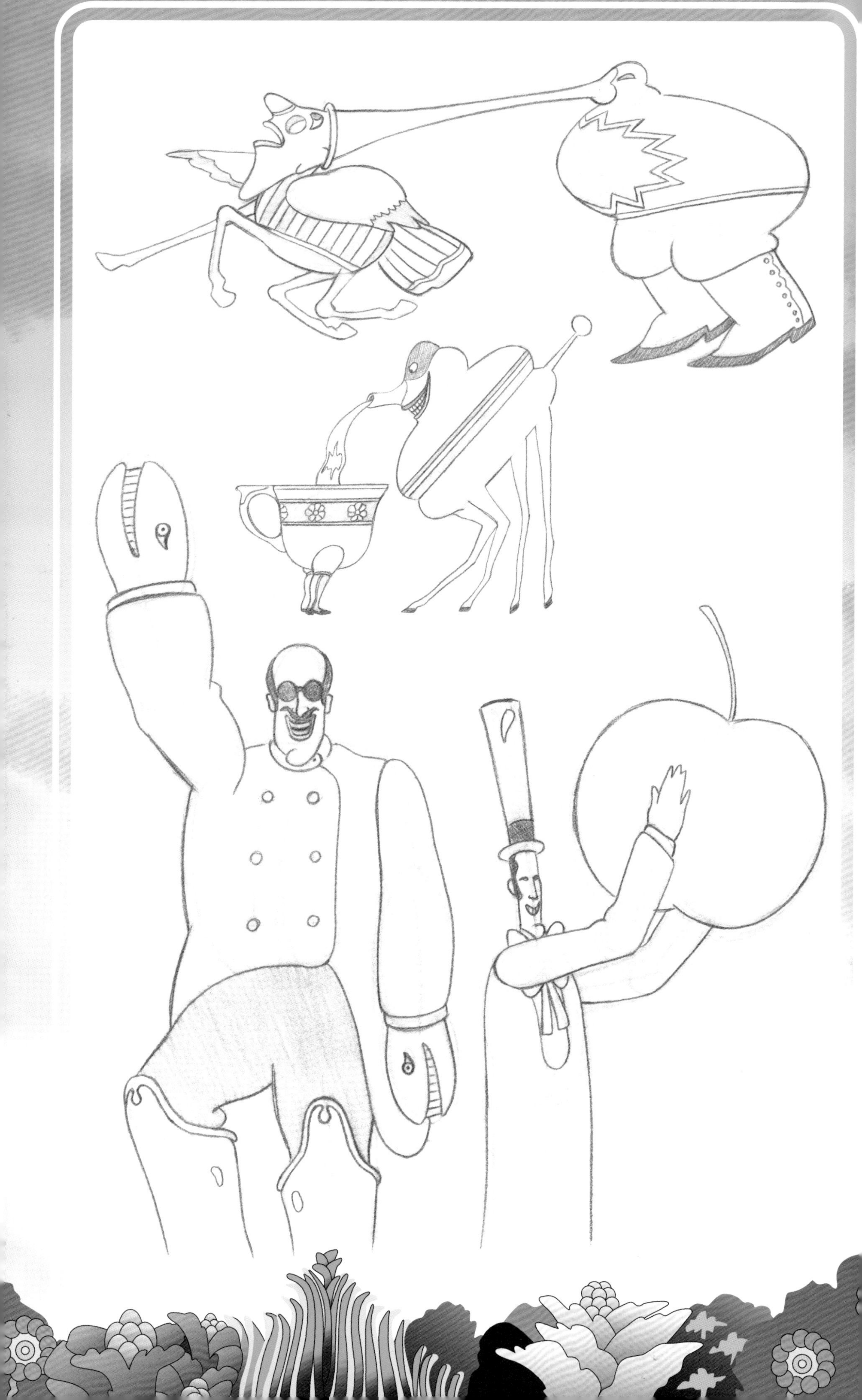

BIOGRAPHIES

Bill Morrison is the co-founder of Bongo comics and the current Editor of *Mad Magazine*. Bill began working as a technical illustrator for Artech, Inc. and went on to work as an illustrator for Disney, where he created promotional art for various titles, including *Bambi*, *Peter Pan* and *The Little Mermaid*. He also created his own comic called *Roswell, Little Green Man*, published by Bongo comics.

Nathan Kane has been working in comics and animation his entire adult life. Starting his career as a colorist, Nathan has also worked as a writer, art director, illustrator, and editor. He's worked on over 500 comic issues for Bongo Comics, where he is currently the Creative Director. Being a part of this *Yellow Submarine* adaptation is a dream come true as it combines his two earliest loves: The Beatles and comic books.

Andrew Pepoy has a long list of comic titles that he's provided artwork for, including *Superman*, *Batman*, *Spider-Man*, *The X-Men*, *Sonic The Hedgehog* and many more. He's also the creator of *The Adventures of Simone & Ajax*.

Tone Rodriguez is an artist who lives in Phoenix, Arizona. He has worked on various titles including *Simpsons Comics*, *Futurama Comics*, and *Snake Plisskin Chronicles*.

Aditya Bidikar is the letterer of multiple comics series, including *Motor Crush*, *Black Cloud* and *Kid Lobotomy*.

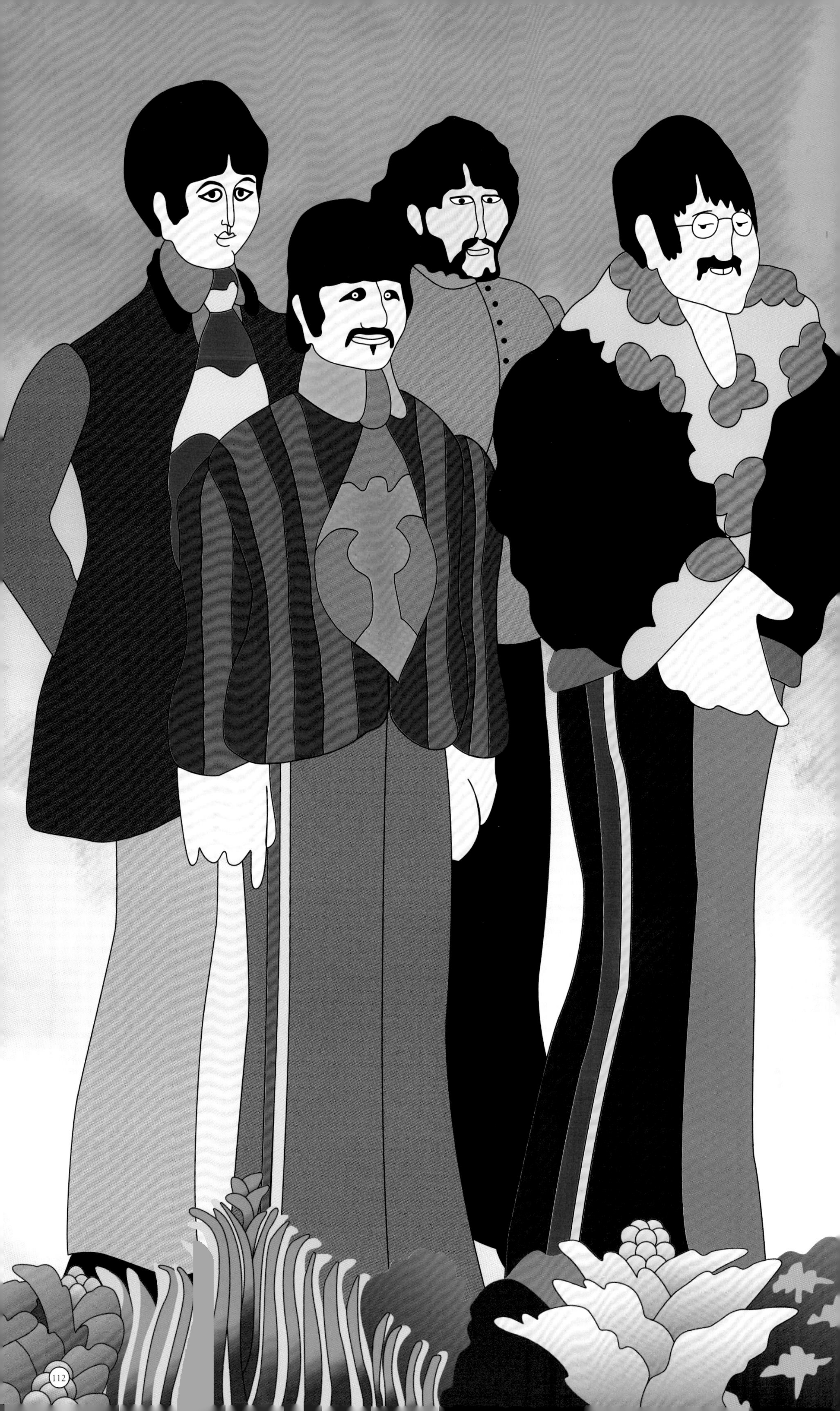

Zachary Z. Packrat
Backpacks the Grand Canyon

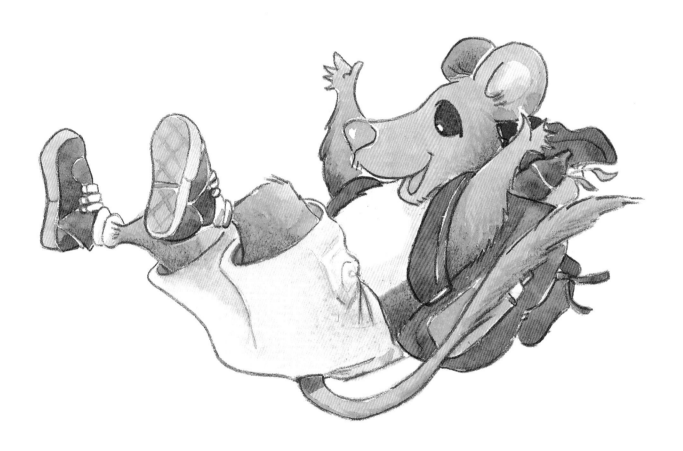

by Brooke Bessesen
illustrations by Jenny Campbell

ARIZONA
HIGHWAYS

Did You Know the Grand Canyon Can Be Seen From Space?

This landmark gorge is a whopping 277 miles (446 kilometers) long, about 10 miles (16 kilometers) across and a mile (1.6 kilometers) deep. It is so enormous that it has been listed as one of the Seven Natural Wonders of the World. And the rocks tell an extraordinary geologic history! There are many ancient rock layers in the Canyon—think of them as a stack of assorted bricks—and the bottom layer is almost *2 billion* years old. The formations were created and shaped by powerful forces of nature, including tectonic shifts (movement of the Earth's plates) and volcanic activity (lava eruptions). For the past 6 million years, the mighty Colorado River has been eroding (wearing away) the terrain, splitting it open and exposing all the layers.

The North Rim is almost 1,000 feet (300 meters) higher than the South Rim, but both slopes are steep. Due to the plummeting landscape, the climate in the Grand Canyon can range from the icy chill of Canada to the blistering heat of Mexico. In fact, there are five major ecosystems from rim to river. *Boreal Forest* is at the highest elevation and receives the most rain and snow. The towering trees in the *Ponderosa Forest* are frequently burned by lightning-ignited fires. Trees in the *Piñon-Juniper Woodland* are much shorter and grow farther apart. *Desert Scrub* is the hottest and driest ecosystem, with summer temperatures over 100 degrees Fahrenheit (38 degrees Celsius). And *Riparian* habitat is found along the Colorado River, where the water supports an abundance of life. Each ecosystem provides for particular plants and animals. Several Grand Canyon species live nowhere else on Earth!

People live here, too. The earliest evidence of humans in the area dates back about 11,000 years. Since then, the Canyon has been home to many native tribes. Some of the most interesting artifacts left by early cultures are petroglyphs (symbols etched by prehistoric people), which were made by chipping off the dark surface of the rock.

The Grand Canyon was designated a national park on February 26, 1919, and listed as a World Heritage Site in 1979. Today, it is an extremely popular destination. Every year, about 5 million people arrive at Grand Canyon National Park to take in the colossal buttes, hike the serpentine trails and raft the roaring river. To protect the natural and historic features, Congress called on rangers "to conserve the scenery and the natural and historic objects and the wildlife therein ... by such means as will leave them unimpaired for the enjoyment of future generations." Which means that for the park's splendor to last, each visitor must leave it as they found it. Tread lightly.

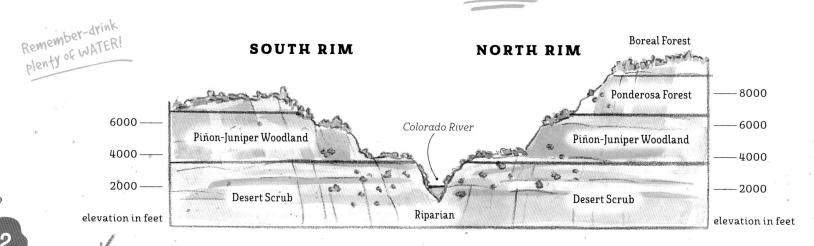

Remember—drink plenty of WATER!

SOUTH RIM
NORTH RIM
Boreal Forest
Ponderosa Forest
Piñon-Juniper Woodland
Colorado River
Piñon-Juniper Woodland
Desert Scrub
Riparian
Desert Scrub
6000
4000
2000
elevation in feet
8000
6000
4000
2000
elevation in feet

Look What Grows in the Grand Canyon

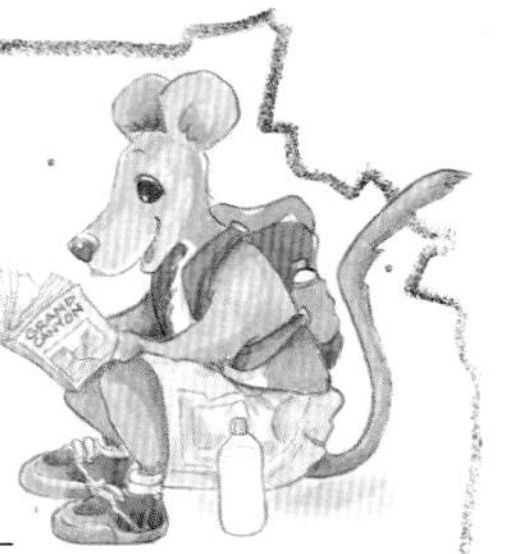

There are about 1,750 species of plant life in the Grand Canyon, ranging from trees to grasses, bushes to wildflowers and prickly cactuses to wetland vegetation.

Banana yucca

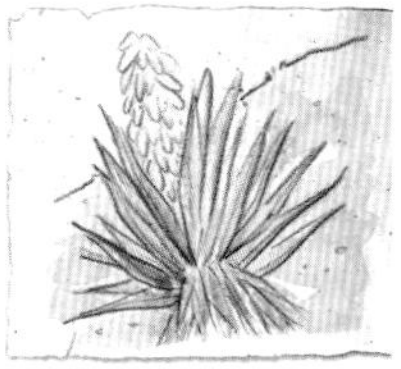

This succulent grows in the Piñon-Juniper Woodland and Desert Scrub. It has long, spiky leaves protruding from its short trunk. The leaf blades were once used for weaving baskets or thinned into needle and thread. Large, creamy-white flowers bloom in the spring, followed by edible banana-like fruit.

Yummy

Blue spruce

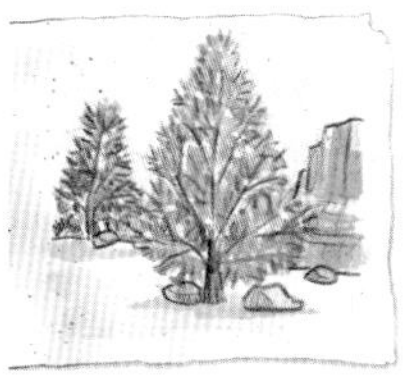

At the Grand Canyon's highest elevations, this evergreen tree can grow up to 100 feet (30 meters) tall and 35 feet (11 meters) wide. It is identified by its silvery blue-green needles and perfect Christmas-tree shape. In the springtime, it produces 3-inch (7.5-centimeter) cones, which have papery, toothed scales.

Cattails

MEOW!!!

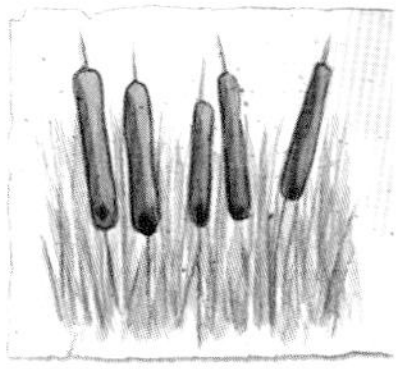

Found in calm, shallow waters along the Colorado River, this Riparian reed grows up to 10 feet (3 meters) tall and can form thick stands. Parts of the plant have been traditionally used by native cultures as a source of food and medicine. Its name comes from the brown flower spike, which looks like a cat's tail.

Coyote willow

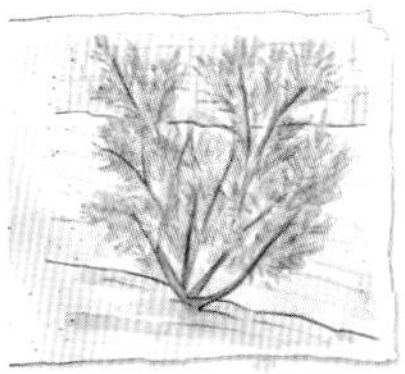

This shrub-like tree forms a dense thicket on the banks of the Colorado River. It has flexible branches and thin green leaves that feed and protect wildlife. Willow was utilized by many native tribes to weave clothes and kitchen vessels, build large structures, create weapons, render dyes and make medicines.

Creosote bush

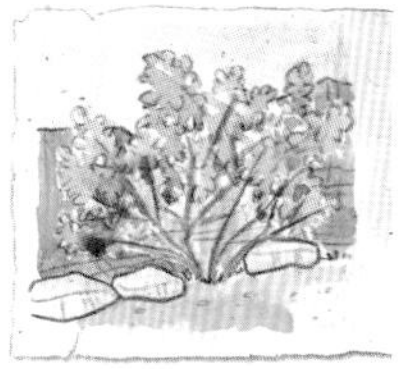

Growing in Desert Scrub, this spindly shrub has a unique aroma that is particularly noticeable after a rain. It is usually 3 to 10 feet (1 to 3 meters) tall and blooms with bright yellow flowers and seeds that are fuzzy white balls. Creosote can sprout new stem crowns as it ages, allowing one colony to live for hundreds of years!

Honey mesquite

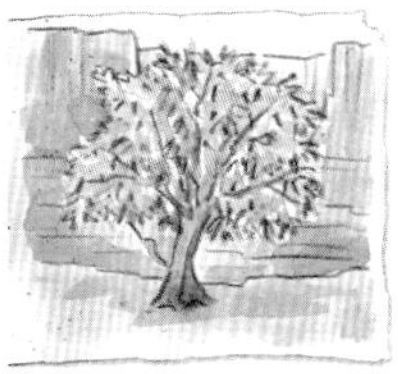

This tree grows near the bottom of the Grand Canyon. It is usually 20 to 30 feet (6 to 9 meters) tall, with drooping thorny branches and feathery green leaves. Its seedpods, called beans, are eaten by both humans and animals, and bees use its nectar to produce mesquite honey, which has a special flavor.

Ponderosa pine

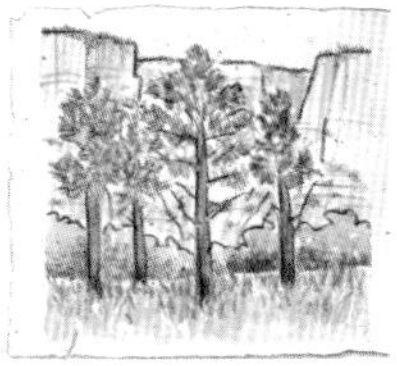

In the Ponderosa Forest, this long-needled tree normally grows 55 to 90 feet (17 to 27 meters) tall and can live for more than 120 years! Lightning often strikes these trees, and fires burn the forests where they grow. The tree's core is protected by cinnamon-red bark as thick as 4 inches (10 centimeters).

The bark smells like vanilla. How cool!!

Prickly pear cactus

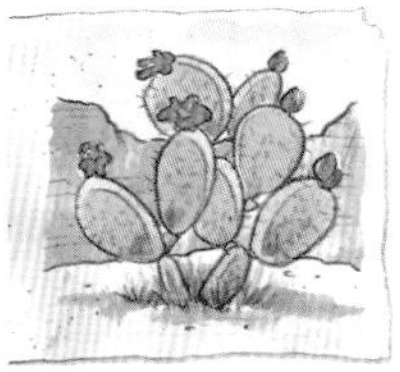

The flat, fleshy pads of this Desert Scrub cactus are covered with clusters of spines. Its pads, called *nopales,* can be cooked and eaten. So can its fruits, known as cactus figs or *tuna,* which are used to make candies, jellies, syrups and fruity drinks. Blooms are a stunning red, yellow or purple.

LOOK!

The Grand Canyon!

A feast for the eyes.

Ruddy red rock against crystal blue skies.

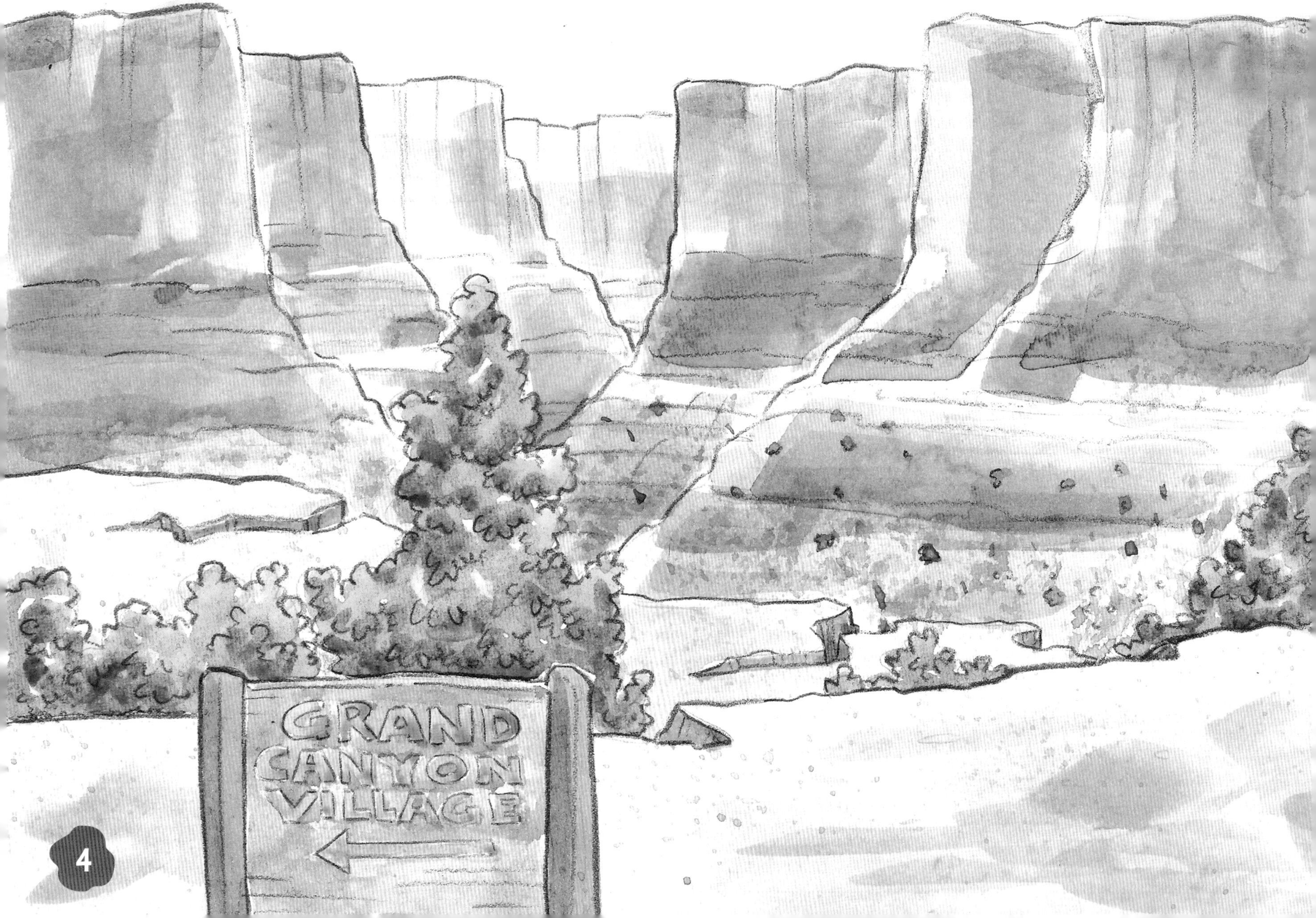
GRAND
CANYON
VILLAGE

To hike this World Wonder, plans Zachary Z.
A real expedition with oodles to see!

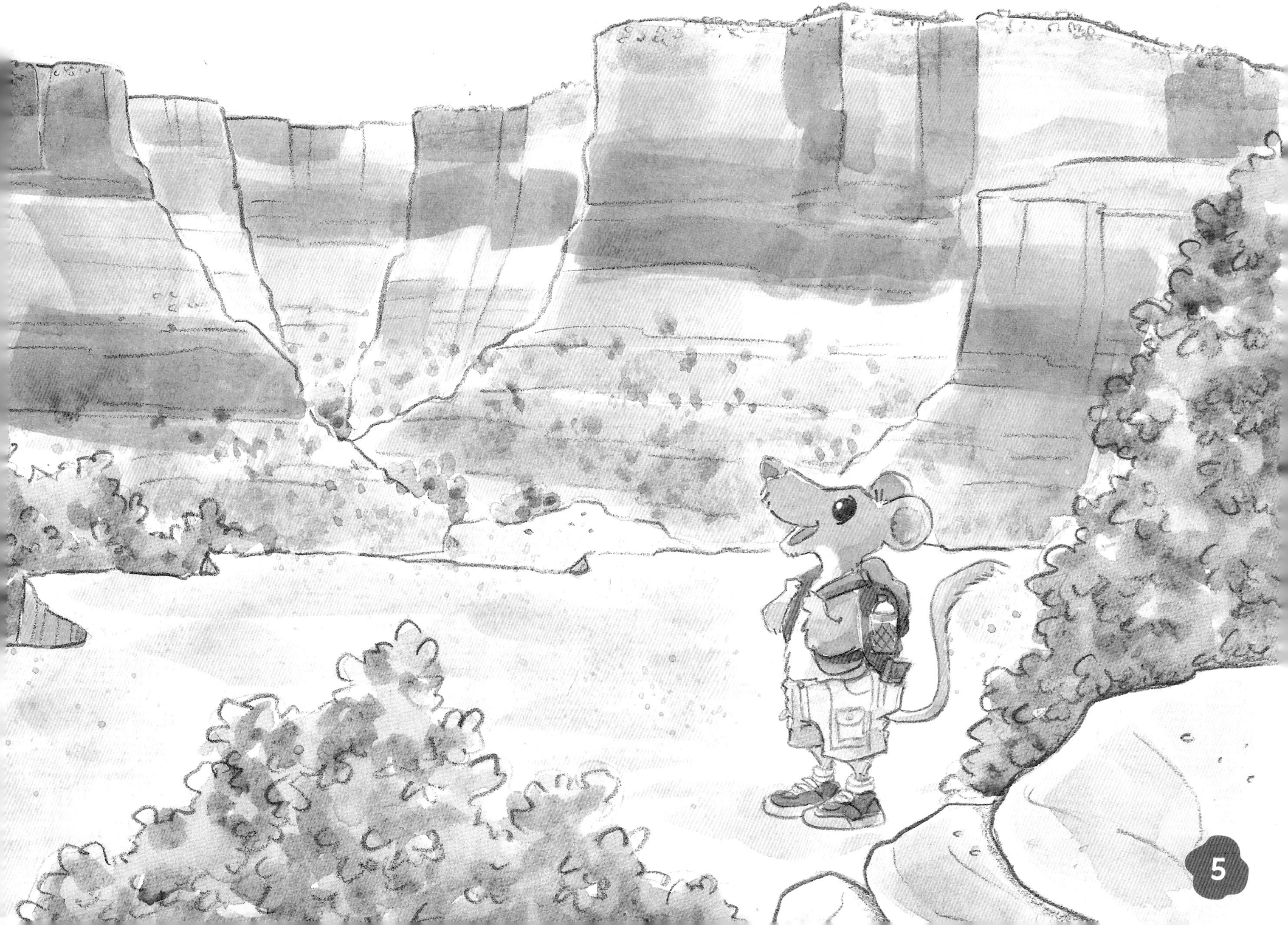

The gigantic gorge gaping out from Zach's feet—
steep and so deep—makes his heart skip a beat.

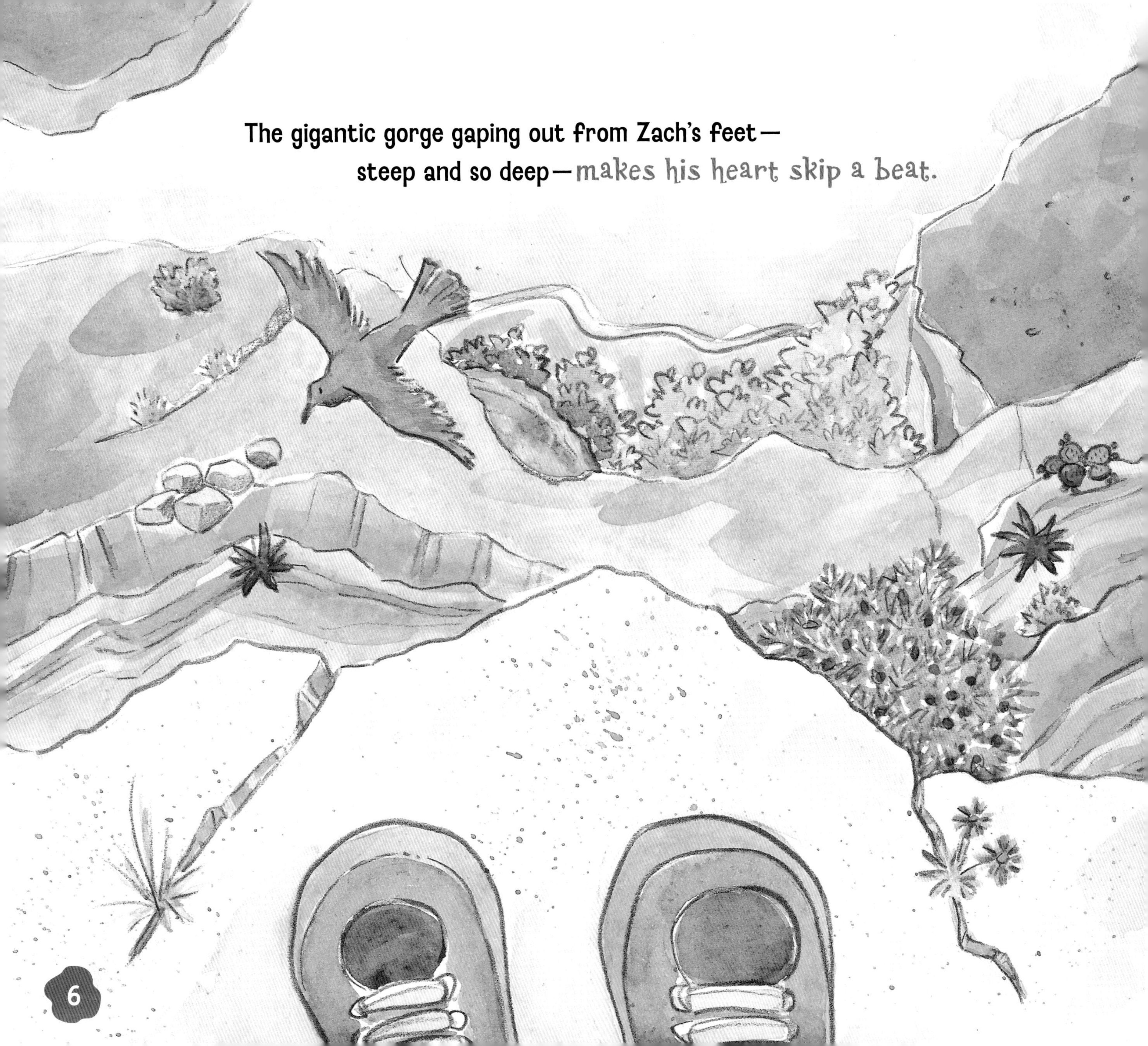

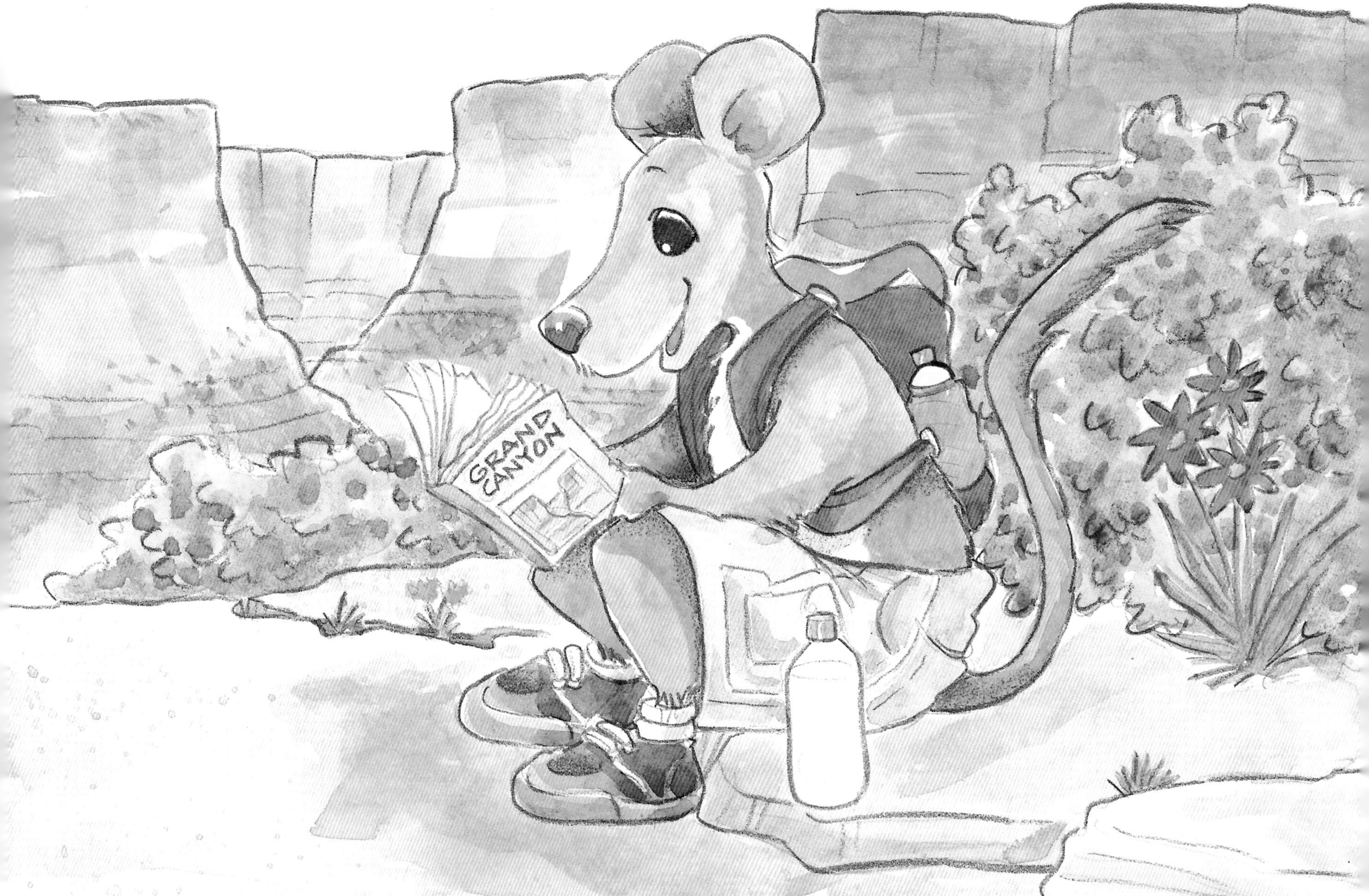
GRAND CANYON

He checks for his guidebook
and studies his maps,
sips from his water and tightens his straps.

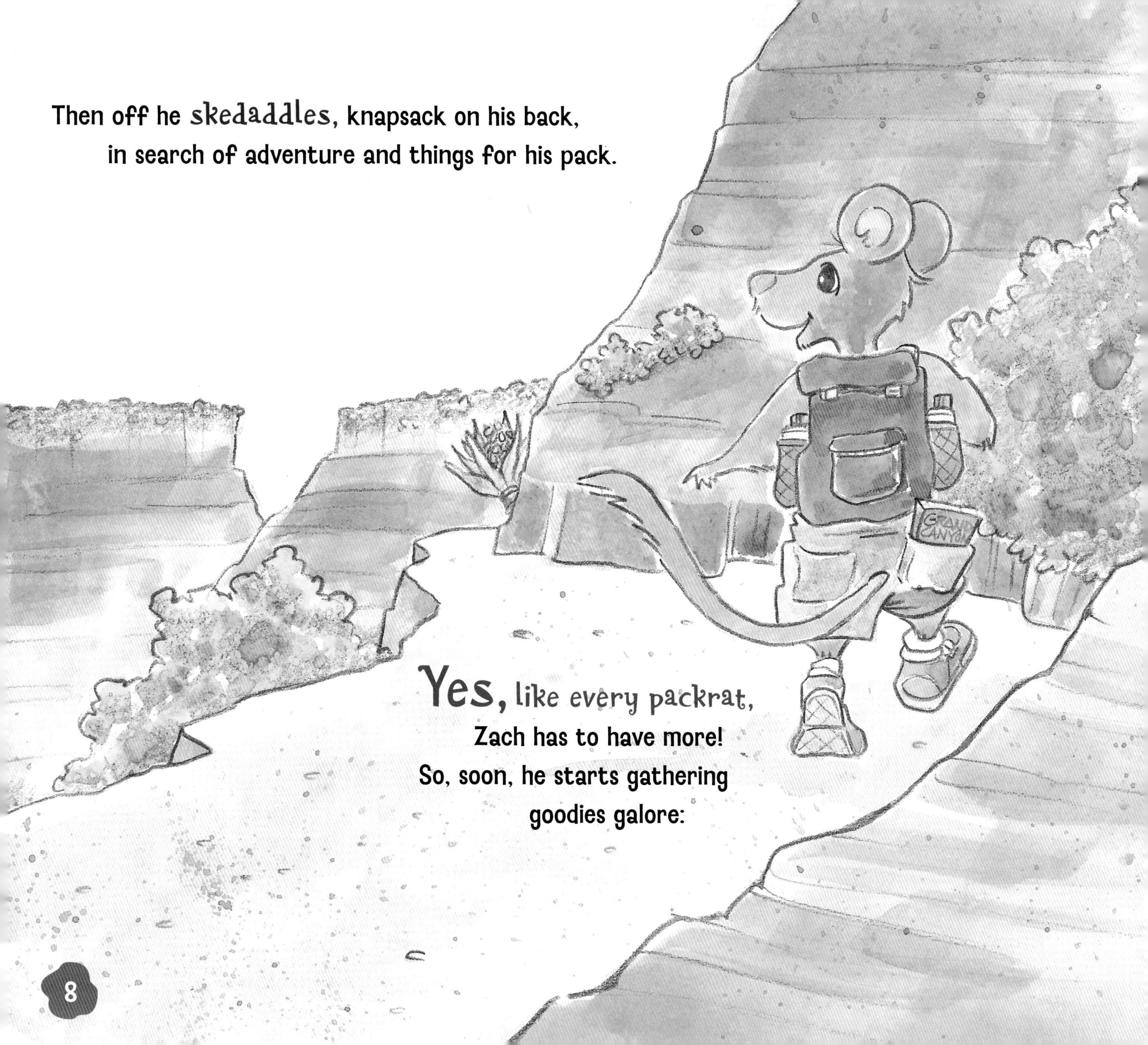
GRAND CANYON

Then off he skedaddles, knapsack on his back,
in search of adventure and things for his pack.

Yes, like every packrat,
Zach has to have more!
So, soon, he starts gathering
goodies galore:

A geode that twinkles,

two twigs in a knot,

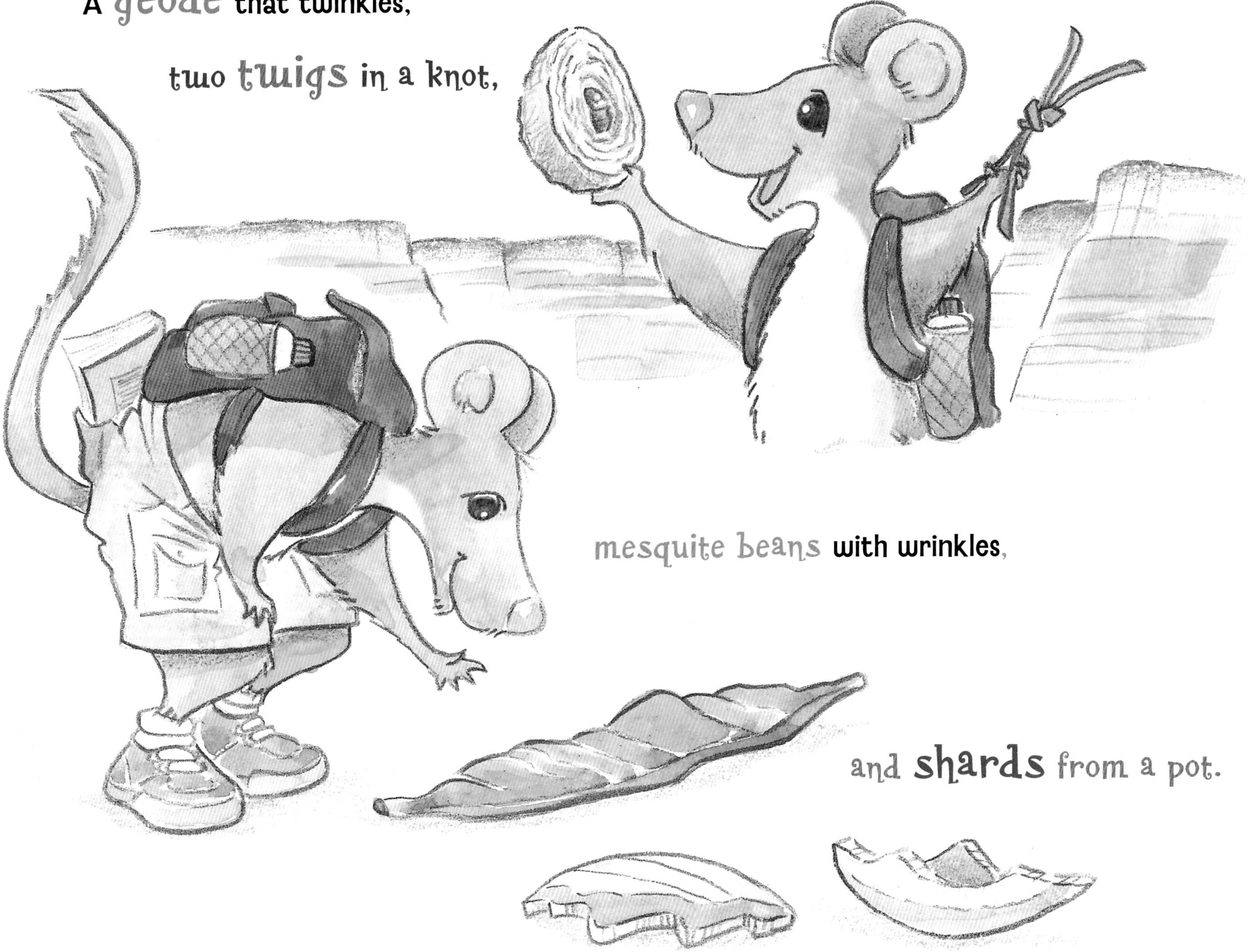

mesquite beans with wrinkles,

and shards from a pot.

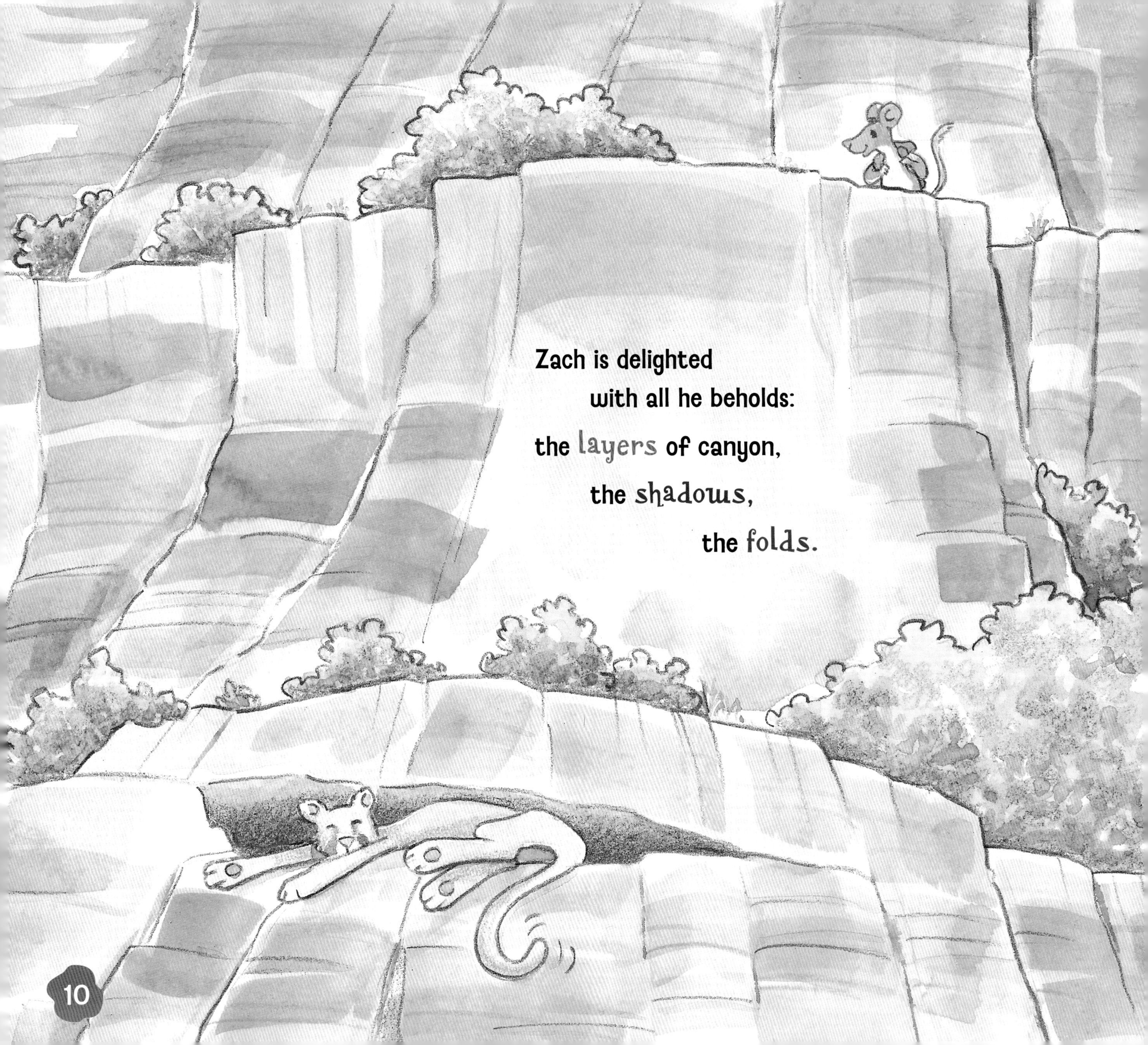

Zach is delighted
with all he beholds:
the layers of canyon,
the shadows,
the folds.

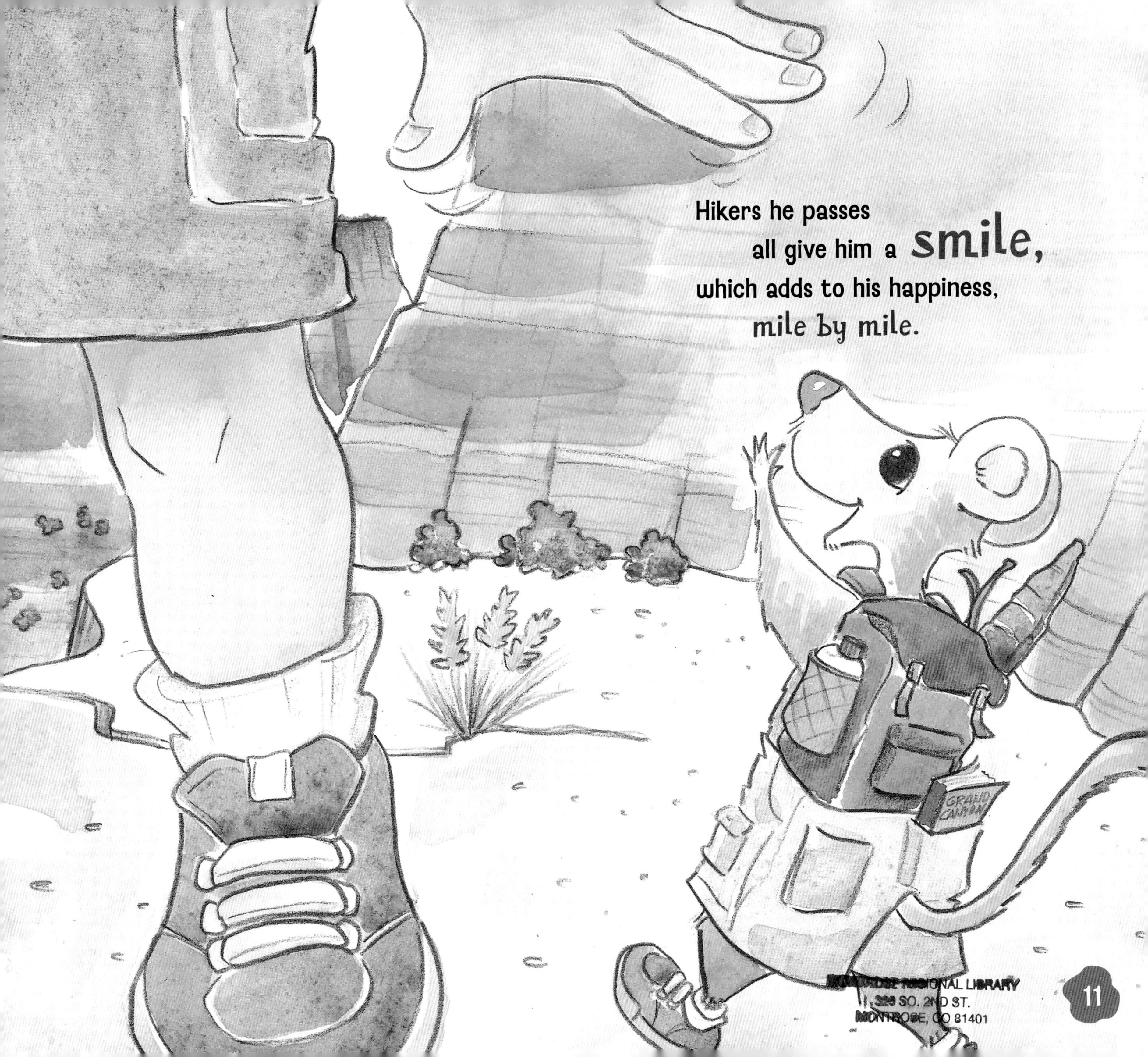
GRAND CANYON

Hikers he passes
all give him a **smile,**
which adds to his happiness,
mile by mile.

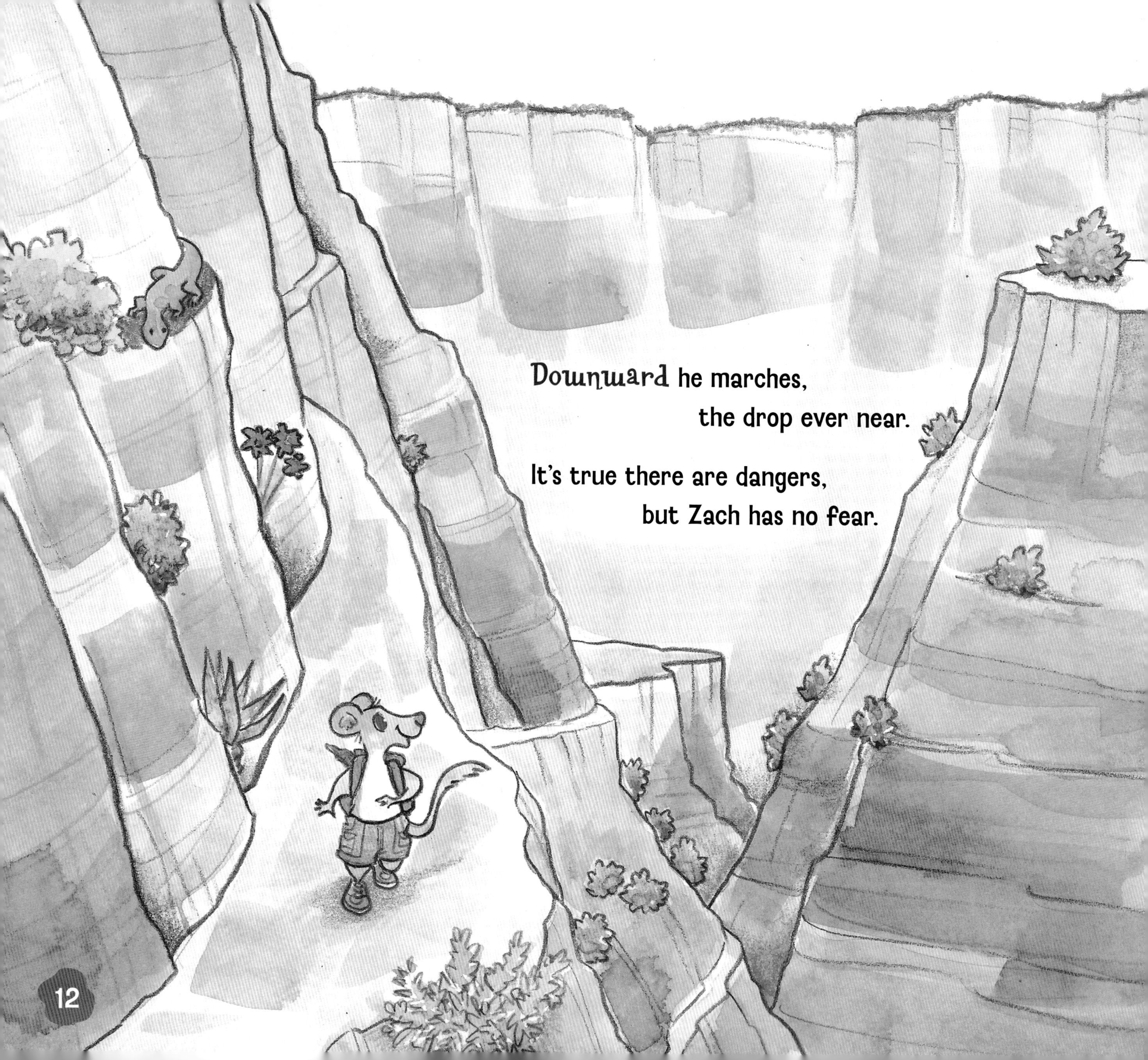

Downward he marches,
the drop ever near.

It's true there are dangers,
but Zach has no fear.

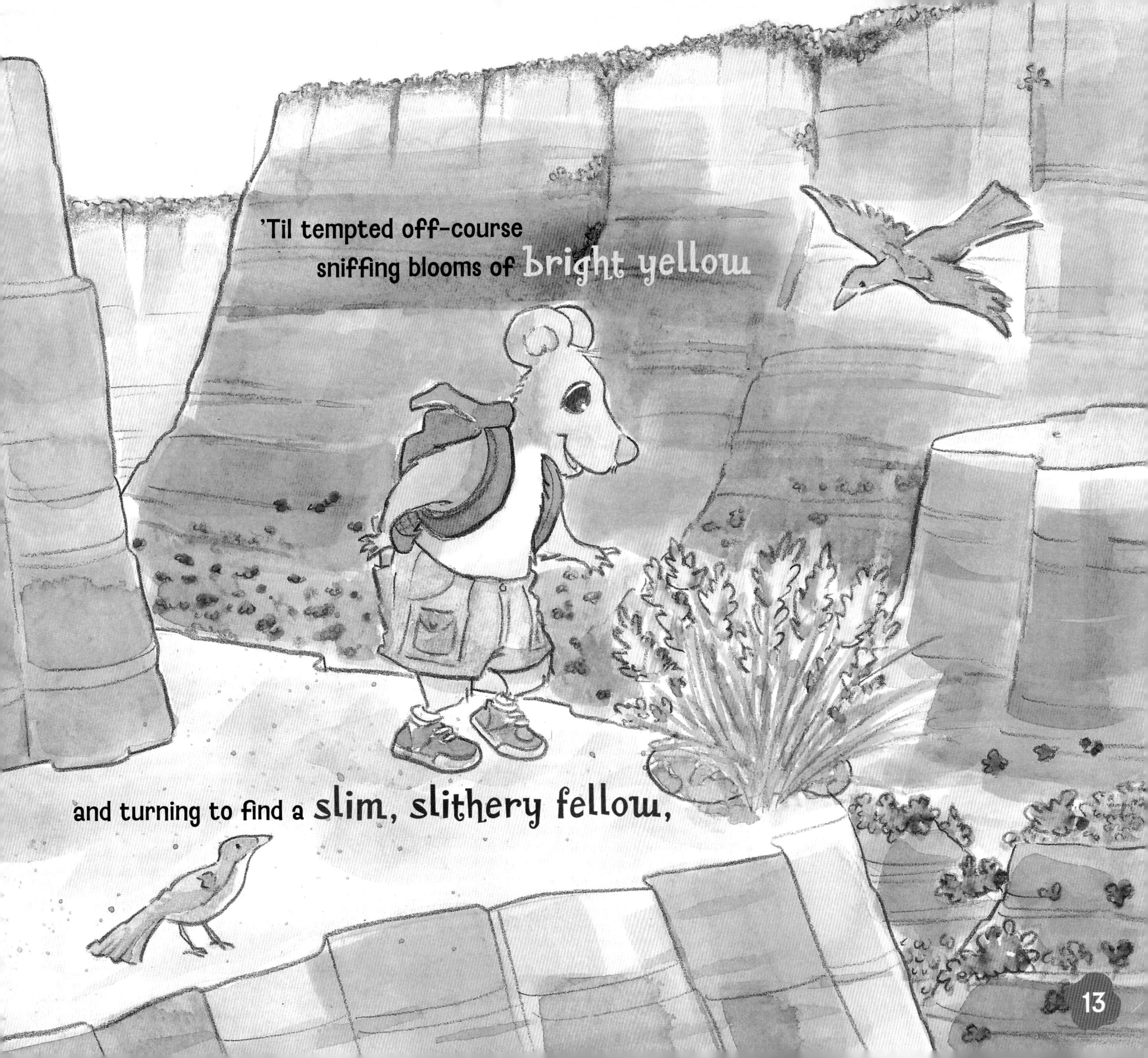
'Til tempted off-course
sniffing blooms of bright yellow
and turning to find a slim, slithery fellow,

Zach stumbles

off sideways and

lets go a BELLOW!

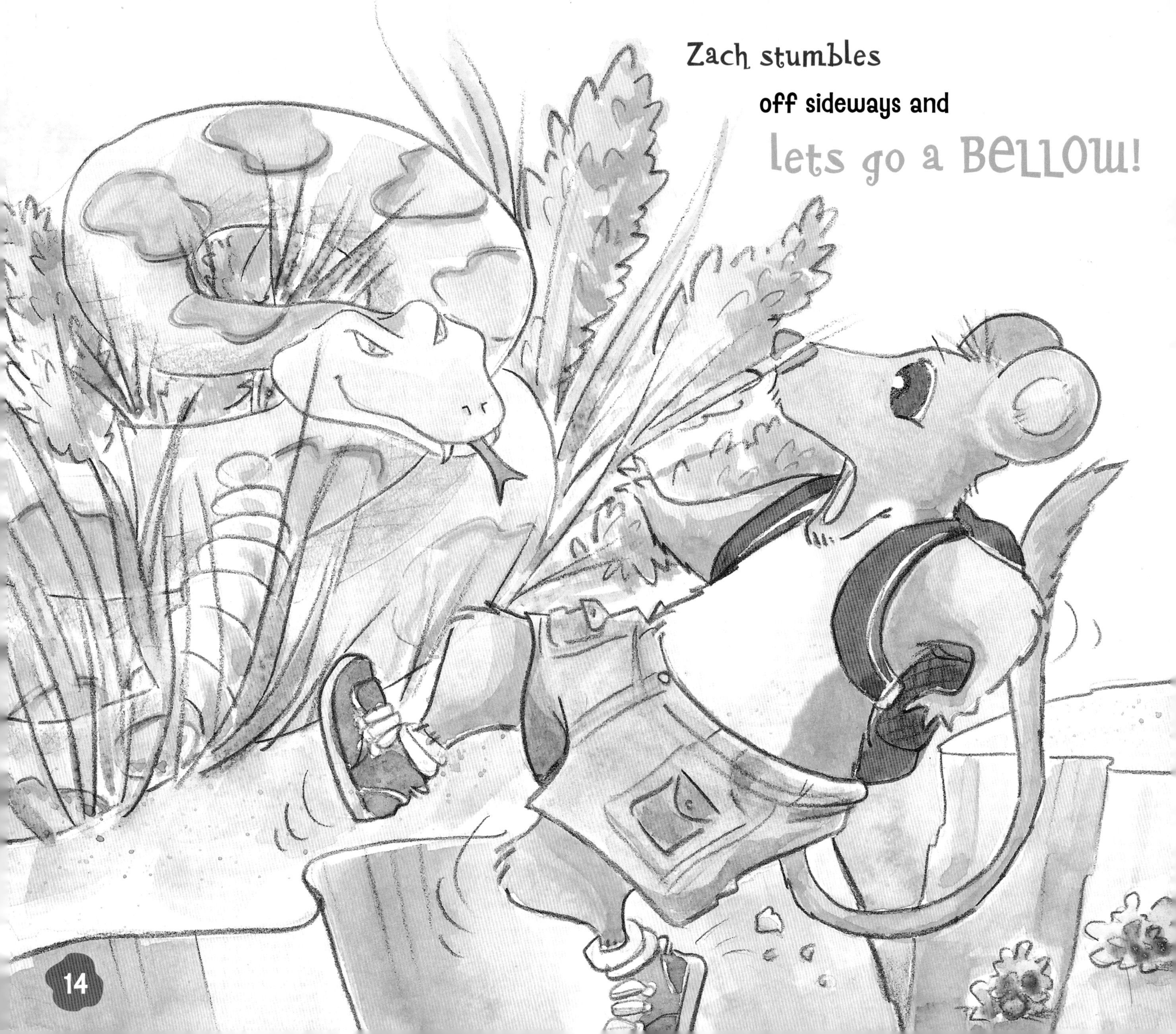

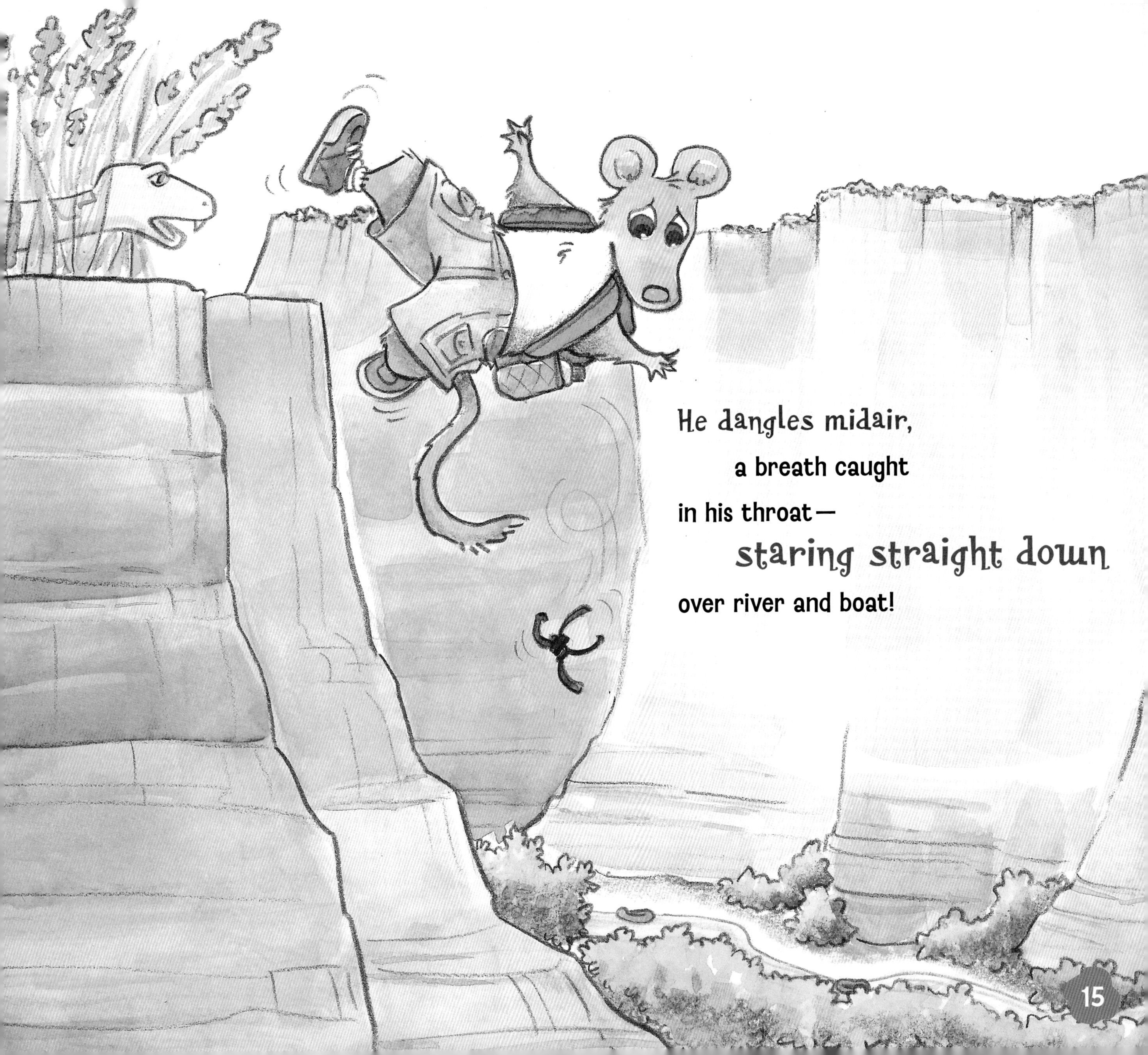

He dangles midair,

a breath caught

in his throat—

staring straight down

over river and boat!

When 10 feet of feathers
come — *whoosh!* — by the cliff.

(Gripped tight at this height,
one will wonder, "*What if?*")

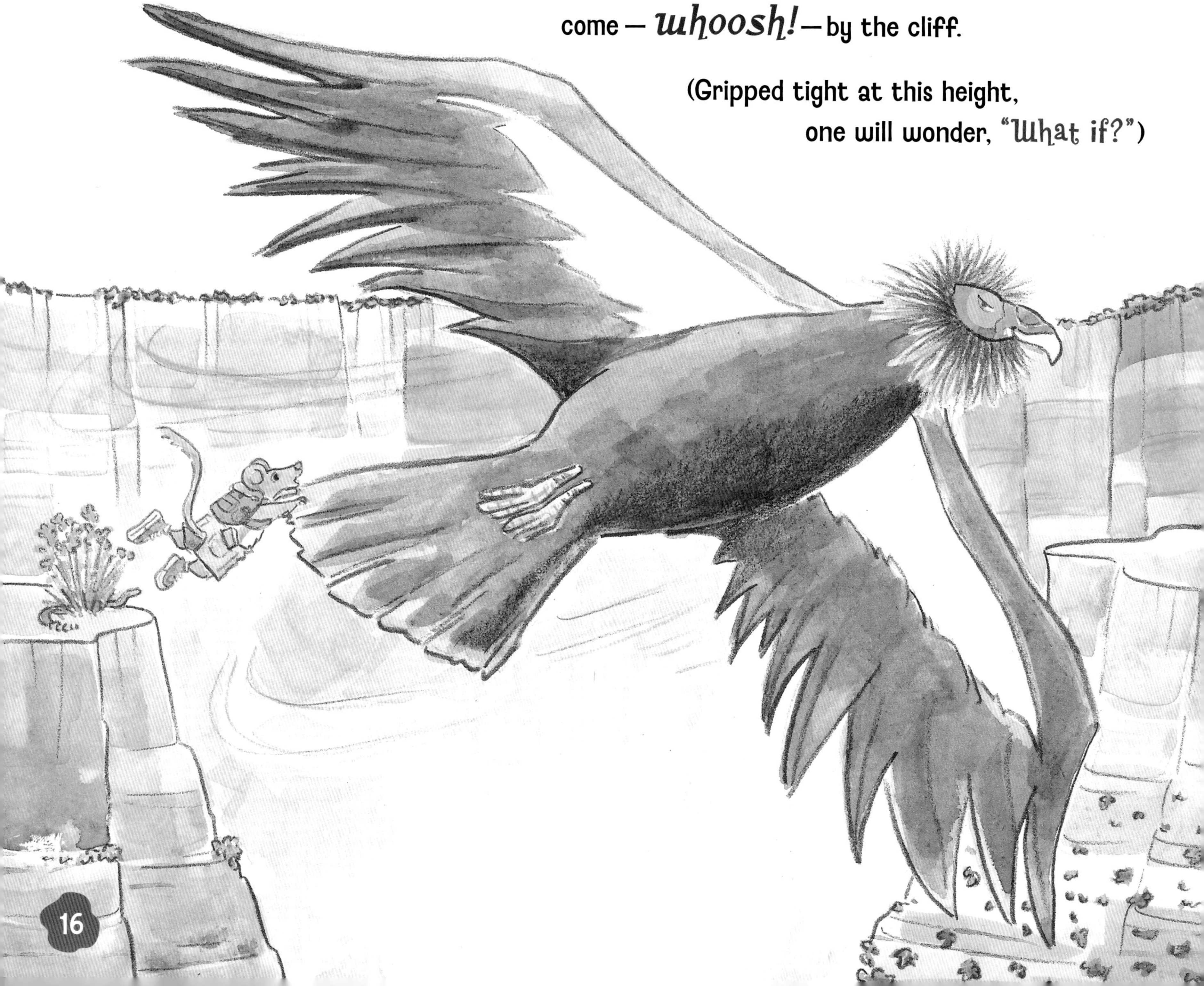

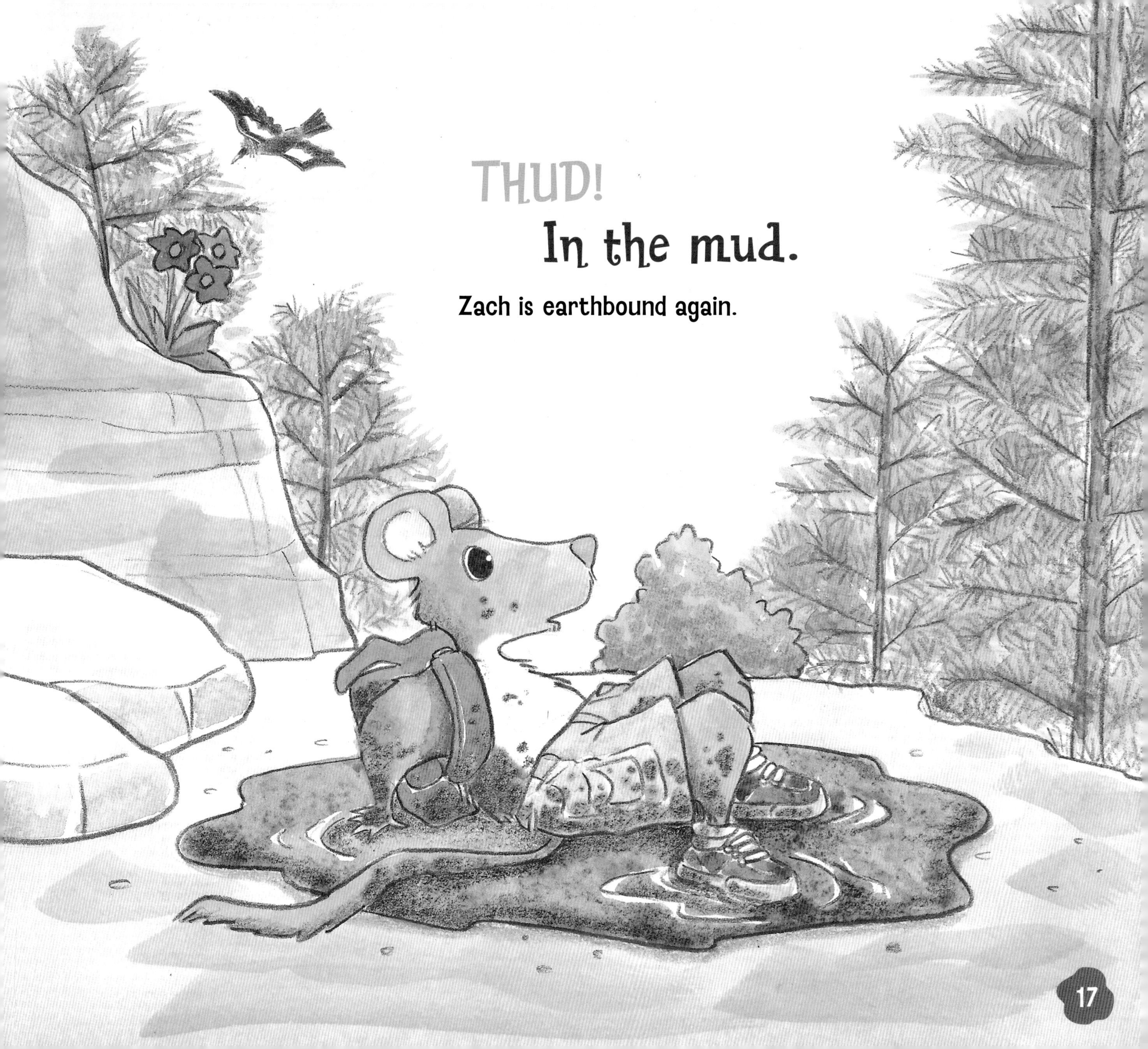

THUD!

In the mud.

Zach is earthbound again.

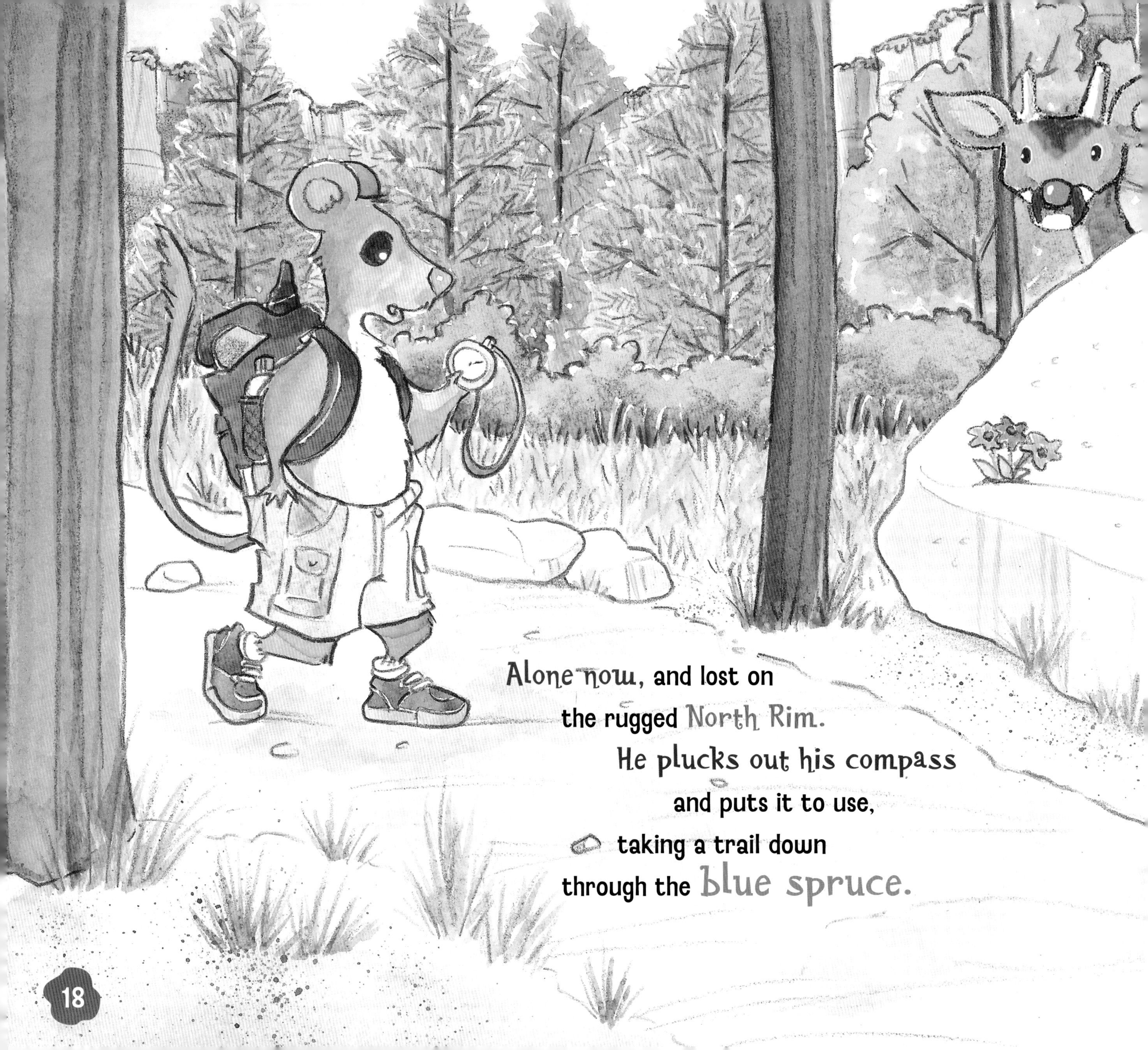

Alone now, and lost on
the rugged North Rim.
He plucks out his compass
and puts it to use,
taking a trail down
through the blue spruce.

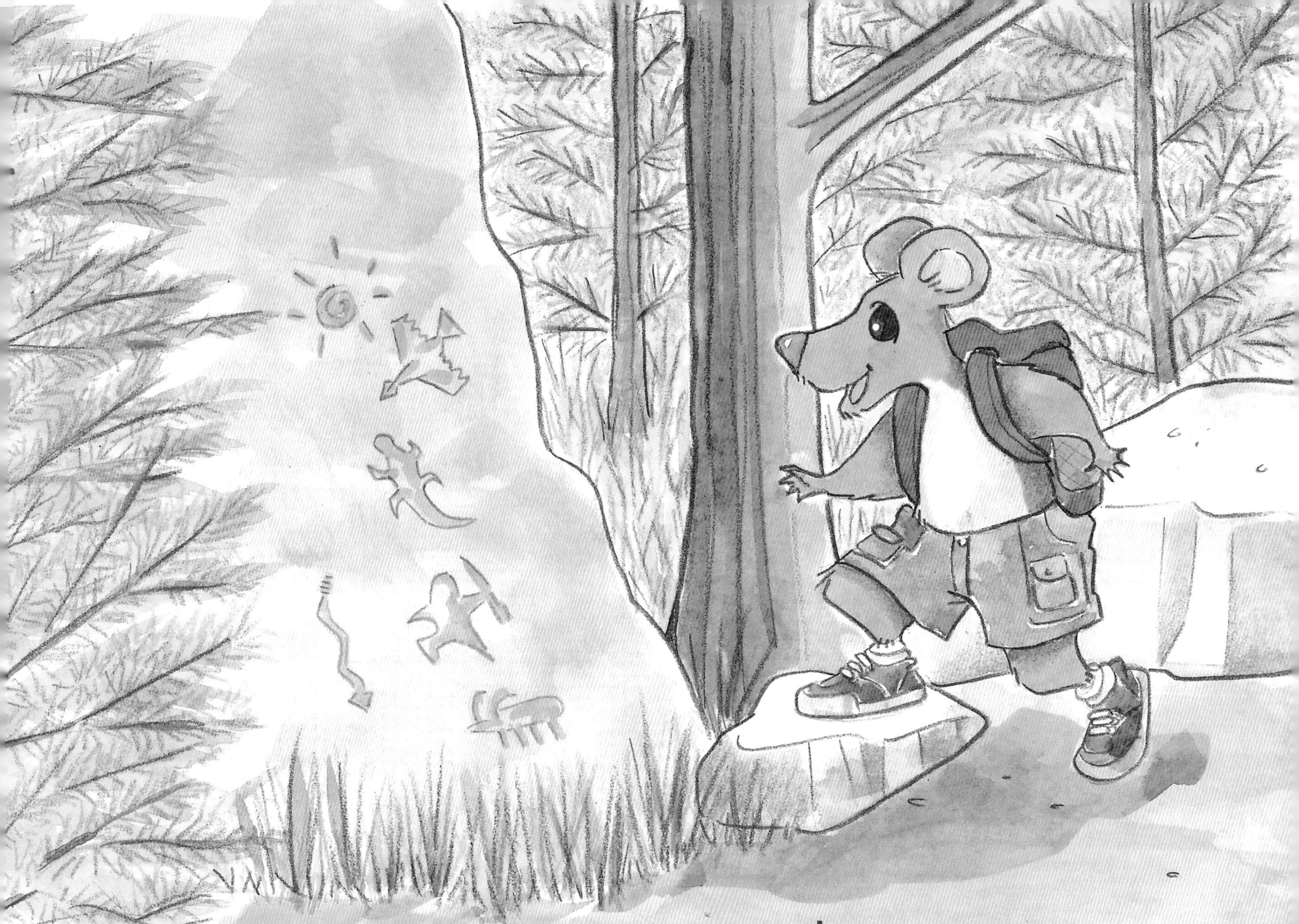

When what does he find? A rare relic indeed!
A sight that would stop even you—guaranteed.
Odd sketchings in stone, carved eons ago.
Exactly what petroglyphs mean, we don't know.

But Zach prefers stuff he can own and adore,
so off he skedaddles to stockpile more:

one funky flat **fossil**,

some chunks
of **soft moss**,

a seed that's **colossal**,

and fox hairs (for floss.)

Ooh, something new...

A brown kangaroo?

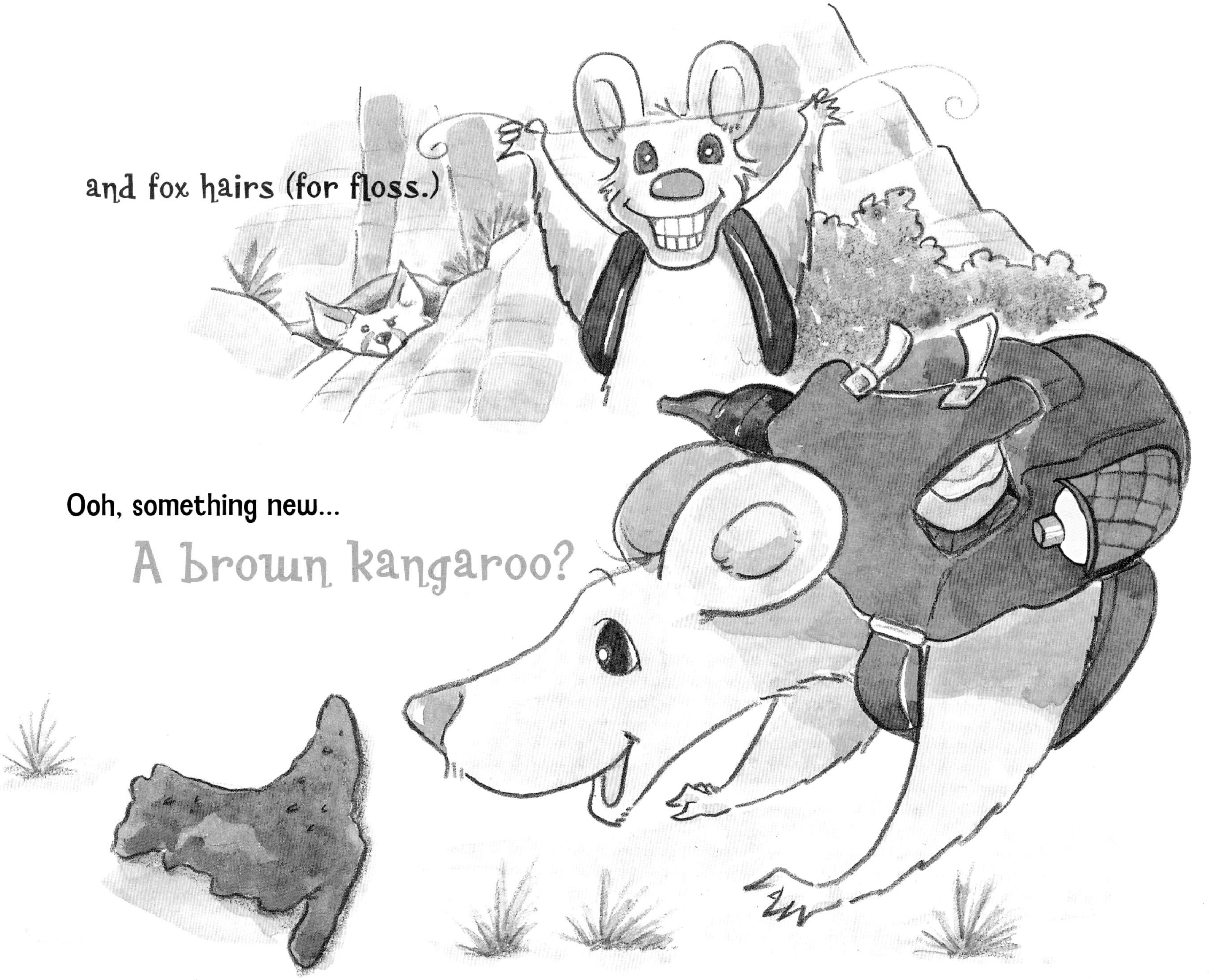

Now that is by far the most oddly shaped poo!

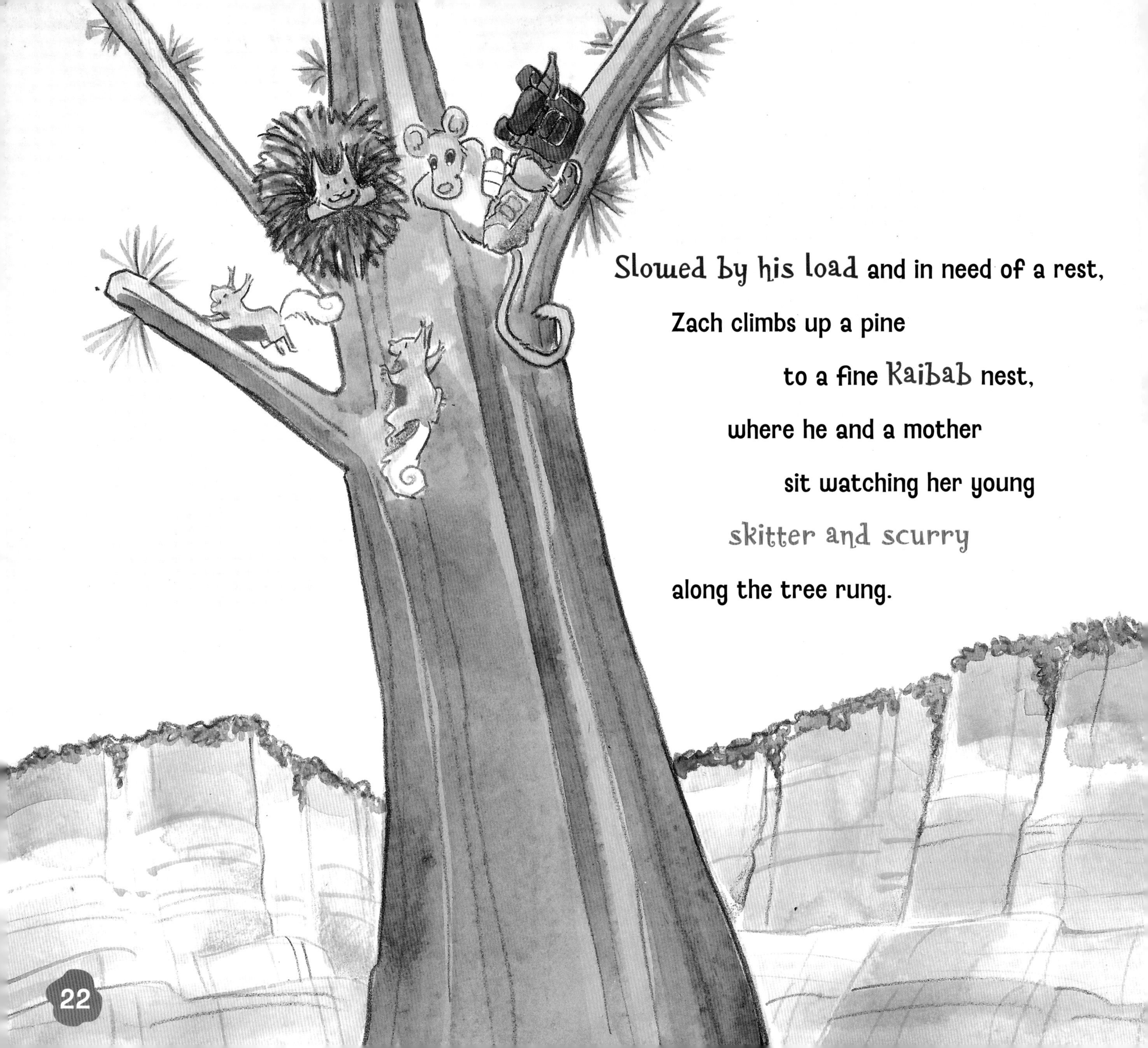

Slowed by his load and in need of a rest,

Zach climbs up a pine

to a fine Kaibab nest,

where he and a mother

sit watching her young

skitter and scurry

along the tree rung.

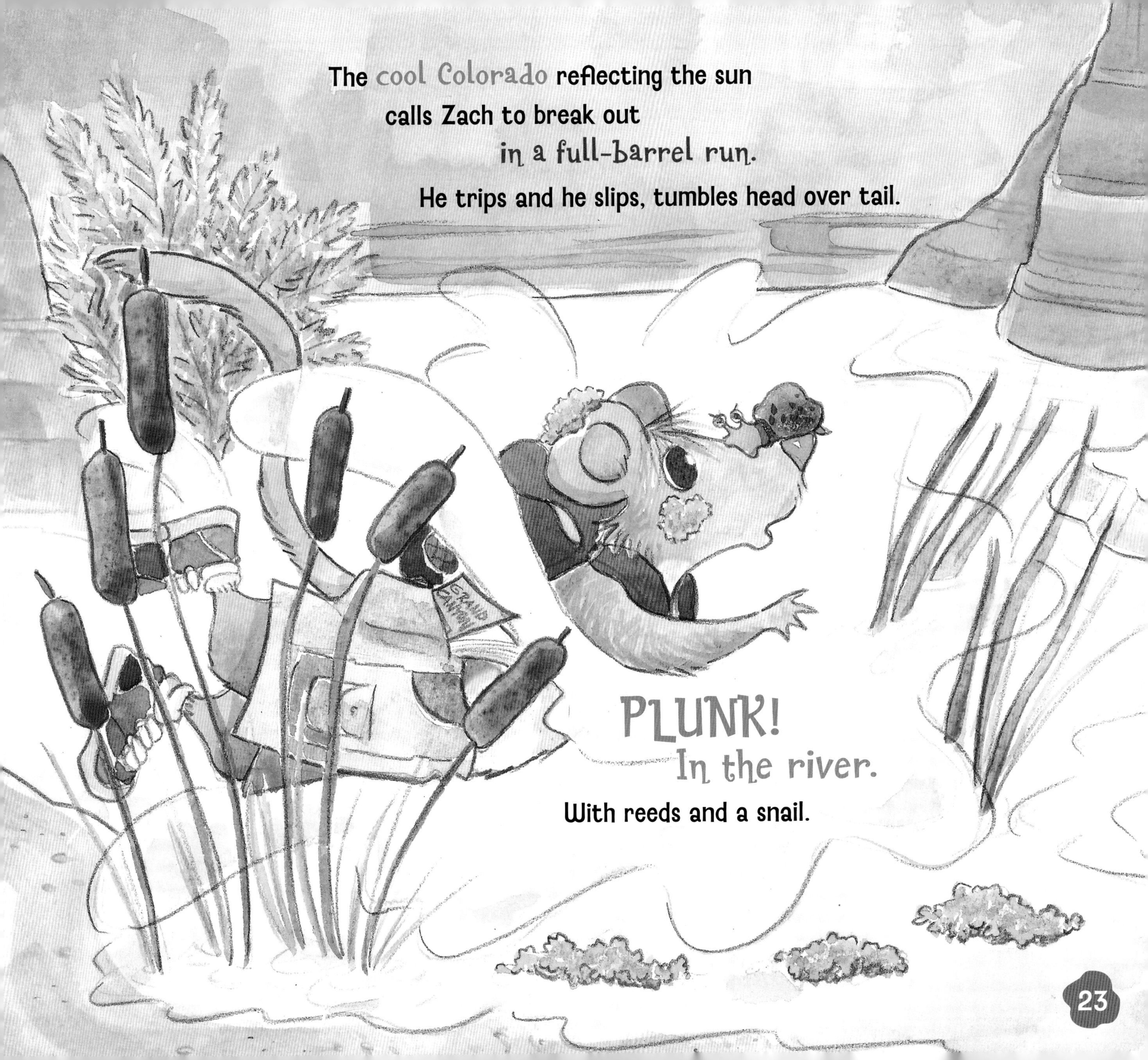

The cool Colorado reflecting the sun
calls Zach to break out
in a full-barrel run.
He trips and he slips, tumbles head over tail.

PLUNK!
In the river.
With reeds and a snail.

It's hard to do much in the heat of the day.

But crafting a raft, he soon gets underway.

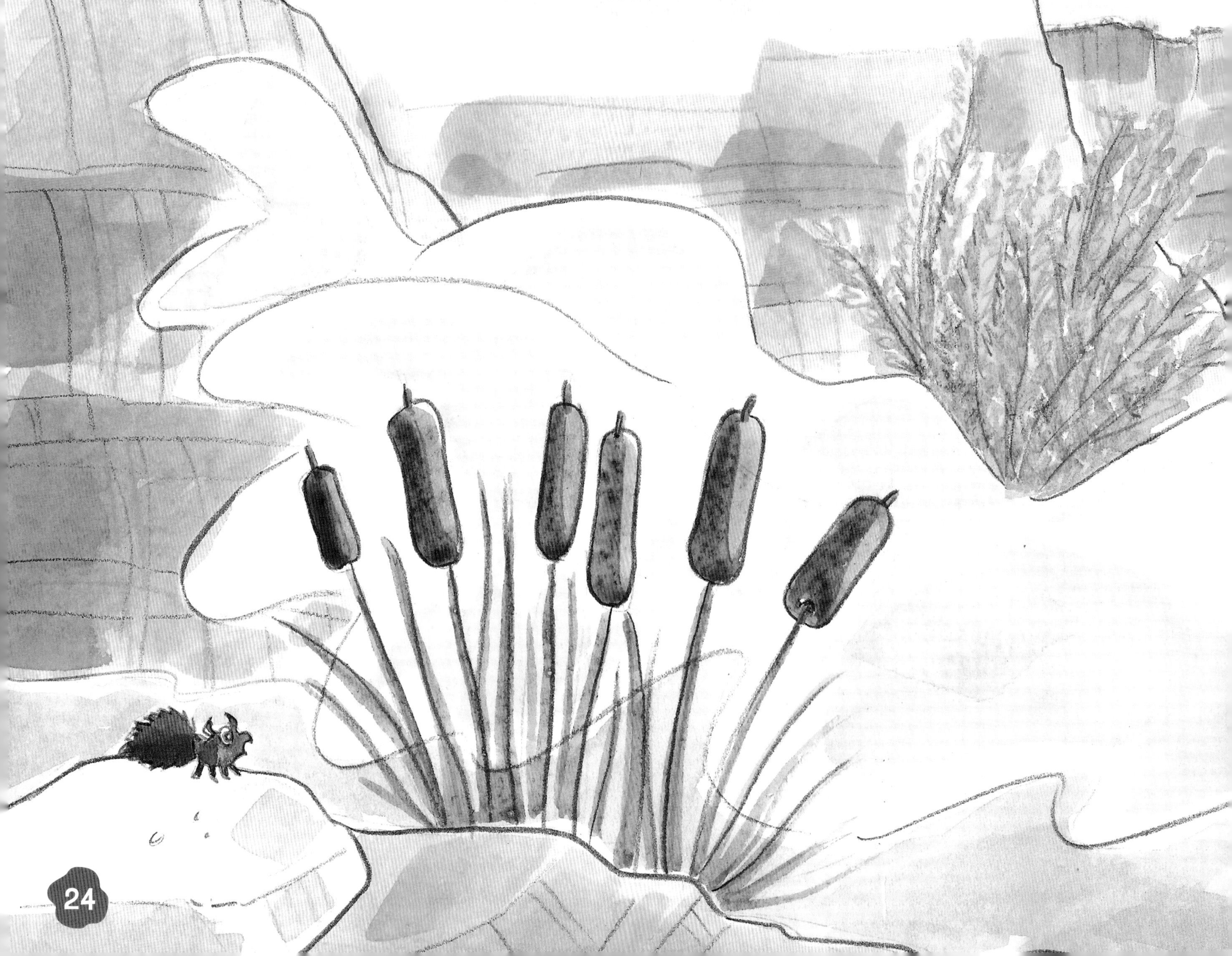

The rapids are roaring — oh boy, what a ride!
He braves wild waves splashing over the side,
a huge hump of CHUB leaping swiftly aside.

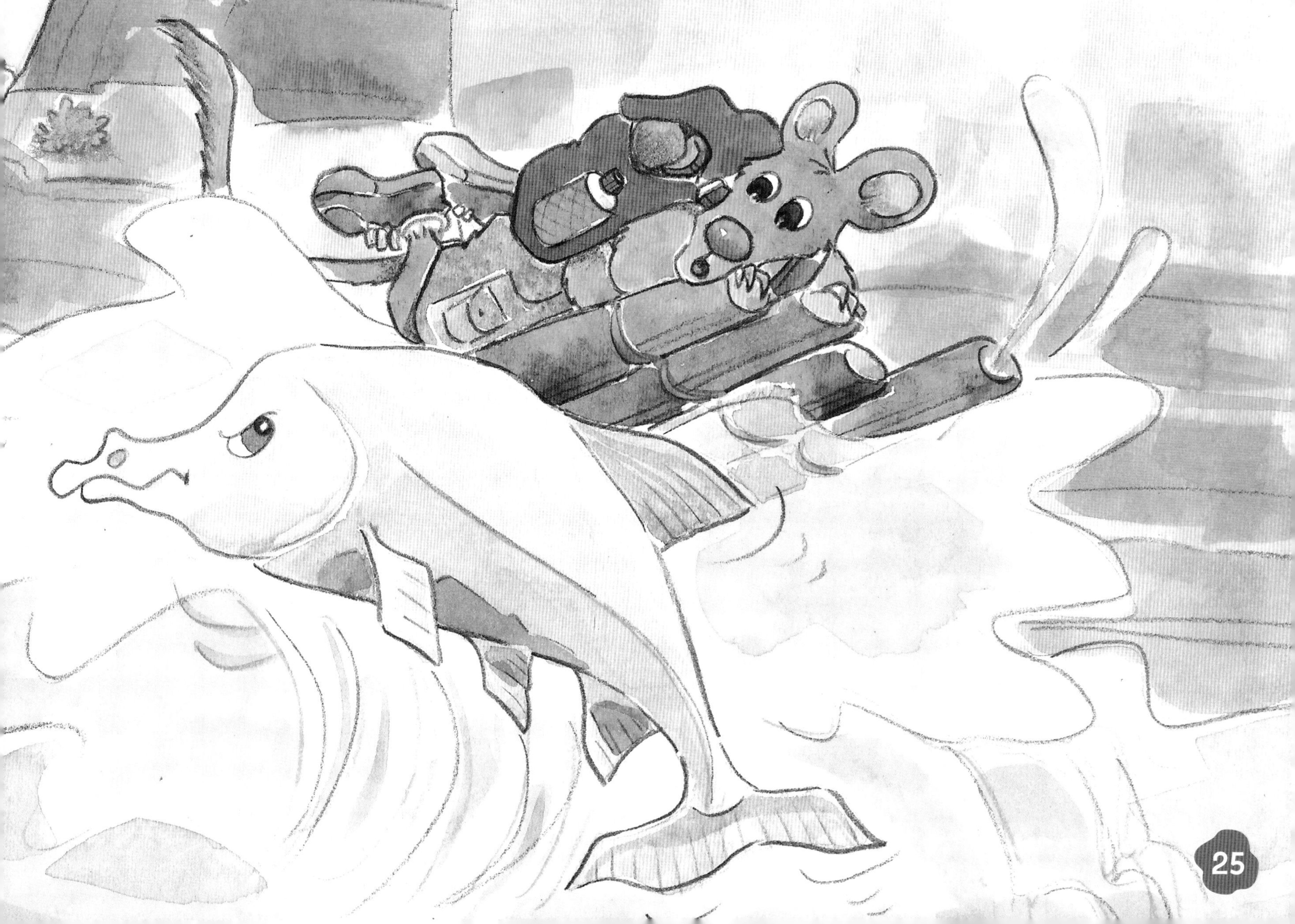

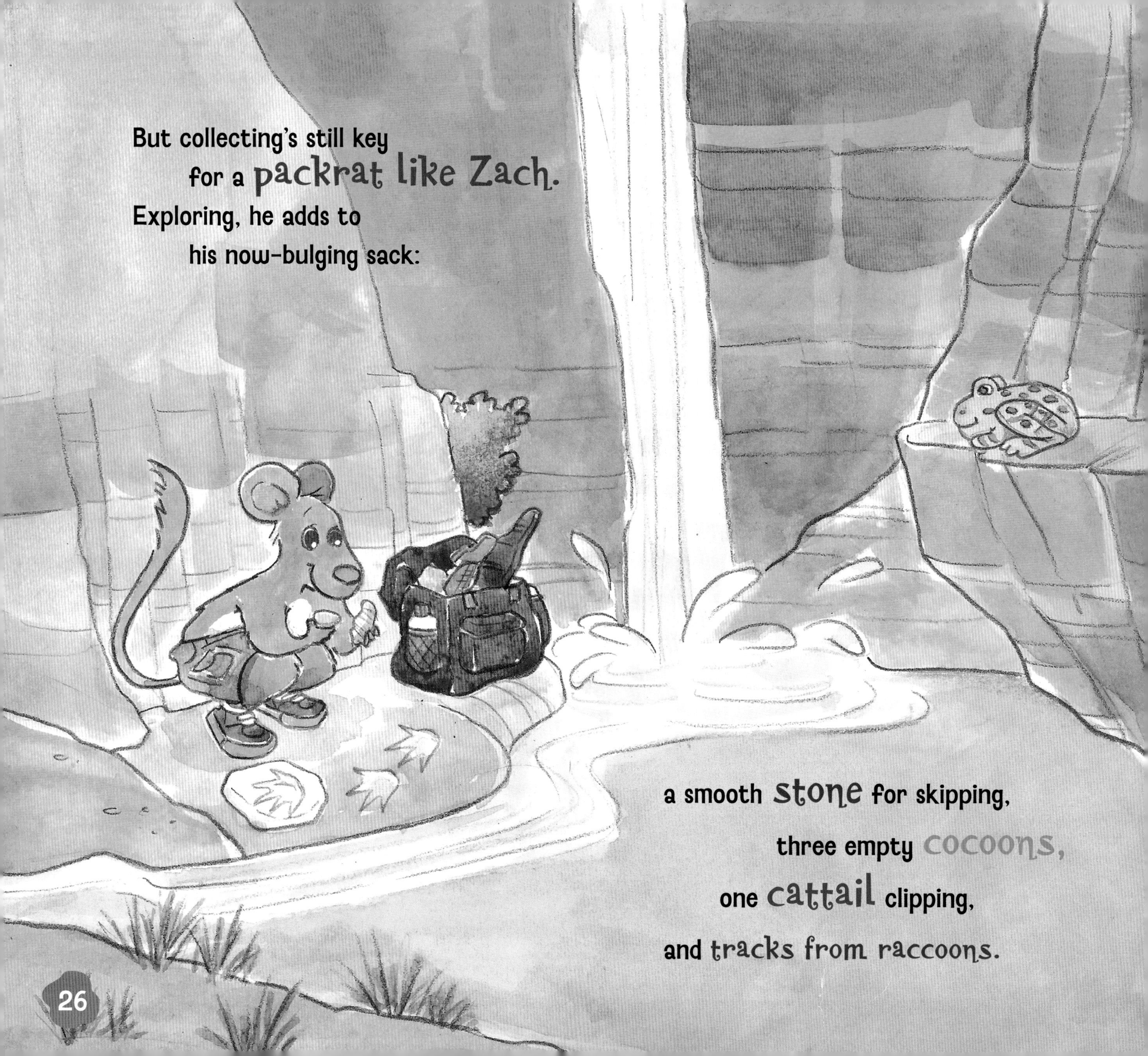

But collecting's still key
for a packrat like Zach.
Exploring, he adds to
his now-bulging sack:

a smooth stone for skipping,
three empty cocoons,
one cattail clipping,
and tracks from raccoons.

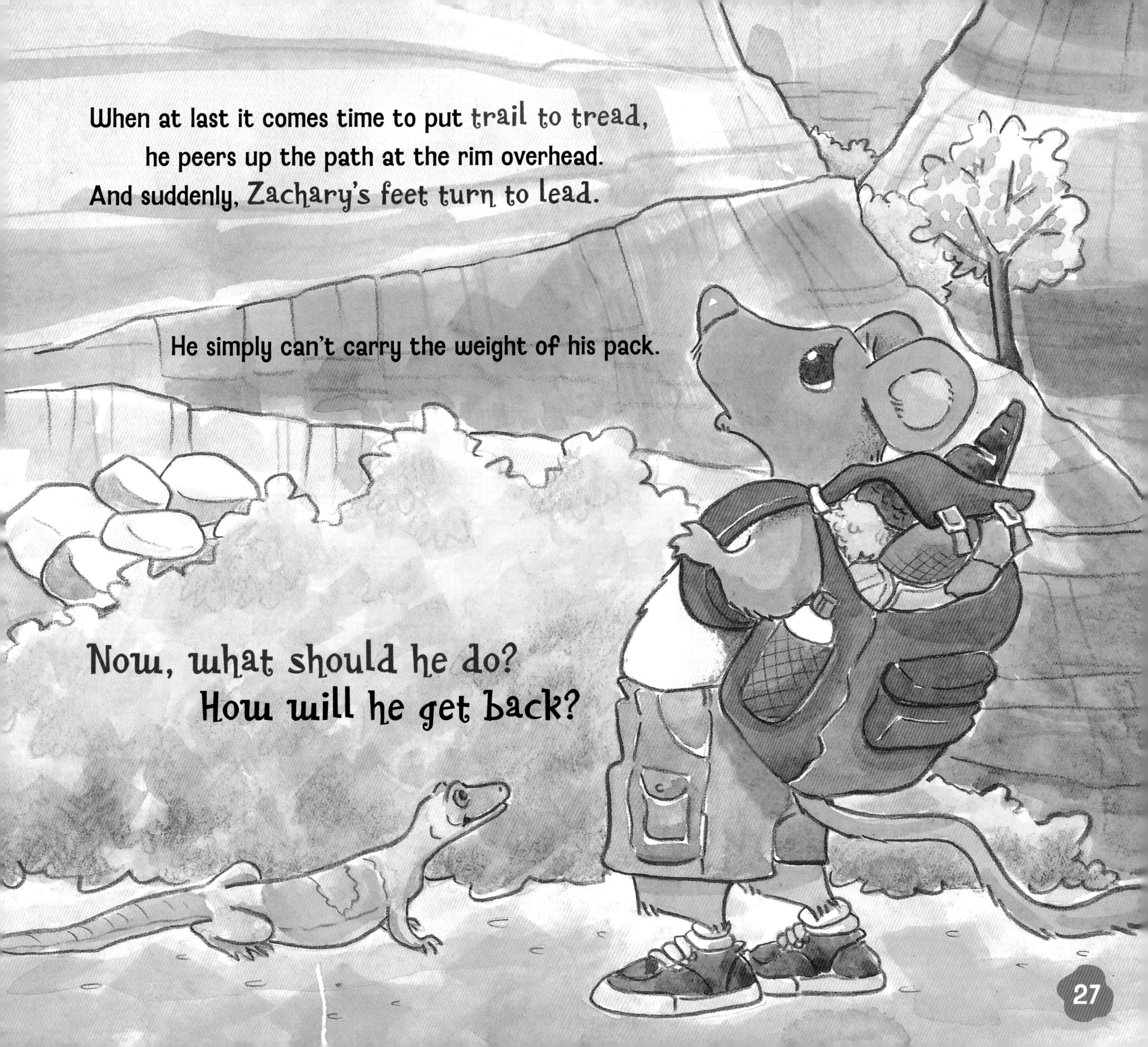

When at last it comes time to put trail to tread,
he peers up the path at the rim overhead.
And suddenly, Zachary's feet turn to lead.

He simply can't carry the weight of his pack.

Now, what should he do?
How will he get back?

Struck by **GOOD LUCK!**

He hears a mule bray ...

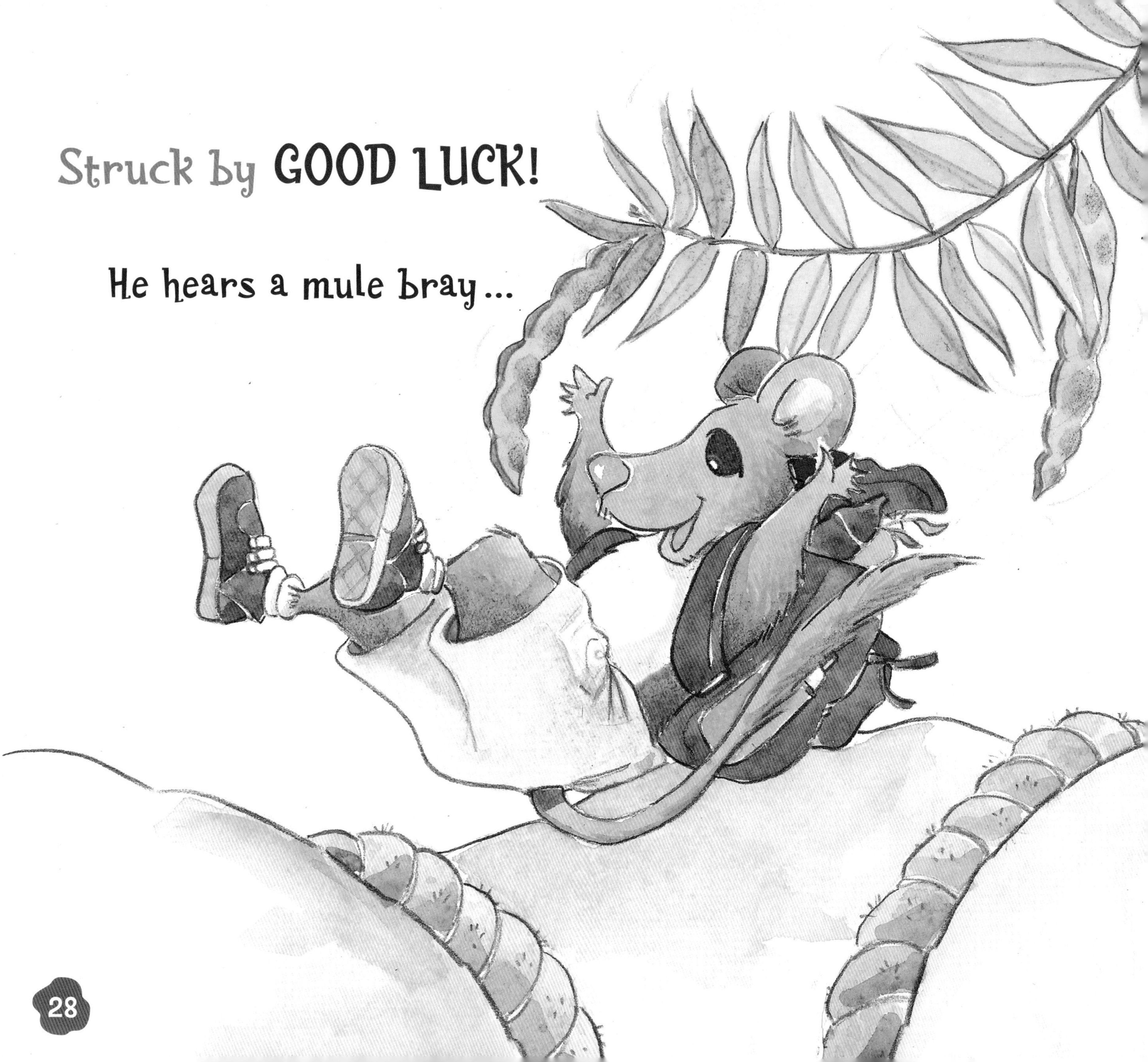

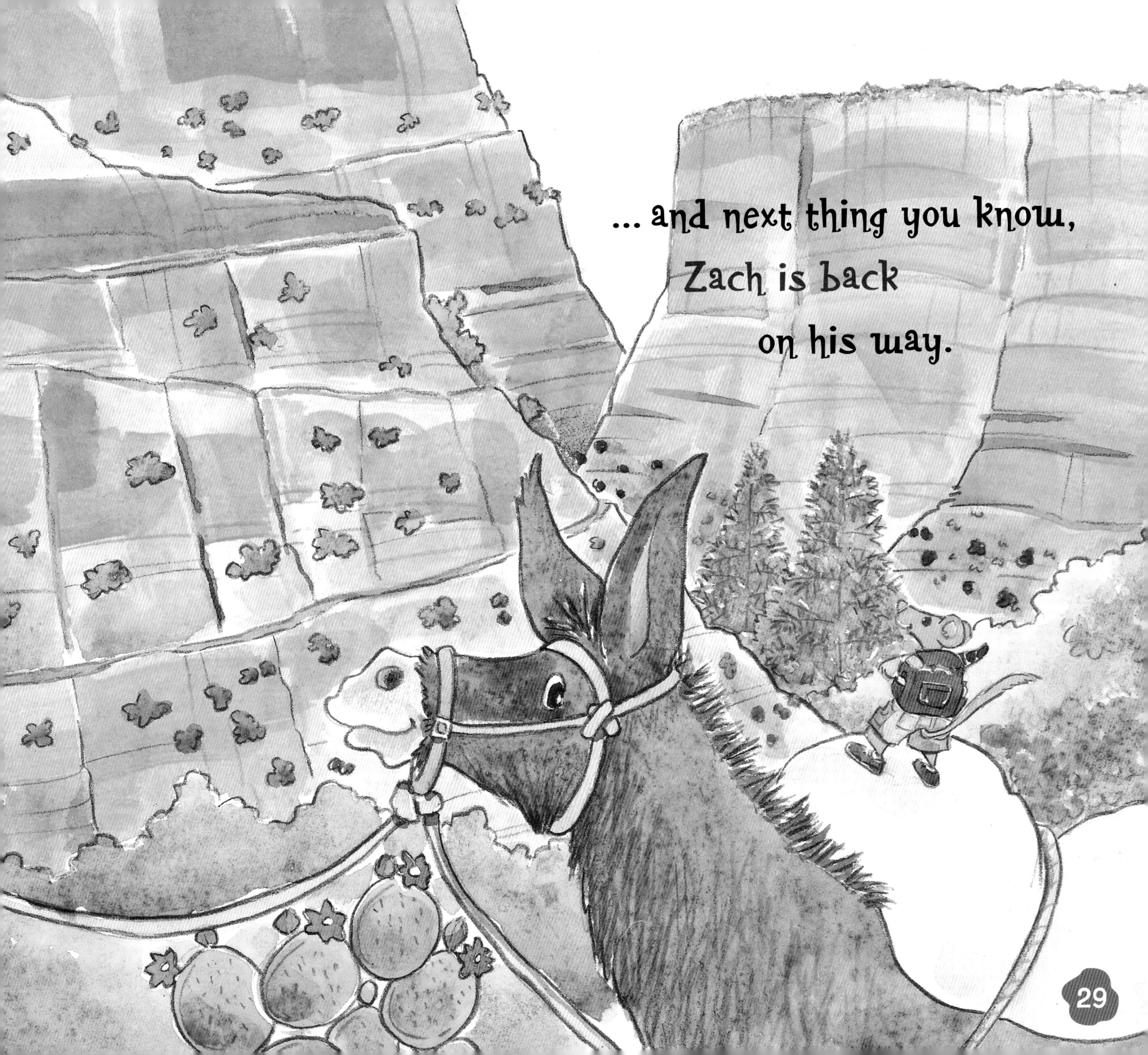

... and next thing you know,
Zach is back
on his way.

Upward he rides, with
eyes glued to the views
of canyon walls rising in colorful hues.
He spots ancient dwellings
up under a ledge,
a proud pair of horns
perching out on the edge.

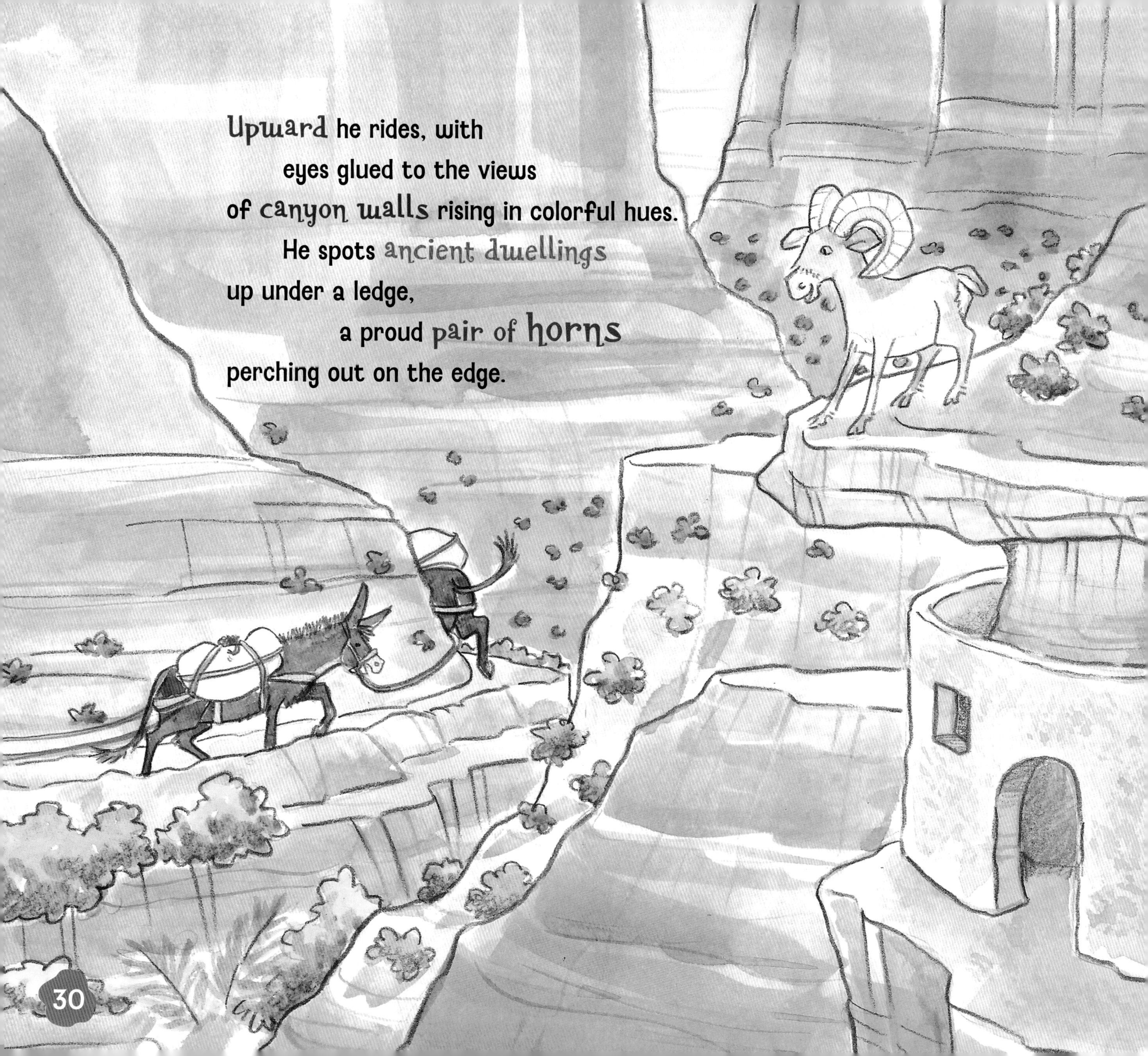

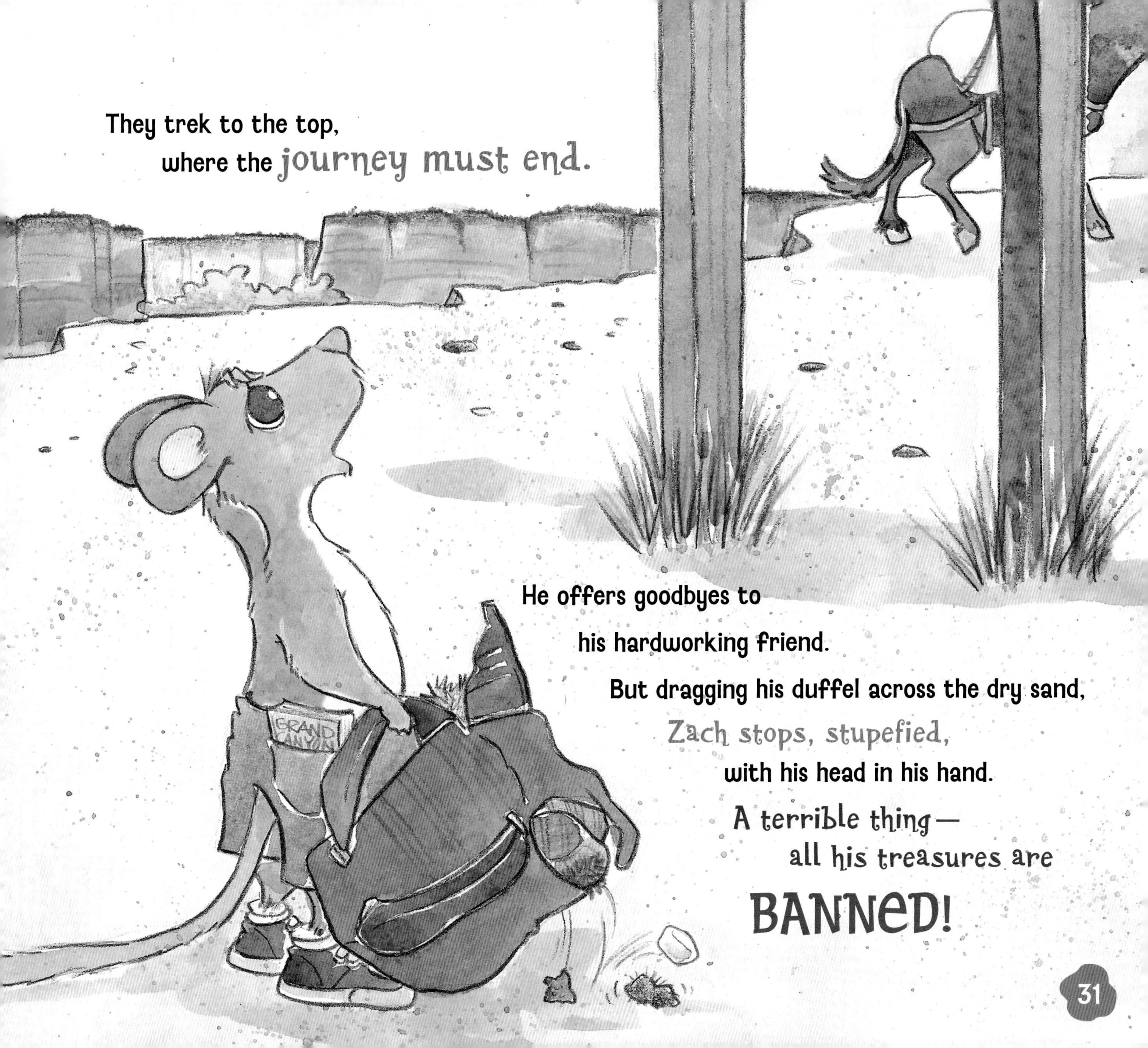
GRAND CANYON

They trek to the top,
where the journey must end.

He offers goodbyes to
his hardworking friend.
But dragging his duffel across the dry sand,
Zach stops, stupefied,
with his head in his hand.
A terrible thing—
all his treasures are
BANNED!

He purges his pack with hot tears on his cheek.

The cost! So much lost!

His knees become weak.

Wistfully wishing for what might have been,

Zach slumps in a lump.

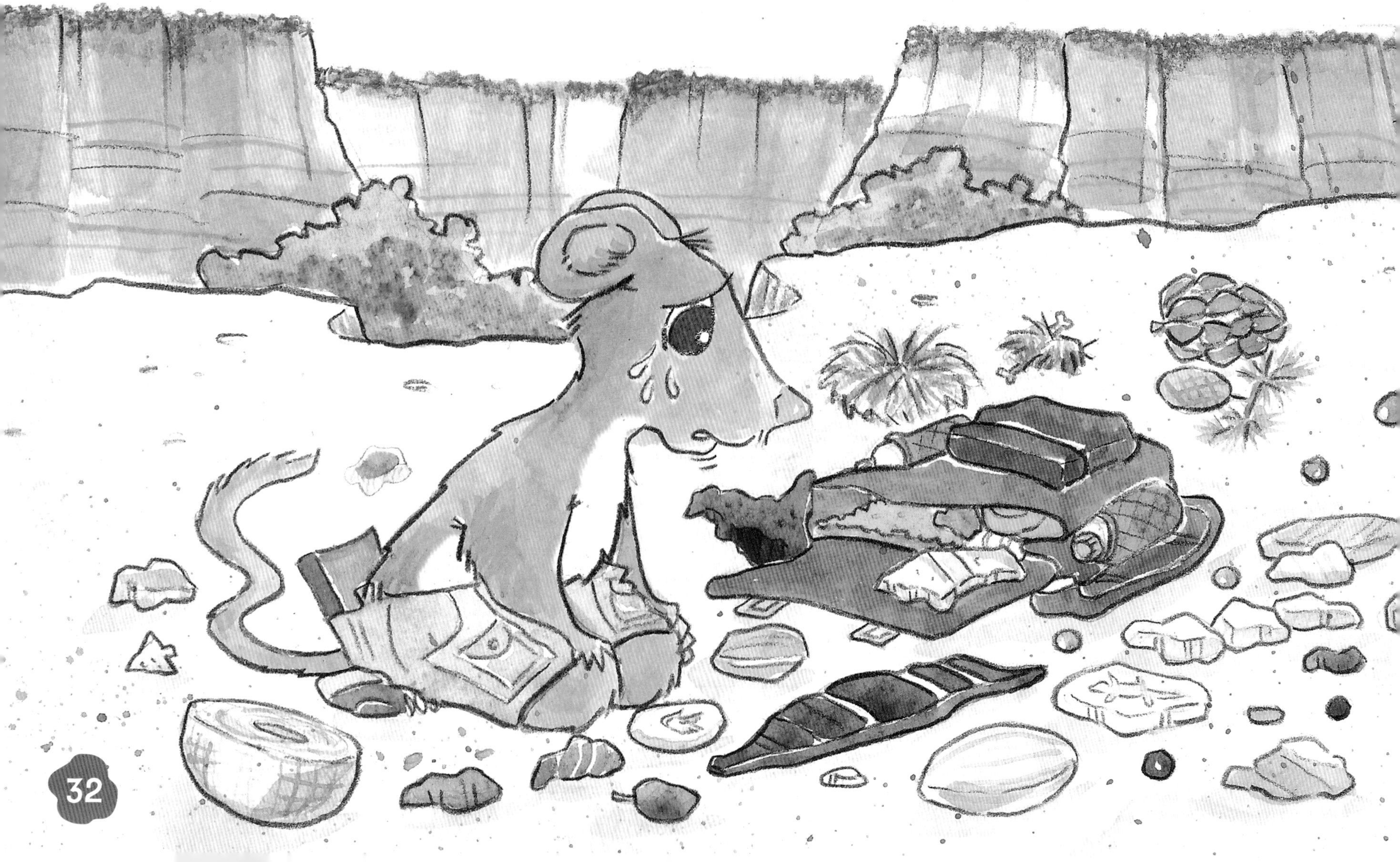

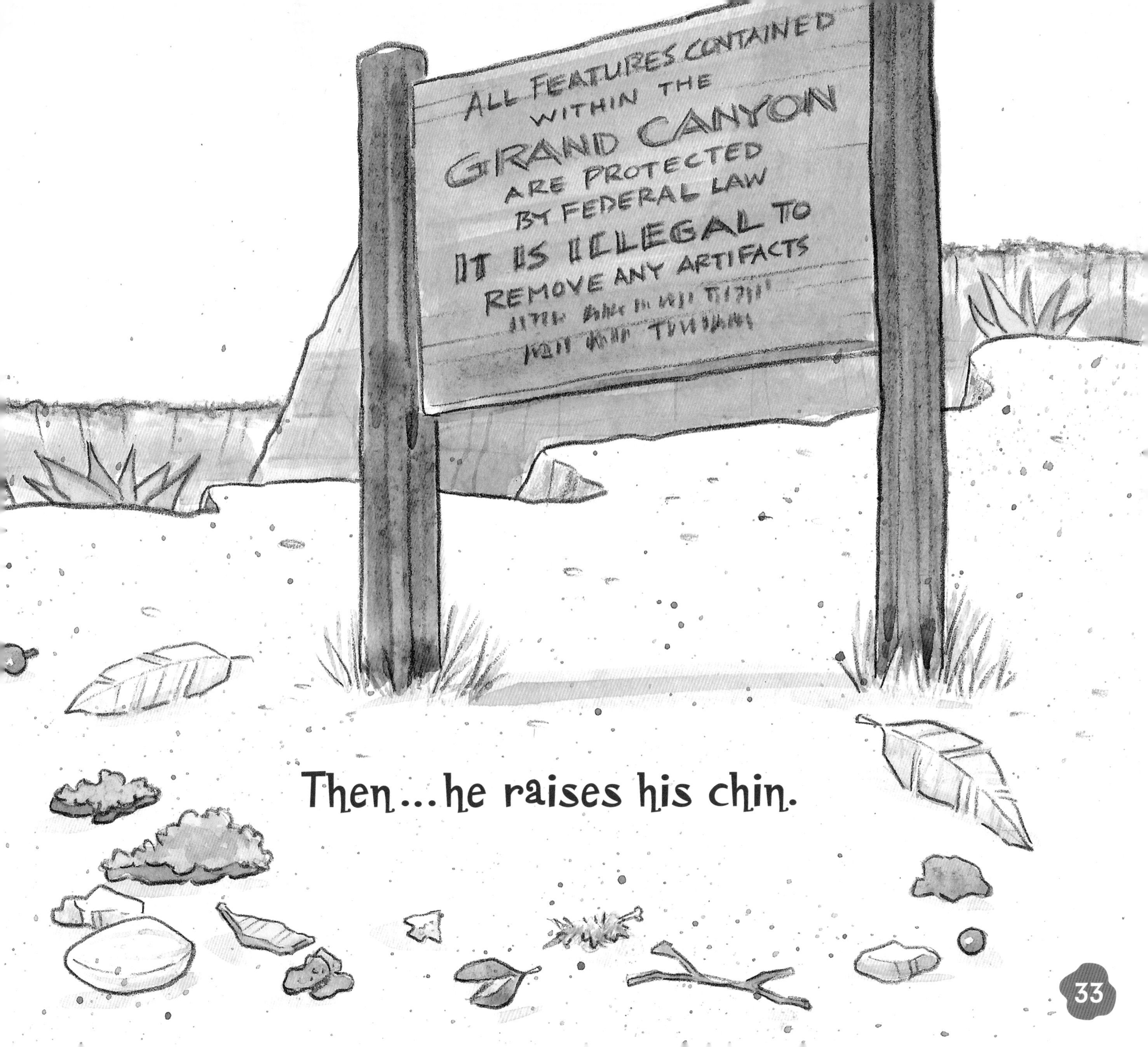
ALL FEATURES CONTAINED
WITHIN THE
GRAND CANYON
ARE PROTECTED
BY FEDERAL LAW
IT IS ILLEGAL TO
REMOVE ANY ARTIFACTS

Then...he raises his chin.

Look!

THE GRAND CANYON!

A feast for the eyes.

Ruddy red rock against crystal blue skies.

He hiked a World Wonder, grins Zachary Z.

A real expedition with oodles to see!

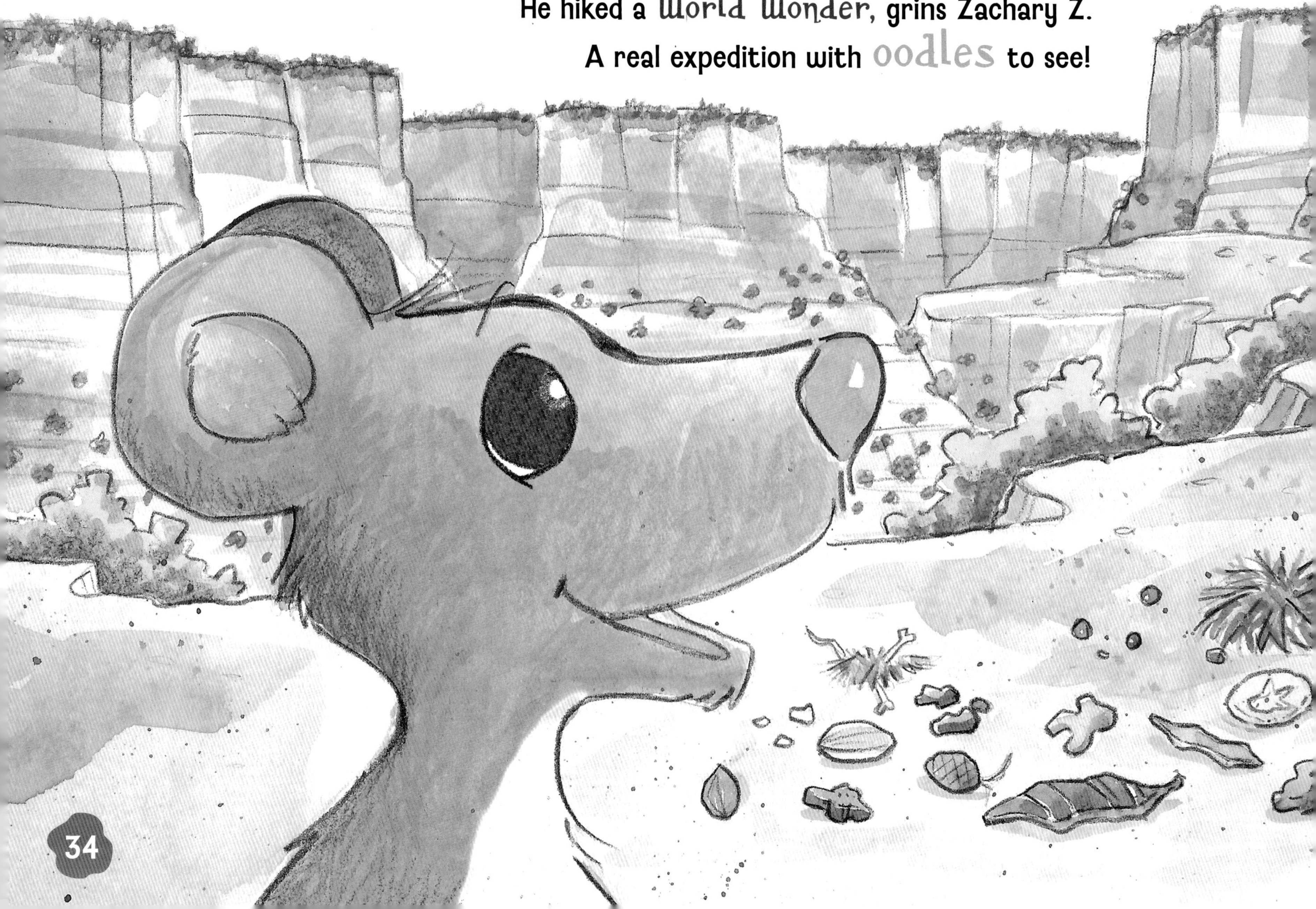

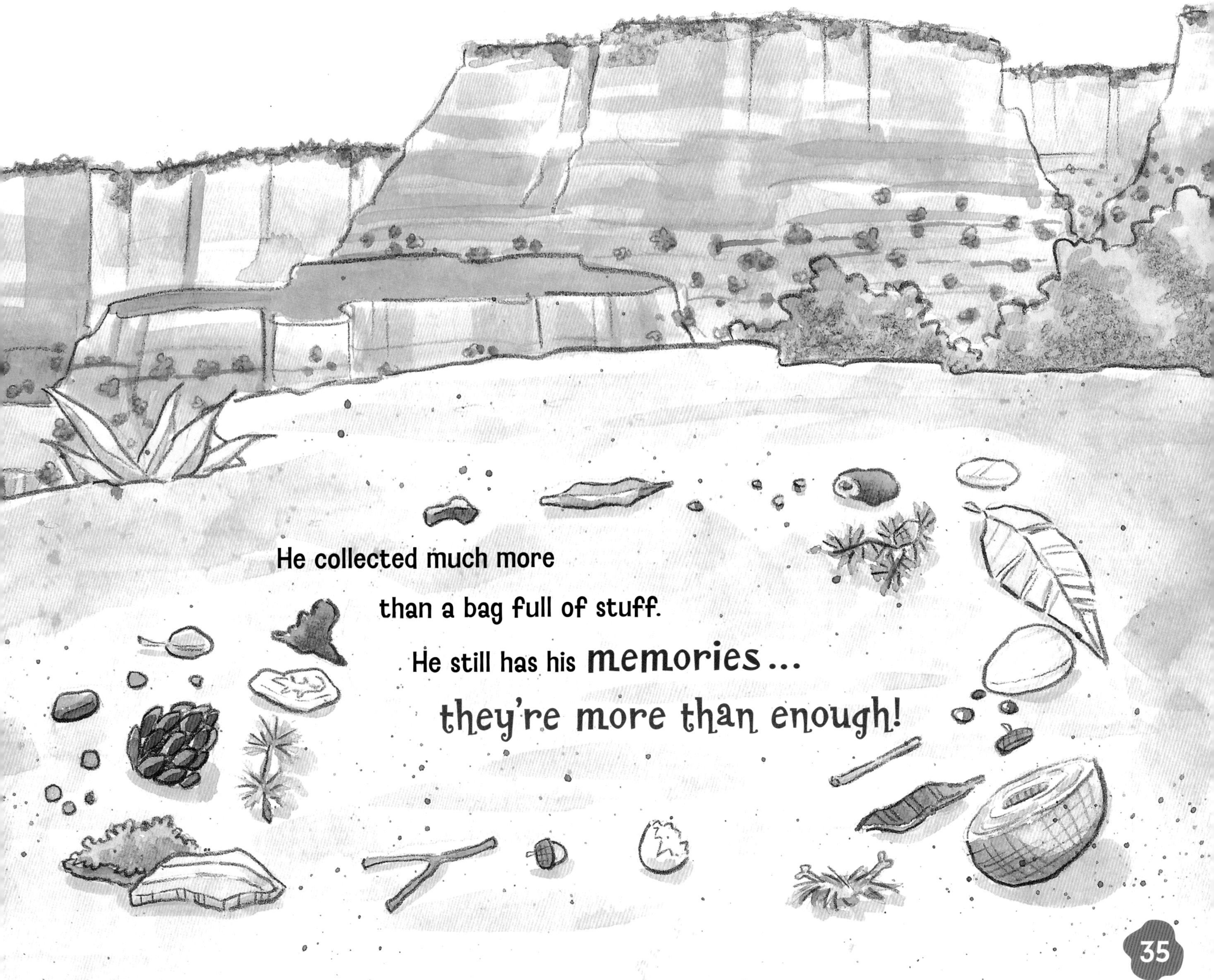

He collected much more

than a bag full of stuff.

He still has his **memories…**

they're more than enough!

Marvelous scenes are now etched in his mind.

Life's take-along treasures—the **most precious** kind!

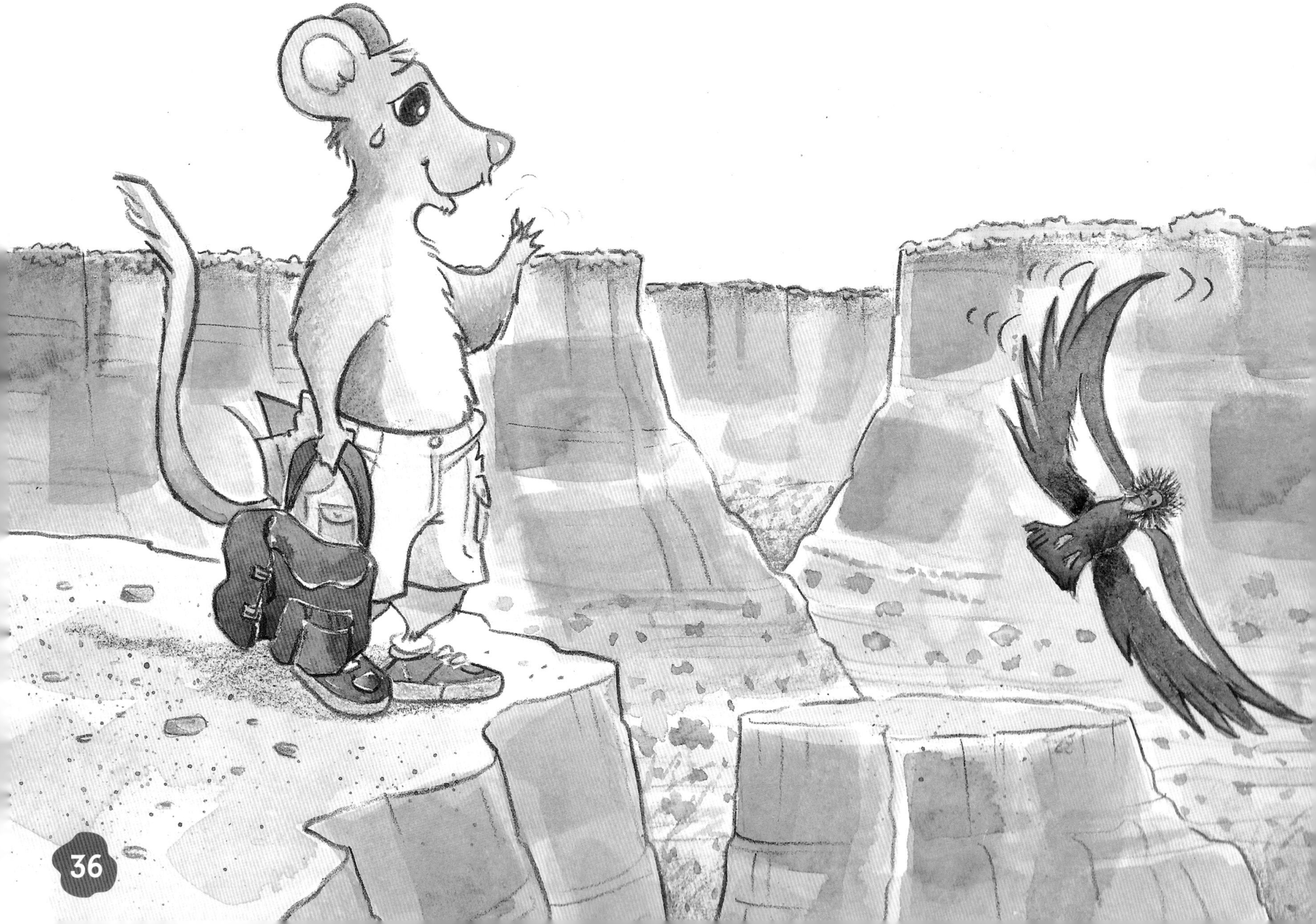

For now, Zach's content

and feels no need to roam.

Knapsack on his back,

a pleased packrat

heads home.

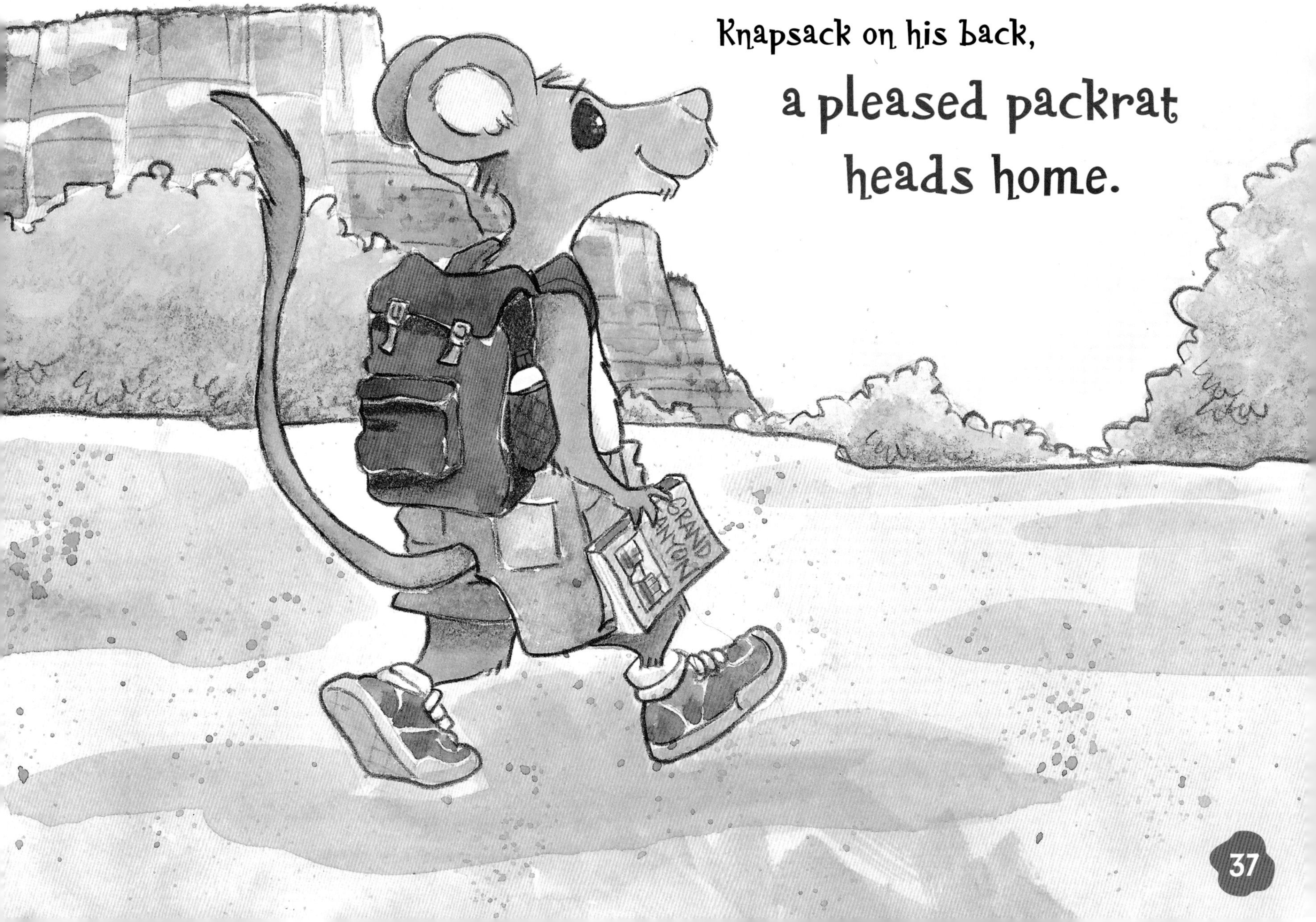
GRAND CANYON

Look Who Lives in the Grand Canyon

There are about 9,000 species of animals living in the Grand Canyon, including about 90 mammals, 350 birds, 60 reptiles and amphibians, 20 fish and more than 8,500 known invertebrates.

Bighorn sheep

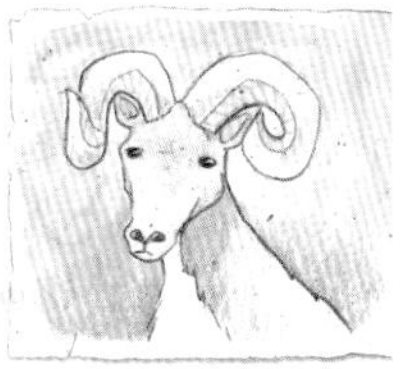

Adapted to life in the Canyon, this stocky sheep has soft-center hooves that help it balance on narrow ledges, maneuver rocky slopes and even leap spans of nearly 20 feet (6 meters)! It grazes on grasses and shrubs. Both sexes have horns, but the males' can curl all the way around and weigh up to 30 pounds (13.5 kilograms).

California condor

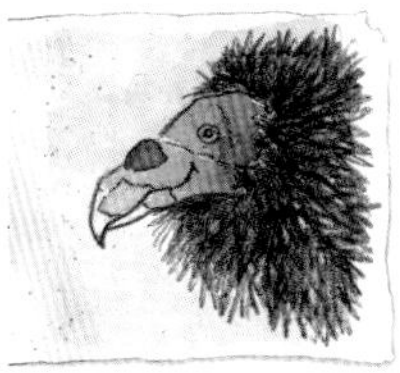

This is the largest flying bird in North America, with a wingspan of nearly 10 feet (3 meters)! The species came to the brink of extinction but can once again be seen soaring in the Grand Canyon. Adults have red heads and white patches under their black wings. As scavengers, they eat nothing but carrion.

YUCK!!

Canyon tree frog

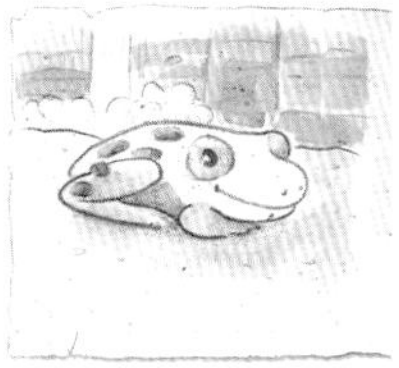

Found in tributaries of the Colorado River, this amphibian dines on insects and spiders. It is about 2 inches (5 centimeters) long — and recognized by its disc-shaped toe pads. Sightings can be difficult because it hides in rock crevices during the day, and its coloring provides camouflage against the stone walls.

Chuckwalla

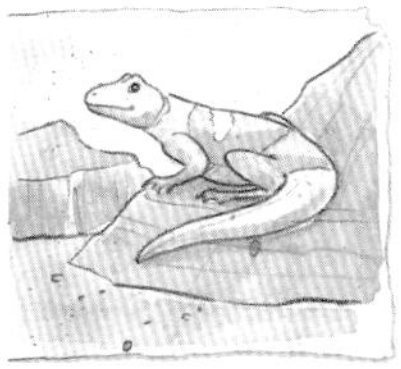

A member of the iguana family, this harmless wide-bellied lizard can grow to more than 15 inches (38 centimeters) in length, including its tapered tail. Active during the day, it is sometimes seen basking on rocks, especially near the river. Males are more colorful than females. Its diet is mostly leaves, fruits and flowers.

Grand Canyon mule

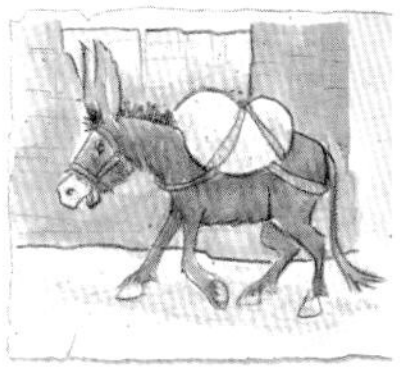

Trusted for their endurance and incredible sense of balance, mules (a cross between horse and donkey) have been carrying people and packs up and down Canyon trails for more than 100 years! These sure-footed animals live in stables at Grand Canyon National Park and are fed and cared for by humans.

Grand Canyon pink rattlesnake

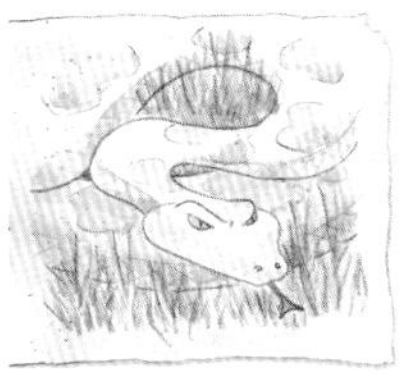

This is the most common rattlesnake in the Grand Canyon. Beware its venomous bite! It is an endemic species (found nowhere else), and its pink color helps it blend into the Canyon landscape. It grows up to 5 feet long and has darker blotches along its back and a rattle at the tip of its tail. It eats rodents.

YIKES!

Humpback chub

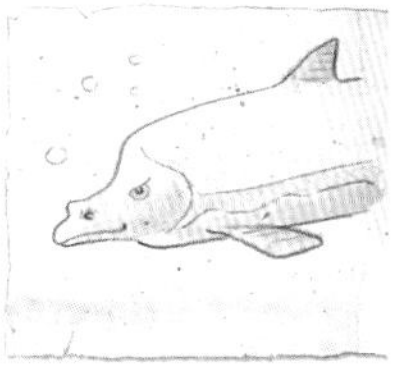

Only found in the Colorado River basin, this endangered fish has a streamlined body, strong fins and a sharply forked tail adapted for fast-running waters. It dines on small aquatic insects and algae, reaching up to 18 inches (46 centimeters) in length. The name comes from the high arch behind its head.

Kaibab squirrel

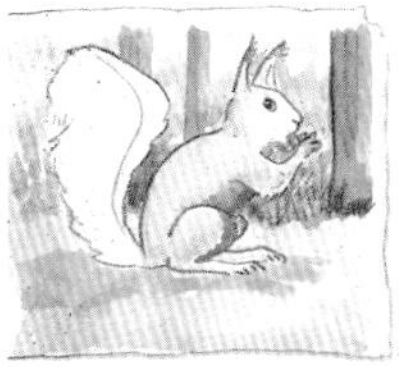

This squirrel is designated a National Natural Landmark because it is an endemic species (found only on the North Rim of the Grand Canyon). It lives and nests exclusively in ponderosa-pine trees, eating mostly seeds, bark and fungi. It can be recognized by its prominent ear tufts, black belly and bushy white tail.

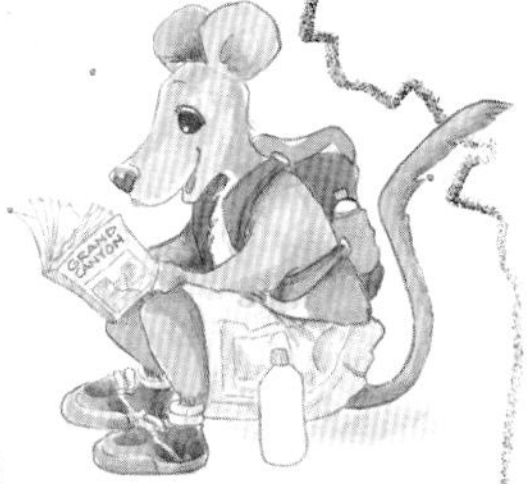

Look for footprints

Kanab ambersnail

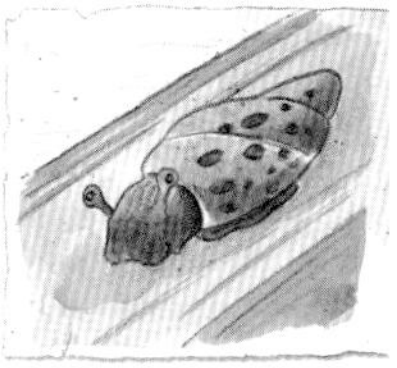

Living in a spring-fed marsh at the edge of the Colorado River, this critically endangered land snail depends on wetland vegetation for food and shelter. The tiny mollusk is less than an inch (2.5 centimeters) long, and its mottled grayish-amber or yellowish-amber shell is dextral (twists in a right-handed spiral).

Kit fox

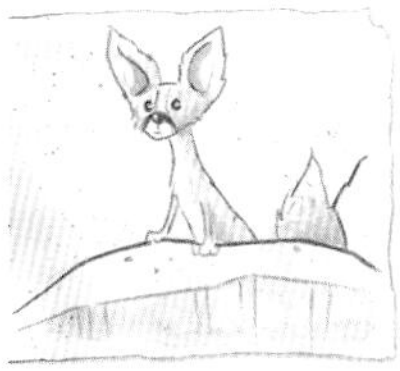

Weighing only about 5 pounds (2.25 kilograms), this small member of the dog family has buff coloring and oversized ears that are used to shed excess body heat. It also has fur on the bottom of its feet for walking across hot desert sand and stone. As a nocturnal hunter, it catches and eats small prey and insects.

Mountain lion

Here, kitty, kitty, LOL!!

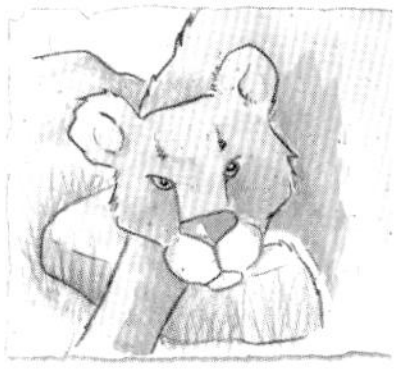

Also called *cougar* or *puma*, this is the largest wildcat in North America, weighing up to 200 pounds (90 kilograms). It can run fast in short bursts but is normally an ambush hunter that uses a silent-stalking approach to capture deer and small animals. It can leap up to 18 feet (5.5 meters) from a standstill!

Mule deer

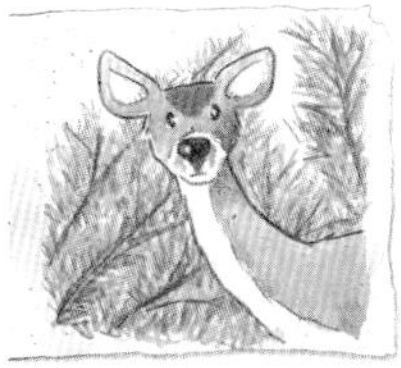

Commonly seen throughout the Grand Canyon region, this large deer mainly browses on leaves, weeds and twigs. It was named for its mule-like ears and has a dark forehead and black-tipped tail. Only males grow antlers, which fork from the main branch. A doe usually gives birth to two fawns in early summer.

Raccoon

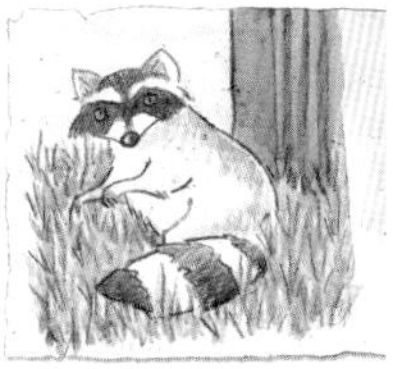

Known for its black mask, ringed tail and plump, gray body, this 8- to 20-pound (3.5- to 9-kilogram) mammal eats an array of food. Because it does not produce much saliva, it must moisten its food in the water. Footprints from its nighttime activities can be seen along the muddy banks of the Colorado River.

Raven

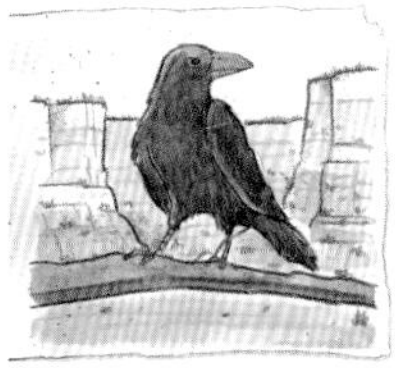

This glossy black bird is legendary for its intelligence, playfulness and aerobatics. It is the largest member of the crow family, often seen soaring with a wingspan over 4 feet (1.2 meters). Although it can mimic many sounds, a gurgling croak is its most common call. As a hunter and scavenger, it eats a wide range of food.

Western scrub jay

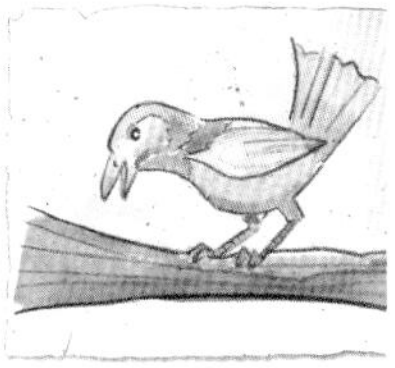

A common sight in the Grand Canyon, this animated bird is about a foot (30 centimeters) long, with a crestless head. Its blue coloring is broken by dusty gray patches, a light belly and a white eyebrow. It has at least 20 known calls. Its diet includes nuts, seeds, insects, berries and small animals such as lizards.

Velvet ant

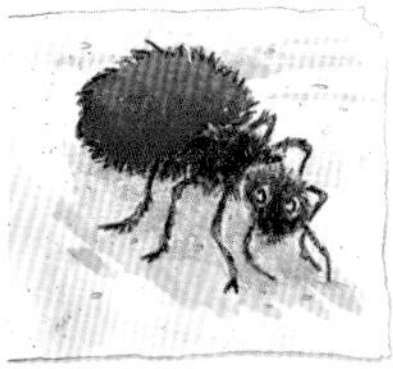

This is actually a wasp. The name comes from the wingless females, which look like giant fuzzy ants. In the Grand Canyon, these insects are usually red or orange, but some are white or gold. They drink nectar. Although not overly aggressive, velvet ants can deliver a painful sting if touched.

Don't touch!!

To Kevin, for 20 wonderful years!
I'm so grateful to be **sharing the journey.** —bb

Text: Brooke Bessesen
Illustrations: Jenny Campbell
Design: Keith Whitney

Library of Congress Control Number: 2013951485
ISBN: 978-0-9887875-5-1
First printing, 2013. Printed in Malaysia.

ARIZONA
HIGHWAYS

Published by the Book Division of *Arizona Highways*
magazine, a monthly publication of the Arizona
Department of Transportation, 2039 W. Lewis Avenue,
Phoenix, Arizona 85009.
Telephone: 602-712-2200
Website: www.arizonahighways.com

Publisher: Win Holden
Editor: Robert Stieve
Senior Editor/Books: Kelly Vaughn Kramer
Senior Associate Editor: Kathy Ritchie
Associate Editor: Noah Austin
Creative Director: Barbara Glynn Denney
Art Director: Keith Whitney
Photography Editor: Jeff Kida
Design Production Assistant: Diana Benzel-Rice
Production Director: Michael Bianchi
Production Coordinator: Annette Phares

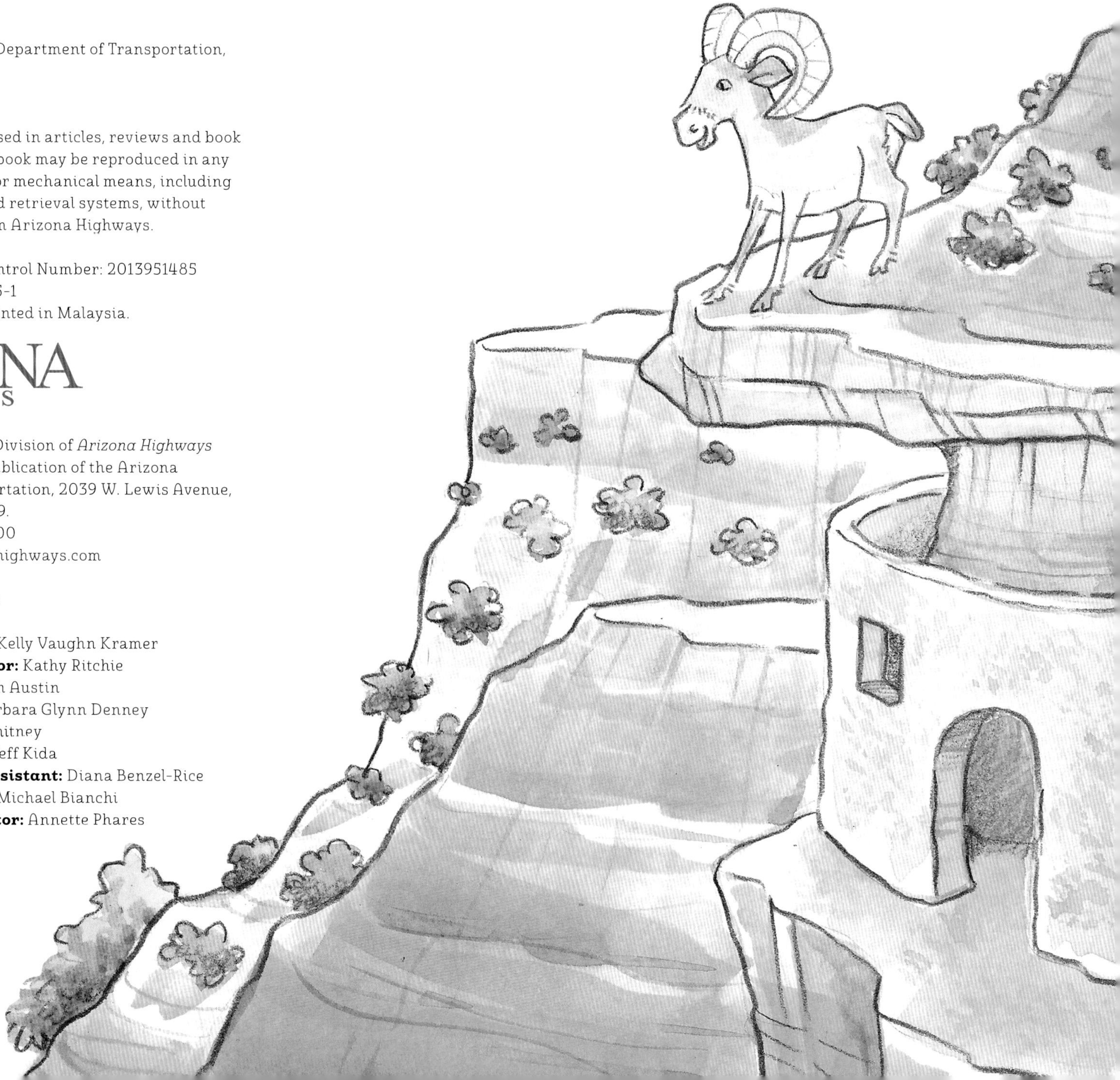